Normalization in World Politics

The notions of normalcy and normalization have been present for some
time in international relations, but there has been little explicit effort to
conceptualize and unpack their meanings in practice. This book explores
the discourses and practices of normalization in world politics. It investi-
gates three distinct types of normalization interventions: those seeking to
impose a new order of normalcy over fragile states, those seeking to either
restore or develop a more resilient normalcy in disaster-affected states, and
those seeking to accept an endogenous meaning of normalcy in suppressive states. The book argues that discourses and practices of normalization have emerged as intervention optimization manifested through selective, uneven, and discordant responses to governing risks and disciplining
states. Accordingly, this book highlights some of the contemporary analytics of interventionism in world politics, particularly the efforts of dominant states to employ normalization technologies to create a society of
docile states that eventually would become passive yet productive subjects,
open to external examination, regulation, and punitive measures, as well
as disciplined and open to transformation and norm taking. By providing
a critical account of the discourses and practices of normalization in world
politics, this book exposes the changing rationales and techniques of intervention and domination among states.

Gëzim Visoka is Associate Professor of Peace and Conflict
Studies in the School of Law and Government at Dublin City
University, Ireland.

Nicolas Lemay-Hébert is Senior Lecturer in the Department of
International Relations at the Australian National University.

Normalization in World Politics

Gëzim Visoka and
Nicolas Lemay-Hébert

University of Michigan Press
Ann Arbor

For questions or permissions, please contact um.press.perms@umich.edu

Published in the United States of America by the
University of Michigan Press
Printed and bound by CPI Group (UK) Ltd, Croydon, CR0 4YY

First published February 2022

A CIP catalog record for this book is available from the British Library.

Library of Congress Cataloging-in-Publication data has been applied for.

ISBN 978-0-472-13289-8 (hardcover : alk. paper)
ISBN 978-0-472-03901-2 (paper : alk. paper)
ISBN 978-0-472-90281-1 (open access e-book)

DOI: https://doi.org/10.3998/mpub.10171116

Front cover: *From the Cape to Cairo*, Udo J. Keppler (1902), from the Library
of Congress, https://www.loc.gov/item/2010652189/

For
Grace, Eira, and Erik
Aurélie, Eva, and Joséphine

Contents

PREFACE ix

1 Introduction 1

2 Mapping Normalization in World Politics 21

3 Imposing Normalcy 55

4 Restoring Normalcy 89

5 Accepting Normalcy 119

6 Toward a Society of Docile States 151

REFERENCES 169

INDEX 197

Digital materials related to this title can be found on the Fulcrum platform via the following citable URL: https://doi.org/10.3998/mpub.10171116

Preface

We started thinking about the concepts of normalcy and normalization in 2016, in what seems like a lifetime ago. Since our first work on the subject (Lemay-Hébert and Visoka 2017), we have spent countless hours tracing various semantic uses of normalization in world politics. The product of all those hours is encapsulated in this book. Its writing has been a long journey, marked by the birth of children, the passing away of loved ones, and countless international and national crises that have made the book all the more challenging to complete and, we hope, all the more relevant to deciphering the new world we are entering.

As we face new challenges from climate change and the rise of populism in Western politics and beyond, there is little doubt that we are entering a new configuration of world politics. Driven by nostalgia for past certainties or fear of what is coming next, references to normalcy have been creeping into political discourse, with people either vying for a return to past normalcy or coping with the new normal. The normal and the quest of normalcy are emerging as central features of how we make sense of the world. After being questioned multiple times by people "hearing it on TV," one political commentator asked recently if normalcy "is even a word" (McNally 2019). While there are widely accepted definitions of the normal and normalcy, associated with the "standard" and the "regular, usual, or typical" (*Oxford English Dictionary*), what is normal can be highly contested. The concept ingrains descriptive and prescriptive features of reality. It signifies order but constantly aims to regularize and discipline life along particular norms. Most important, it tends to include and exclude, to homogenize and heterogenize, ways of being, seeing, and acting in the world.

These features of normalcy are omnipresent in the world now like never before. With the focus on climate security, it certainly feels as if we are living in a new, abnormal world—normalizing a state of affairs that was considered highly abnormal just a few years ago. In that regard, it is telling that normalization has become a new political battleground between agents of change on both sides of the climate equation, trying to (re)conquer this new world molded by changing standards of normalcy. As we wrote this book, one of us was living in the Australian capital, Canberra, which was covered in thick clouds of smoke for months due to a "historical" bushfire crisis. For Australian Prime Minister Scott Morrison, the implications of that crisis as of January 2020 meant that "we have to prepare for the new normal," an understanding immediately challenged by the leader of the Labor opposition, Anthony Albanese, who tweeted, "We can't just sit by and accept this as the new normal." On another front, the effort to control the evolution of the novel coronavirus (COVID-19) led to new governmental strategies, with one-third of the world's population under some form of lockdown at the start of the pandemic. In turn, critical theorists such as Giorgio Agamben lament the growing tendency to use the state of exception as a normal paradigm of government. At the same time, states impacted by the epidemic have tried to reassure others (and themselves) that there will be a "return to normalcy." What is normal and what is accepted as such are increasingly at the center of politics, creating new fault lines and disrupting old ways of doing politics. Some believe the pandemic has given us a once-in-a-generation chance to remake societies and build a better future, with a more just and sustainable normalcy. Others fear that it may simply lead to an increase in existing injustices, returning to an old familiar normal state. Around the same time, the Black Lives Matter movement picked up steam after the killing of George Floyd in May 2020, with growing calls to "normalize equality."

A further example of the political battleground of normalcy is the rise of populism in politics, pushing people to question how political discourse has disrupted past normal settings. Donald Trump's rise to US presidential power is itself a testimony of a new battleground of normalcy, paradoxically presenting a contestation of a specific normal state of affairs—normalizing what was previously highly abnormal—while promoting the return to a "normal," romanticized past. In a very public way, Trump threw out of the window all pretense of normalcy in everyday politics (especially acting "presidential"), while simultaneously making a central claim, throughout his campaign and term in office, to return to a previous normal, a nostalgic and romanticized past of unfettered American domination ("making America great again," or making normalcy normal again). Populist parties have gained votes and seats in many countries and entered government coalitions in eleven Western democracies, including in Austria, Italy, and Switzerland, disrupting "normal politics." Examples also abound outside the West. Brazilian President Jair Bolsonaro redefined normalcy in Brazil, otherizing segments of the Brazilian population with statements such as "leftists do not deserve to be treated like normal people," while vying to reconnect with tactics of the past military dictatorship. Philippine President Rodrigo Duterte posed a drastic challenge to what is considered normal in Filipino politics, promoting his own brand of illiberalism and using swear words never printed previously, leading to emulation by government officials and a reconfiguration of everyday life. What is normal is being redefined constantly, often by drawing on discourses about old normalcy, increasingly redefining the political landscape around us, and thus imposing new meanings of normalcy.

This book aims to trace various discourses and practices associated with normalcy in world politics. Mostly, we here focus on how dominant states and international organizations try to manage global affairs through imposing normalcy over fragile states, restoring normalcy over disaster-affected states, and accepting normalcy over suppressive states. We try to show how discourses and practices come together in constituting normalization interventions and play a role in shaping the dynamics of continuity and change in world politics. That the challenges of climate change and the rise of populism are not tackled explicitly in this book should not be taken as a statement about what we consider central or more important in world politics. The book's focus simply highlights the specific topics, most notably the thematic of international interventions, that are our areas of mutual and relative expertise. More work remains to be done to highlight other forms of normalization in world politics, and do hope that this book will open up new research avenues for students and scholars interested in normalization discourses and practices.

Many colleagues read part of the manuscript and gave us frank advice. We thank Pol Bargués-Pedreny, David Chandler, Jonathan Fisher, Luke Glanville, Elisa Lopez Lucia, Elisa Randazzo, and Katrin Travouillon for their comments on early drafts. We benefited from feedback provided by colleagues when we presented draft chapters at the Ninth Pan-European Conference of the European International Studies Association in Sicily (2015), at the International Studies Association's Fifty-Eighth Annual Convention in Baltimore (2017), at the conference "The Practices, Politics, and Paradigms of IO Peacebuilding" organized by the Austrian Study Centre for Peace and Conflict Resolution (2017), at a research seminar organized by the School of Law and Government at Dublin City University, and at a manuscript workshop held in the Department of International Relations at the Australian National University (2019). We are specifically grateful to Mary-Louise Hickey for providing thorough feedback on the manuscript and facilitating the copyediting process. We thank the Faculty of Humanities and Social Sciences at Dublin City University for partially supporting the completion of this book. Finally, we are grateful to Elizabeth Demers and Haley Winkle at the University of Michigan Press for their generosity and support throughout this project and to the two anonymous reviewers who provided constructive and encouraging feedback.

Gëzim Visoka, Dublin

Nicolas Lemay-Hébert, Canberra

December 2020

1 ✦ Introduction

In December 2012, the United Nations (UN) concluded its peacekeeping operations in Timor-Leste, declaring that the country had reached normalcy, self-sufficiency, and resilience. Since 1999, the UN had administered and monitored the country in its transition to independent statehood and had played a major role in building the state from scratch. The rationale for international intervention in Timor-Leste, as well as its progress toward recognized statehood and self-sufficiency, was based on the capacity of that fledgling state to demonstrate "democratic normality," to achieve "institutional normalization," and to be able to "return to normalcy" after political turmoil (UN Security Council 2009a, 2009b, 2012). International actors have used multiple discursive frameworks for justifying interventions in world politics, from maintaining international peace and stability to enhancing resilience and promoting human rights and the protection of civilians. Among those frameworks, the discourse of normalcy and normalization has been mobilized to justify interventions in societies affected by conflict or disaster. For instance, in Kosovo, the mandate of the UN mission was to build a normal society; in Afghanistan, normalcy has been used interchangeably as a measure of peace, stability, and post-conflict reconstruction; and in Georgia, normalization is understood by the European Union to be an instrument of conflict management and stabilization. In disaster-affected countries, the quest for restoring normalcy underlies the rationales for emergency relief and post-disaster recovery. Gradually, calls for adjusting to the normalcy and accepting the permanence of crises are gaining prominence in political and academic discourse about a range of concerns, from terrorist attacks and protracted violent conflicts to natural disasters caused by climate change, the rise of populism, and global pandemic outbreaks. How can we make sense of those invocations of normalcy? How and to what effect do different actors mobilize the vocabulary of normalcy? Has normalization become another global rationale for framing and governing multiple forms of international interventions?

The concepts of normalcy and normalization have been defined variously in different disciplines, making the notions essentially contested and contingent on semantic interpretations. The normal is associated with the ordinary, average, and acceptable state of affairs, whereas normalcy is associated with order, stability, and acceptability. In turn, normalization signifies the process and range of techniques, tools, and mechanisms employed for imposing, restoring, or sustaining normalcy. Normalization operates through a dual mode of intervention: constructing the abnormal through a preconceived notion of what ought to be normal and imposing new meanings and practices of normalcy through prescribing what should be normal. The notions of normalcy and normalization have been present for some time in world politics, but there has been little explicit effort to conceptualize and unpack their meaning(s) in practice. Mostly, those notions have been used interchangeably with the concepts of peace, stability, safety, and order, as well as recovery and reconstruction of relations and affairs between and within states affected by war, disaster, and other events deemed unusual and unacceptable. In other words, normalcy is associated with a good and desired state of affairs, something to be aspired to in general. Normalization has been studied widely in broader social science disciplines, which provide fertile grounds on which we construct our analytical framework of normalization in world politics. However, what is normal is contingent on relational perspectives; therefore, there is no single truth about normalcy. The permanent struggles for normalization result in shifting the meaning of what is normal in the social and political realm. At best, exploring normalization practices sheds light on competing rationales and technologies for constantly producing new ways of seeing and acting in the world.

The purpose of this book is to make sense of contemporary normalization discourses and practices in world politics. The meaning of normalcy is context-specific and contingent on the discursive frameworks that precede and follow interventions in targeted societies. Therefore, we do not privilege a particular understanding of what is normal and what should constitute normalcy. Instead, we identify tensions and contradictions inherent in the various normalization discourses and practices prevalent in world politics. We are well aware that there is no singular understanding of what constitutes normalcy. We try to problematize the technologies of power implicated in imposing, restoring, or accepting normalcy in societies labeled as abnormal. Doing so reveals that the practices of normalization are intertwined deeply with the discursive knowledge in which they are situated. The motive for normalizing turbulent societies may be rooted in geopolitical or ideological interests, may be a response to external events and processes that trigger the necessity for intervention to impose or restore normalcy in abnormal societies, or may even coexist with different understandings of normalcy. Thus, the purpose and technology of normalization correspond to how abnormality is framed. That correspondence is at the heart of the paradox of a selective understanding of normalcy. The abnormalization is constructed and sustained through knowledge production in the form of reports, metrics, and statistical analysis, which categorizes state performance across different scales. In short, the very act of normalization makes certain practices abnormal, which serves as the locomotive for justifying intervention and maintaining unequal power relations.

This study offers a reflective overview of various registers of normalizing interventions in the contemporary world, problematizing the constitutive politics of international hierarchical order that privileges certain states and marginalizes and locks others into a complex regime of docility. By bringing together three clusters of discourses and practices of normalization—imposing, restoring, and accepting normalcy—we highlight interventionary dynamics mostly obscured, until now, by other international relations paradigms. Whereas the discourse and practices of normalization have largely been subsumed into other frameworks or paradigms and not given specific treatment in existing scholarship, we aim to reveal the normalization logics that are structuring world politics. Furthermore, this work contributes in a new and innovative way to the existing scholarship by bringing together interventionary dynamics that tend to be treated separately in the literature. An undue focus on singular forms of interventions—liberal interventionism, resilience building, or even noninterventionism—overlooks the delicate balancing act in which powerful actors find themselves. We posit that the mobilization of specific semantic categories by powerful actors responds to a logic of optimization of interventions, following a "science of the possible," so to speak.

PROBLEMATIZING NORMALIZATION IN WORLD POLITICS

The question of normalization is central to understanding the ever-shifting rationales and techniques of intervention in world politics. Existing accounts tend to approach normalcy as a desirable state of affairs linked to the concepts of peace, order, stability, and progress, regarding normalization as a gradual process of returning to an optimal condition of normalcy. When the international order is stable and operating according to a fixed set of principles and rules agreed by most, the configuration of world politics is understood as being "normal" or at least operating in a normal way. Any deviation to that perceived norm triggers reactions that involve labeling other states and actors as abnormal. That labeling further legitimizes various disciplinary and punitive measures, ranging from derogatory labeling to various forms of stigmatization, subjugation, examination, and subordination. Perceived deviation from a specific order of normalcy at the international level is handled through a wide range of measures, involving various actors, as well as the mobilization of different interventionary mechanisms and tools. Until now, the loose international architecture of normalization has been studied through the separate lenses of preventive diplomacy, sanctions, peacekeeping, conflict management, military and civilian interventions, peacebuilding, disaster relief, humanitarian assistance, and mechanisms of human rights protection. Looking at normalization efforts through those lenses fails to capture adequately the politics and analytics behind normalization in world politics. In particular, it remains puzzling how normalcy as a typical state of affairs is constructed in practice and then applied unevenly across different states and societies deemed abnormal. Moreover, we have limited understanding of the normalization technologies employed to impose, restore, or accept meanings of normalcy.

In our work, we seek to offer a rich account of normalization in world politics, not by putting forward a single and unified account of the normal, but through an analysis of the multiple meanings, complex attributes, and various features of normalization across different scholarly and policy debates. What constitutes normalcy is highly political and contested, subject to a multitude of discourses, practices, institutions, and relations propagated by state and non-state actors. We posit that discursive knowledge and practices of normalization go hand in hand, jointly constituting a social reality and the grounds for determining the techniques and the scope of interventions. Prior to examining the discourse–practice nexus of normalization intervention, it is important to highlight what we think foregrounds contemporary interventions. We posit that interventions are linked to a will to normalize other states, which is based on the assumption that for an international rules-based society to emerge and operate under certain common norms, regulations, and institutions, states have a responsibility to engage in normalizing other states—and sometimes themselves—and to ensure that perceived anomalies, deviancies, and misconduct are handled through various technologies of power and disciplinary mechanisms. Behind normalization interventions lies an assemblage of states, institutions, structures, and alliances governed by a set of evolving socio-legal, political-diplomatic, and military norms, standards, and practices that justify interventions not so much to protect the abnormal states but to maintain the normal and stable parts of the world. Notably, the quest for normalization among the intervening states originates from their ontological insecurity about anticipating, mitigating, and managing perceived risks to their norms and way of life as well as entrenched geopolitical, economic, and institutional privileges abroad. That origin raises an important question: are normalization interventions foregrounded on a region-specific meaning of what a normal state should look like, and if so, how possible and ethically viable is it to impose such an order of normalcy on other regions and parts of the world? This question is central to our analysis, as, in the present time, the dominant figure of normal state and infrastructure of political, normative, and social features of normalcy is the Western model of statehood associated with peace, stability, democracy, liberalism, human rights, and the market economy. Other states that do not fit that civilizational, ideological, and organizational model of political communities often risk being labeled as deviant, fragile, failed states and thus become subject to various normalization interventions.

The practices of normalization are embedded in the predicaments of transformative change, entailing the reorganization of systems of political authority and institutions, norm constitution, and social identities (see Adler 2019). At the same time, the purposes and technologies of normalization correspond to how abnormality is framed. Therefore, it is crucial to examine how the abnormalization of states is constructed and sustained through knowledge production in the form of reports, metrics, and statistical analysis, which categorizes state performance across different scales. As Nicholas Onuf (1989: 23) posits, "categories derive from a consideration of language as enabling people to perform social acts and achieve ends by making statements of assertion, direction, and commitment." Semantic categories are tied, in turn, to what Michael Barnett (2010: 11) calls "productive power," showing "how underlying discourses produce social kinds, make possible, imaginable, and desirable certain kinds of actions, and distribute unevenly social capacities to actors that are situated in distinct social positions." That uneven distribution is tied to international hierarchies, with more powerful actors contributing to shape "what is 'normal,' 'natural,' 'abnormal' or 'unthinkable'" (Suzuki 2017: 221). However, this process is not linked to one single, unified understanding of (ab)normalcy and (ab)normalization. Exploring the plurality of normalization practices opens up possibilities to research the different ways of seeing and acting in world politics, with a different graduation of normalization strategies as disciplinary techniques designed to respond to very specific sets of issues at hand for powerful actors. As the following analysis shows, the discursive knowledge of targeted states has a direct role in legitimizing particular forms of normalization. The intersection of both "worlds"—the policy and academic spheres—enables the constitution of the meanings of normalcy and normalization practices identified in this study. Thus, analyzing normalization in world politics as a spectrum of discourses and practices sheds light on the complex governmentality arrangement where dominant states mobilize different bodies of knowledge to portray specific situations or polities as abnormal and to enable different forms of interventions.

At the domestic level, normalization intends to create subjects with rights and obligations to obey the normal legal, political, social, cultural, and economic order. In the international context, the motives of normalization cannot be easily decoded. One way of making sense of the rationales for normalization is to trace their wider effects. The dynamics of state normalization undergo a process of intentional disempowerment by external actors to ensure their transformation and re-empowerment along new modes of state behavior, adopted norms, institutional structures, and codes of domestic and international conduct. Does the process of normalization in itself lay the foundations of protracted fragility and inability for progress, autonomy, and emancipation in states labeled as abnormal? The very process of normalizing others—which often requires an initial abnormalization of others—results in preserving and reproducing the intervener's normalcy, branding it as a universally exported mode of life, which, in turn, enhances the hierarchical status and improves its international moral, political, and military standing. Consequently, societies that undergo normalization interventions are entrapped into systems of prolonged external examination and imposition that take different institutional and knowledge configurations. Normalization through external interventions becomes ingrained in social and political institutions, whereby recipient societies should constantly be disciplined, constrained, and transformed from outside as well as through internalized cultures of self-normalization, self-transformation, and self-restraint. States subject to external normalization interventions thus develop a different form of knowledge about themselves as being less worthy than others, less autonomous and sovereign, or less equal.

Accordingly, problematizing normalization discourses and practices in world politics requires gathering multiple analytical tools as well as drawing on and challenging a broad range of scholarly knowledge. So far, scholarly debates in International Relations (IR) have discussed normalization almost in passing, with no systemic treatment of the theme (see Barston 2013; Wille 2013). We have rich accounts of different and case-specific interventions, but there is a lack of broader understanding of global dynamics of normalization interventions. In this book, we fill the gap by drawing on Michel Foucault's (2003) analytics of normalization (summarized in his lectures on the abnormal) to study contemporary interventions in world politics. While Foucault's work on normalization has been applied mostly to studies of disciplinary power at the domestic level (such as criminal justice, education, health care, and social life), it has insufficiently applied to international relations. Moreover, Foucault's work on governmentality, security, and biopolitics has had a profound influence on the scholarly debates in various IR fields, such as international organizations (Joseph 2012), human security and resilience (Duffield 2001; Jabri 2006; Joseph 2013), critical security studies (Dillon and Neal 2008; Peoples and Vaughan-Williams 2010; Aradau et al. 2014), and critical peace and conflict studies (Richmond 2010; Chandler and Richmond 2015). Foucault's critical analytics has contributed enormously to contemporary studies attempting to disentangle and problematize power, governance, institutions, agency, and resistance (Kiersey and Stokes 2011). That contribution notwithstanding, Foucault's work has been criticized for embedding elements of Eurocentrism and racism and for a disregard of the non-Western world (see Howell and Richter-Montpetit 2019; Lewis 2017; Visoka 2019). However, his work on normalization has had only a limited exposition in IR, with the exception of a number of limited studies that have applied it as an analytical framework for specific case studies (see Zanotti 2006, 2011).

Foucault's work on the technologies of governmentality provides valuable insights for conceptualizing different technologies of normalization in turbulent societies affected by and prone to conflicts and disasters. His conception of the technologies of sign systems and power captures how we use "signs, meanings, symbols, or significations" to justify particular types of normalization interventions, as well as to understand the conduct and submission of individuals "to certain ends or domination" (Foucault 1988b: 18). The knowledge production and practices of normalization operate on an optimization logic, whereby "the field is left open to fluctuating processes" (Foucault 2008: 259–60), which permits the selectivity of what states consider normal and abnormal in other societies. For Foucault, the concept of normalization represents the most "advanced" form of intervention in society by imposing precise norms without having to resort to punishment. As such, we agree with Onuf (2017: 26) that Foucault's "greatest contribution to social theory" is "his treatment of normality," especially his analysis of how disciplinary mechanisms relate to bodies of knowledge that produce standards of intelligibility.

Tracing normalization interventions necessitates identifying the disciplinary techniques and the modes of (ab)normalization through knowledge production and direct intervention in the internal affairs of targeted states. Foucault suggests three disciplinary technologies of power that result in a normalizing order. The first technology is hierarchical observations, where the examiner surveys and tracks the conduct of the subject in relation to the norm. The second disciplinary technique entails normalizing judgment, a process that seeks to use various putative and corrective measures to ensure conformity with the norm. The third technology is examination, which entails a ritualized process of visible observation of social practices, relations, and hierarchies and requires making judgments and differentiations between them. Those three technologies of power contribute to "sediment" norms to the point where they are uncritically accepted and thus become normalized. Beyond the "traditional" Foucauldian perspective, our work also contributes to the study of world politics by providing an innovative theorization of the social practices of normalization in world politics. We seek to offer a rich account of normalization in world politics, by not looking for or prioritizing a single and unified history and account of what is deemed "normal" but, rather, searching for the multiple meanings, complex attributes, and various features of normalization across different scholarly debates.

THE ARGUMENT

In this book, we explore how discourses and practices of normalization have emerged as an overarching rationale for optimizing international interventions. The optimization of interventions entails selective, uneven, and discordant responses to governing risk through different normalization analytics and technologies. Normalization has become a fluid rationale, a regime of truth, as well as a disciplinary technology to govern other states and societies through calculable and optimized techniques that maximize effects, minimize resistance, and enhance the hierarchical power of states without them bearing special responsibilities for the outcomes. Thus, we approach nor-

Table 1. An Outlook of Normalization Interventions in World Politics

State label	Category	Technology
Fragile states	Imposing normalcy	Liberal interventionism
Disaster-affected states	Restoring normalcy	Resilience and disaster management
Suppressive states	Accepting normalcy	Confessionary practices

malization in world politics as discursive practices and social interventions whose meaning and application is determined through different analytics and technologies of power. We argue that normalization interventions lie at the intersection between the technologies of domination of others and those of the self and that the interplay between the two enables different actors to create the subjects of interventions as well as to legitimize specific forms of international interventions. We organize our argument around three key conceptual components: (1) state labeling, (2) categories of normalization, and (3) technologies of normalization (see table 1).

The first component focuses on state labeling as the discursive basis for justifying different forms of normalization interventions. We argue that to understand the technologies of normalization, we must focus on the discourses that define the normal, exceptional, and abnormal and must trace different discursive regimes that make such "truth games" possible. The discursive regimes expressed in the form of metaphor that we use in this book derive from the figures of the "abnormal individuals" as analyzed in Foucault's (2003) lectures on the "Abnormal." The three figures of the abnormal—the monster, the incorrigible, and the onanist—are constructed through a distinct discursive framework and handled through distinct social, political, judicial, medical, and technocratic mechanisms constituting a continuum of normalization technologies. We mirror those figures of the abnormal with similar state labels in world politics. Failed states are linked to the figure of the "monster," defying the laws of nature and society. Disaster-prone states are linked to the figure of the "incorrigible," which is regular in its irregularities, but which the social institutions know how to discipline. Finally, we find parallels between suppressive states that are nevertheless part of the broad "international community" and the "onanist," which appears to be a universal individual that breaches social norms but, at the same time, is still accepted by all. Through these labels, we are able to explore how toponymies of statehood construct a discursive basis for advancing the normalization process. In particular, we analyze how labeling of other states as failed, disaster-prone, or suppressive permits the dominant states (mostly concentrated in the Western world) the right to intervene, tolerate, assist, and punish others. Though existing discourses of normalization in world politics differ from colonial incursions, occupations, and exploitations, they are still embedded in cultural imperialism when determining the original point and positionality of normalcy against which other targeted societies are examined. Resemblances of cultural imperialism are evident especially when non-Western historical conditions and understandings of normalcy are not regarded as sufficient for advancing justice, order, and peace in world politics.

Our argument's second conceptual component focuses on three categories of normalization—imposing, restoring, and accepting normalcy—which correspond to the three state figures labeled and outlined above. We argue that the contemporary technologies of normalization involve imposing normalcy over failed or fragile states to tame their illiberal monstrosity, restoring normalcy over disaster-prone states to manage their incorrigibility, and, finally, accepting the normalcy of suppressive states to strategically forge self-normalization, recognize alterity, and cope with difference. Contemporary normalization interventions are characterized by the deployment of optimal disciplinary technologies for reconfiguring other states along three trajectories: mirroring the self through imposing normalcy, balancing the self and the other through restoring normalcy, and maintaining difference through accepting normalcy. In the following chapters, we link each normalization category with its own technology of intervention and with specific transformative aims. Societies that are labeled as monstrous and unable to self-normalize are subject to external intervention. Imposing a new normalcy over failed states aims to socially transform them into well-behaved actors in world politics through peacebuilding, statebuilding, and social reconstruction. Restoring normalcy aims to improve resilience capabilities of disaster-prone states while bringing back normalcy or "bouncing forward" to a more sustainable normal through assistance in disaster management. Finally, accepting normalcy of suppressive states operates through confessional narratives and the politics of alliance, accepting irregularities as constitutive of the world order.

When discussing the imposition of a new normalcy, we focus on contemporary examples and cases of international interventions aimed at resolving conflicts, building peace, and reconstructing political order and state institutions in societies that are labeled as fragile or failed states. Although that specific area has been widely studied, our engagement with it is crucial to reconceptualize international interventions from the view of disciplinary normalization efforts. Failed states in world politics have been labeled as extreme abnormal subjects that not only fail to respect international norms and rules but also challenge core values of humanity. Countries such as Somalia, Bosnia and Herzegovina, Kosovo, Timor-Leste, Afghanistan, and Iraq are taken as illustrative cases of imposing normalcy, which takes place through hybrid forms of intervention, mixing elements of enforcement through international military and policing deployment, as well as through complex missions in peacebuilding, statebuilding, and social reconstruction. While normalization technologies in fragile and conflict-affected states operate through the politics of care and choice, they set a state of dependency where external normalizers transfer their exceptional rights, knowledge, power, and material means to local subjects in order to normalize those subjects into new norms, codes of practice, and organizational cultures. Normalization works through the progressive disempowerment of local subjects voluntarily accepting external norms, rules, and cultures of governance. Imposed normalcy thus represents some of the most intrusive forms of disciplining political subjectivities and creates new political orders in conflict-affected societies.

In exploring instances for restoring normalcy, we focus on a number of contemporary examples and cases of states and societies affected by disasters and other humanitarian emergencies, such as Typhoon Haiyan in the Philippines, Hurricane Katrina in the United States, and the 2010 earthquake in Haiti. The conditions underpinning disasters and other humanitarian crises have come to be seen as incorrigible and thus subject to containment and management rather than to profound correction and transformation. In this cluster of interventionary practices, normalcy is understood as a willingness of disaster-affected societies to return to antebellum social, political, and economic conditions and is linked simultaneously to local and international perceptions of what constitutes "stability" in a disaster-affected context. The narrative of resilience is mobilized to normalize a permanent state of crisis and instability where the affected subjects should learn to live vulnerably and cope with anticipated and permanent crises. In such instances, instability is not viewed as necessarily abnormal, and disasters are seen not as deviations of the normal state of affairs but, rather, as inherently constitutive of the reality many underdeveloped countries face on an everyday level. Consequently, interventions are not confined to exceptional situations but acknowledge the continuities and discontinuities between crisis and normalcy. We argue that the narrative of resiliency and the back-and-forth logic of normalization is a gradual withdrawal symptom from the liberal aspirational politics of global progress and positive transformation of the human condition, preserving the old, fluid interventionary practices without the burden of local acceptance and global legitimacy.

Finally, we explore how a strand of states who are widely labeled as suppressive and authoritarian toward their own populations continue to be accepted as normal regardless of such perceived abnormal features. We find that although suppressive states possess the conditions of the previous two types of state labeling, they are spared normalization interventions, due to an interplay of the politics of alliances and confessionary politics within multilateral organizations. In tracing the discourses and technologies of accepting the normalcy of suppressive states, we look at three contemporary cases that are implicated in serious human rights abuses but have avoided external intervention: Israel, Bahrain, and Myanmar. In each case, we find that these and like-minded states are part of wider political alliances and have a special relationship with dominant states who protect them regardless of their abuse of international norms and rules. We look at how the discourses of noninterference, pluralism, and coexistence with difference are mobilized to provide space to suppressive states to preempt intervention and permit minor self-normalization through truth-telling and confession mechanisms delivered within international multilateral bodies or through special commissions of inquiry. In those instances, accepting the normalcy of suppressive states enables the dominant states to strengthen their pastoral role and expands the leverage of the targeted states. Acceptance of suppressive states achieves maximum effect (namely, pursuing the globalization of a regional-specific normalcy through toleration of difference and illiberalism as pull factors for self-transformation along liberal norms and values) and permits those states membership in the society of states, where they can pursue normalization through international mechanisms. The practice of accepting normalcy also represents a pragmatic response to the power of dominant states fading away in a transitional international order where alternative norms and conditions of non-Western normalcy are emerging.

By showing how normalization discourses and practices emerge and unfold in each set of cases examined in this book, we seek to problematize both academic and policy-based boundary-making logics surrounding different categories of turbulent states that are treated unevenly and exposed to different regimes and techniques of normalization. The art of what is politically possible underlines the choice of optimal intervention, be that to impose an external order of normalcy, restore the previous order of normalcy, or accept the existing order of normalcy. In the age of normalization, strong and sovereign states are seen as problematic, as they challenge dominant powers and thus are capable of resisting external norms and rules. Perceived as a condition of strength, sovereignty becomes a weakness that can mobilize some states to abnormalize others, discursively and through other diplomatic and coercive methods. In turn, abnormalization enables normalization interventions. An iterative process prolongs the condition of abnormalcy, because the less sovereign a state is, the more likely it is to be disrespected and abnormalized by other states and hence to become the subject of external intervention. The global disciplining structures seek to discipline states, optimize their capabilities for self-reliance, tame their sovereignty, increase their usefulness and docility, and integrate them into the neoliberal economic system. Our work highlights some of the contemporary analytics of power, particularly the efforts of dominant states to create a society of docile states who are passive yet productive, disciplined, and open to external examination, regulation, punitive measures, transformation, and norm taking.

Moreover, by looking at the discourses and practices of normalization, we are able to reflect on the broader dynamics of international politics. Our analysis shows that the international community is bonded together by its quest to safeguard its normalcy while simultaneously seeking to expand its influence by imposing on others the rules, institutions, and values that ensure the retention of its privileged status. Most interactions between states and other transnational actors are about maintaining optimization of a particular normative order, with various other underlying geopolitical, economic, and personal intentions. In that context, the abnormalization of certain states by labeling them as conflict-affected, disaster-prone, or suppressive contributes to the (re)constitution of hierarchies of norms, power, and relations between states. In particular, the politics of normalcy has strong implications for generating different hierarchies of authority and power, where difference, pluralism, and nonconformity are considered pariah-like and delegitimized in some cases but accepted as normal in others. By default, those who label other states as normal and intervene to impose, restore, or tame a specific version of normalcy reproduce their own identity and position themselves as normal and responsible states with much wider entitlements and ordering capacity than other states. Dominant powers often exempt themselves from normalization regimes. There is a growing consensus that the international liberal order is gradually on the way out, with powerful actors displaying less appetite for the ambitious international interventions characterizing the

1990s and early 2000s. While we agree that, generally speaking, the liberal international order is waning, we argue that we should take a wider view of interventionary dynamics and not simply focus on broad military interventions. The process of normalization is not imposed through military and coercive methods (although they have been used in some specific circumstances); rather, the process works through a complex technology of incentives and conditions and through observation, judgment, examination, and supervision, which make local societies dependent and docile toward external forces. As the following analysis shows, normalization interventions represent fluid, remote, and ambiguous forms of social interventions in world politics, which simultaneously combine forms of ad hoc military intervention with deep state and society transformation. Normalization can be seen as the dominant states' attempt to retain their global status and relevance at a time when the liberal international order is unraveling.

By offering a Foucauldian reading of normalization practices in world politics, our study complements and challenges a number of assumptions and scholarly knowledge about international interventions, statebuilding and peacebuilding, resilience and disaster management, as well as multilateralism, human rights protection, and political alliances. For instance, our analysis problematizes different nuanced approaches to normative order in world politics, from the most obvious interventionary and imposing nature of norm-building and norm-diffusion arguments to more encoded normative takes on norm localization, translation, and contestation. In our reading, those different theoretical strands are part of a sophisticated epistemological technology of normalization, which ultimately seeks to impose norms with or without the consent of the affected subjects or through disciplinary power and democratic deliberations. Existing accounts recognize the two-way process of normalization but do not engage sufficiently with the power-ridden intentions behind norm promotion, which is more of a disciplinary and governing regime than an expansion of normative sameness around the world.

Discourses on normalization are products of the knowledge production industry, such as policy think tanks and other research institutes whose function is to produce indexes, annual reports, and gradings of state performance on specific norms, themes, or issues. Throughout our analysis, we problematize the role of those measurements that have direct implications for the normalization of certain states and, by default, the abnormalization of other states. That knowledge is often portrayed as being objective, scientific, and impartial. Examining how it informs and justifies various technologies of intervention clarifies, however, that such knowledge seeks to globalize and impose a region-specific version of normalcy at the expense of sidelining and delegitimizing alternative ways of knowing, being, and acting in the world. Therefore, it is crucial to question the ethics and expose the power and implications of knowledge production in shaping international interventions.

Our analysis complements existing critical perspectives on peacebuilding and statebuilding, as our findings demonstrate the double effects of imposed normalcy and the limits of top-down approaches. Further, our analysis offers new insights into peace and conflict studies, by problematizing the role of bottom-up approaches to peacebuilding and state formation. It highlights how local ownership and agency of reconstruction processes and civil society movements, along with the alternative metrics and analytics for knowing and building peace, are co-opted by an external intervener's quest to implant a self-sustaining politics of "care of the self" while retaining privileged access for external examination, regulation, and intervention. In relation to discourses and scholarly work on disaster management and resilience, our analysis situates their debates in a wider web of interventionism, highlighting their function in justifying and enabling fluid interventions in world politics. Finally, our analysis exposes the dark side of multilateral organizations and political alliances, as pastoral spaces where suppressive states retain or reaffirm their international normalcy through confessionary practices and are enabled to retain their acceptability through the promotion of strategic narratives and alternative truths. We demonstrate the politicization and cooptation of human rights mechanisms for selectively determining the normalcy of states, often to the detriment of the facts on the ground.

There are some potential objections to this analysis of international interventions. Some could say that it dilutes the study of international interventions in world politics, broadening the concept to the limit of its usefulness. Others might perceive our analysis as ahistorical. We claim, however, that interventions are an integral feature of world politics and that focusing solely on one form of intervention, no matter how prominent it is, obscures how powerful actors operate in world politics, mobilizing different bodies of knowledge to legitimize a register of actions. Military interventions clearly shape world politics, and we do not claim that we should not carefully analyze them. Chapter 3 carefully disentangles the logics of liberal interventionism in world politics through a study of imposing normalcy practices. But our analysis ties normalization practices operating in high-profile, top-down interventions with other forms of normalization practices operating in different yet complementary registers—resilience building (restoring normalcy) and confessionary politics (accepting normalcy). As we have focused only on external aspects of normalization (largely because domestic normalization technologies have already been covered), there is scope for future research to expand the analysis to look at national and local dynamics of normalization. In particular, a significant and clearly traceable endogenous quest for self-normalization through external intervention has not been covered in this book.

We have focused mostly on describing various techniques of normalization in world politics. That our analysis does not examine how the targeted societies respond to external tendencies for imposing, restoring, or accepting normalcy could create the impression that, much as the literature on socialization to international norms depicts, normalization occurs along a one-way process of normalization, from the normalizer to the normalized. Our focus only on international and transnational dynamics of normalization interventions could form the impression that elites or local subjects in conflict-affected and disaster-prone societies lack power, agency, and sovereign capacities. As we have shown in our other work (Lemay-Hébert 2011; Lemay-Hébert and Visoka 2017; Visoka 2016), local dynamics and agency are central to the success or failure of international interventions. There is also a solid basis for looking at the constitution and contestation of normalization practices, which offers a more nuanced reading of the transactional nature of normative contestation in world politics. That the analysis in this book problematizes and criticizes international practices of normalization might create the impression that we have endorsed anti-liberal norms or, at best, were unable to develop an explicit articulation of our normative positionality. Certainly, adopting a Foucauldian outlook of normalization discourses and practices can lead to normative confusion. Moreover, as we have not looked at the internal dynamics of normalization, there is scope to perceive our analysis as partial or too critical of Western states. There is further scope to explore the normalization visions and practices of emerging and peripheral powers. In particular, there is scope to look further at the Chinese ideology and vision of harmony and harmonization.

THE OUTLINE

This book consists of six chapters. In chapters 2–5, we establish the theoretical framework and then separately analyze three clusters of normalization discourses and practices in world politics. Chapter 2 represents the theoretical backbone of the project. In the chapter's first section, we analyze how normalization is conceived of in social and political theory. In particular, we explore Foucault's seminal work on normalization, to develop the conceptual contours for studying normalization in world politics. We focus on how the three figures of the abnormal mobilize different analytics and technologies of normalization. In the second section of the chapter, we map out the conceptual contours of our study. Each figure is associated with a specific type of state in world politics (fragile or failed, disaster-affected, and suppressive), a category of normalization (imposition, restoration, and acceptance), and a normalization technology (liberal interventionism, disaster management, and confessionary practices). Finally, chapter 2 outlines the methodological aspects of this study, elaborating on the suitability of the method of problematization and discourse analysis.

Chapter 3 explores the normalcy externally imposed on societies in a wide range of conflict-affected and fragile states. The chapter's first section examines the historical, normative, and political features of the discourse of failed states as monsters in world politics. It explores how knowledge production mobilizes and justifies a distinct set of practices and techniques of normalization. The second section looks at the normative and organizational features of liberal interventionism as an ideology for imposing normalcy in failed states. The third section focuses on peacebuilding and statebuilding interventions, looking at the top-down and bottom-up features of imposed normalcy in cases such as Somalia, Kosovo, Bosnia and Herzegovina, Timor-Leste, Afghanistan, and Iraq. Chapter 3 illustrates the most radical forms of imposed normalcy in the contemporary world, through a complex set of discourses and technologies of intervention employed to tame failed states and turn them into docile subjects. In addition to describing and cataloging different discourses and practices of normalization, chapter 3 offers critical observations on the inconsistencies and limits of the efforts to impose normalcy and on the wider implications for both intervening and targeted states.

Chapter 4 explores a set of discourses and practices of normalization labeled here as "restoring normalcy," which aim to facilitate the return to conditions before the eruption of a crisis—namely, to a situation deemed normal and acceptable for international and local actors. The chapter's first two sections look at the discursive features associated with disaster-affected societies, exploring how knowledge about disaster management, complexity, and resilience presupposes the incorrigibility of affected states mobilizing distinct techniques for restoring the conditions of relative normalization that partially resemble the pre-crisis and post-crisis features of good-enough normalcy. The third section considers three separate disasters (Typhoon Haiyan in the Philippines, Hurricane Katrina in the United States, and the 2010 earthquake in Haiti) and discusses how the discourses and techniques for restoring normalcy unravel in practice. Chapter 4 concludes by discussing the promise, significance, and wider implications of the politics of crisis containment and optimization of interventions.

Chapter 5 looks at a set of discourses and practices that revolve around accepting normalcy of states that are labeled as suppressive and in breach of human rights norms. The chapter's first section looks at the politics of state acceptability in world politics, focusing on both the normative aspects and the political manifestations. The analysis looks at the narrative on noninterference, pluralism, and respect for difference in IR as manifested in practice through strategic narratives, state alliances and friendships, and the acceptance of normalcy by confessionary regimes. The second section delves deeper into the politics of state confession and truth-telling as a confessionary space to forge its version of normalcy and prevent external intervention. It looks at the universal periodic review of human rights compliance of suppressive states, such as Israel, and the role that international multilateral regimes play in promoting liberal norms, human rights, and values, as well as whitewashing abuses and permitting normative discord among member states. The third section looks at other instances of accepting normalcy of states, through commissions of inquiry and fact-finding missions that enable suppressive states great scope for claiming self-normalization and the politics of the care of the self to avoid external impositions. It looks at the role of such bodies in challenging and accepting the normalcy of suppressive states such as Bahrain and Myanmar without challenging their international standing. Through these examples, chapter 5 seeks to problematize the discourse and practices of accepting normalcies, questioning if acceptance signifies the optimization of interventions in such a way that the "abnormal" state of affairs is accepted and legitimized internationally when imposing or restoring normalcy is not possible.

Finally, in chapter 6, we discuss the broad implications of our argument and findings. We look at elements of continuity and change in world politics, analyzing how "traditional" interventionary dynamics meet newer forms (and discourses) of interventions. Concepts of normalcy and normalization defy conventional siloing and ask for a broader understanding of interventionary dynamics. The three clusters of normalization practices—imposed, restored, and accepted normalcy—have distinct logics but, at the same time, reflect a spectrum of possibilities for powerful states. The optimization of international strategies dictates which body of knowledge is being mobilized to respond to a specific call for normalization. We conclude this book's discussion with a number of insights about the prospects for creating a society of docile states that would be subject to both self-normalization and external intervention.

2 ✦ Mapping Normalization in World Politics

The concept of the normal, the state of normalcy, and the process of normalization are central to making sense of contemporary societies. Normalcy is a polymorphous concept. It has been variously defined in different disciplines, making the notion essentially contested and contingent on semantic interpretations (Davis 1995). As discussed in the introduction of this book, normalcy denotes a specific condition of being, which is closely linked to conformity to specific norms and codes of conduct, whereas normalization entails the process of imposing, creating, restoring, maintaining, or accepting a specific order of normalcy. Evoking a pluriversal engagement with social reality, normalcy simultaneously describes and prescribes a specific state of social affairs. The concept of normalcy plays a central role in understanding social and legal norms and discourses, political power, order and authority, agency, structure, institutions, and social transformation. A broad review of different social science disciplines shows that what is normal is contingent on relational perspectives; therefore, there is no single definition, meaning, and truth about normalcy, and this book does not pretend to offer one. Presenting an overview of how normalization is conceived in social and political theory, this chapter particularly employs Michel Foucault's seminal work on normalization, to develop the conceptual contours for studying normalization in world politics. By default, the very process of defining what is normal is complicit in producing new subjectivities and, in the process, marginalizing other actors and processes. Yet we argue that exploring normalization practices sheds light on competing rationales and technologies that impose certain ways of seeing and acting in the world.

In this chapter's first section, we examine the sociological and political meaning of the concept of normalcy. To develop a more critical take on normalcy in world politics, we focus on Foucault's analytics of normalization. Foucault's concept of normalization is a central feature of his critical theory of sociopolitical power as well as technologies of discipline and control. He offers reflexive grounds for making sense of the disciplinary power of norms, standards, and rules in shaping social conduct and the organization of collective institutors and structures of governmentality. He regards normalization as the most advanced form of governance, where the subject serves as the enforcer of its own conduct without needing additional external intervention. Foucault places the practices of social exclusion—namely, abnormalization—at the heart of defining the normal. He categorizes the figure of the abnormal along three graduations, according to which the monster, the most extreme example of abnormality, is followed by the incorrigible and, finally, the onanist, the most common form of abnormalcy in society. Additionally, Foucault maps out the discourses and techniques of normalization along three disciplinary mechanisms: hierarchical observation, normalizing judgment, and examination. While Foucault's work on normalization offers the richest critique of that concept to date, it has not been examined sufficiently in international relations. We know a great deal more about intrastate normalization than we know about international or interstate normalization.

In the second section of this chapter, we propose mapping normalization in world politics according to a framework mirroring Foucault's thoughts on the abnormal and normalization. We argue that exploring normalization in world politics requires tracing dominant discourses and practices that are implicated in labeling states along different gradations of normalcy, justificatory discourses, and the disciplinary techniques for interventions aiming to impose, restore, or accept normalcy of states under scrutiny. By looking at different normalizing interventions and the discourses, ethics, institutions, and mechanisms that enable them, we can see how the international system operates, how inequality and hierarchies unfold, and how power structures are disguised and optimized. This chapter concludes with a note on the methodological orientation of this study.

FOUCAULT AND DISCIPLINARY NORMALIZATION

Western sociology associated with positivism has played a major role in constructing knowledge about the normal and abnormal phenomena in order to serve governments with tangible knowledge for sociopolitical intervention (see Misztal 2015). The sociology is rooted in Auguste Comte's positivism, aiming to identify the "normal state" from the pathological, finding the one, true type of society that is deemed valid. That understanding of normality has deeply influenced a generation of scholars, including Émile Durkheim. For Durkheim (1982: 104), the duty of statesmen is to "work steadily and persistently to maintain the normal state, to re-establish it if it is disturbed, and to rediscover the conditions of normality if they happen to change." In positivist sociology, the normal took central primacy, pathological conditions were seen as a deviation from the normal, and interventionary socioeconomic and medical measures were seen as curation and return to normalcy (see Hacking 1990).

In sociology, normalcy represents a central objective for explaining how we generate knowledge about how societies should function (Misztal 2015). In most of its invocations, the normal is associated with "the common, the ordinary, the usual, the standard, the conventional, the regular" (Cryle and Stephens 2017: 1), which holds the key for explaining social order and continuity, as well as social acceptance and recognition. For symbolic interactionists, for whose movement Erving Goffman (1983) served as figurehead, normality is about predictable and ordinary social interactions that give society a sense of safety and stability. As Barbara Misztal (2001: 313) shows, "sociologists tend to identify the normal with the present, average, or factual state, on the one hand, and with a desirable state, on the other." As such, the normal becomes synonymous simultaneously with conformity to a standard as well as exemplarity (Cryle and Stephens 2017: 1). Moreover, normalization is not entirely about government intervention and control; rather, social interactions and conformity, as bottom-up processes, have a much stronger normalizing power (see Misztal 2015: 56). While sociological perspectives offer important insights for understanding the social and political functions of normalcy, they tend to overwhelmingly adopt an uncritical and unproblematic view of those concepts.

There is a plethora of alternative social and political theories that engage more critically with the question of the normal and normalization practices. Recently, critical scholars have challenged classical securitization studies (or the Copenhagen school) by noting the skewed notion of "normal politics" in key foundational texts (Howell and Richter-Montpetit 2019: 7), a claim that has been challenged by the key scholars behind the Copenhagen school (Wæver and Buzan 2020: 27–30). Feminist analysis and praxis question and interrogate the socially and bodily constructed normalcy of heteropatriarchy, racialized and gendered inequalities, family structures, and labor relations (see Spade and Willse 2016; Sandoval 2000). The work of Judith Butler (1990) clearly shows how norms come into being, are normalized and internalized through performative actions and constructed narratives and forcible citation of norms, and are enforced through social disciplinary regimes and punishment. Similarly, critical race studies (CRS) examine how racial groups are categorized into hierarchies of privilege and exclusion (see Delgado and Stefancic 2013). Normalized racial inequalities are seen as regimes of injustice and sources of social discrimination. Those that hold privileges define the norm, and others outside that racialized privileges are seen as abnormal. In that regard, the function of CRS is to problematize normalized racial norms, oppose oppressive practices, and promote racial justice. Similarly, disabilities studies have widely engaged with the social construction and enforcement of normalcy, particularly questioning how the human body and physical (dis)abilities are subject to categorization, judgment, and intervention (see Davis 1995). The biopolitics of life, bodily shape, and social ability are ranked through different scales that become productive of social norms and thus constitutive of what is labeled as normal and abnormal. While we draw on those critical social and political theories when accounting for normalization discourses and practices in world politics, we use Michel Foucault's rich analytical repertoire as the main conceptual guideline. Foucault's analytics have informed many of those critical social and political theories on the dynamics of governmentality, biopolitics, disciplinary normalization, and resistance to repressive practices (see Goldberg 2001).

We argue that Foucault's critical account of the historicity of normalization practices offers a unique take on the external dimensions of normalization through the prism of different disciplinary technologies of knowledge and practice, which will help develop a more cohesive conceptual framework for analyzing normalization in world politics. While IR and peace and conflict studies have extensively applied Foucault's work on governmentality and biopolitics (see Kiersey and Stokes 2011), they have examined his work on normalization only indirectly, as a by-product of those related concepts. Yet, as Jon Simons (2013: 311) holds, "given its broader framing of political technology, many of the power relations reviewed . . . under the rubric of discipline, normalization, and biopower can also be analyzed in terms of 'governmentality.'" Most important, Foucault's work on normalization deserves more attention precisely because, as Cressida Heyes (2007: 16) argues, it "offers a more complex account of normalization, as a set of mechanisms for sorting, taxonomizing, measuring, managing, and controlling populations, which both fosters conformity and generates modes of individuality." Foucault's take on normalization is crucial for understanding not only the micropolitics of power but also the standards and the structure of social meaning and emergent ethics that underpin such an order (Taylor 2011a). For Foucault, normalization emerged as a hidden governance of social relations in the wake of modernity and the perceived necessity for governing all aspects of society. Defining normalization as "a system of finely gradated and measurable intervals in which individuals can be distributed around a norm—a norm which both organizes and is the result of this controlled distribution," Foucault adds that "a system of normalization is opposed to a system of law or a system of personal power" (Rabinow 1984b: 20). Normalization represents the final stage in the institutionalization of the norm and what counts as normal as a derivative of that disciplinary and judicial-epistemic process. Reaching normalcy through normalization technologies requires the creation and classification of anomalies and deviations, isolating them through corrective or therapeutic interventions.

One of the central theoretical contributions of Foucault is the usage of power for normalizing certain discourses and practices through a disciplinary technology (Paternek 1987). For Foucault, discipline, biopower, and normalization are the key forms of power that help us understand governmentality mechanisms (Simons 2013: 307). Foucault defines the technologies of power both as "a form of social and political control that should be subject to critique" and as "a solution to a number of previously unacknowledged limitations in understanding power relations" (Behrent 2013: 56). In short, technology is a term intended to describe power relations and interventionary practices that seek to shape conduct and produce certain effects while averting others. Disciplinary power often takes the shape of pastoral power, which is concerned with ensuring, sustaining, and caring for the lives of individuals and their obedient conduct. Foucault held that the idea of normalization, to impose norms without having to resort to punishment, represents the most advanced form of interventionism in society. The purpose of disciplinary technology is to ensure the compliance of society with certain norms, where punishment is hidden in the institutional mechanisms of governance. Disciplinary normalization does not openly exclude or repress subjects. Foucault (1991: 194) states, "It produces reality; it produces domains of objects and rituals of truth. The individual and the knowledge that may be gained of him belong to this production." The origins of normalization lie within the management of social knowledge organized around norms and the process of normation. Foucault (2007: 85) argues,

> Disciplinary normalization consists first of all in positing a model, an optimal model that is constructed in terms of a certain result, and the operation of disciplinary normalization consists in trying to get people, movements, and actions to conform to this model, the normal being precisely that which can conform to this norm, and the abnormal that which is incapable of conforming to the norm.

Thus, disciplinary normalization undertaken in the name of promoting sameness reveals power dynamics and the constitution of exceptions. Who decides on the normal stands out as the exception, which is entitled to suspend the rule itself (see Schmitt 1985: 13). As Giorgio Agamben (1998: 18, 19) put it, "the sovereign decision of the exception is the originary juridico-political structure on the basis of which what is included in the juridical order and what is excluded from it acquire their meaning."

Normalcy can have both descriptive and prescriptive functions. It can describe observable material and social facts while also prescribing specific qualities attributed to them. In that sense, normalcy entails repeatability—the predictable reoccurrence of events and situations—and even projected and anticipated social behaviors and attitudes (Titchkosky 2015). The repeatability of normalcy concerns the expectation of how a state and society ought to be ordered (Yalcin 2016). Social disciplinary mechanisms of normalization also involve social expectations, of how we and others ought to behave. For instance, Norbert Elias situates normalization in the context of civilizing processes, involving "a change in the balance between external constraints, constraints by other people and self-constraints, the balance tilting towards the latter in the control of behavior in the average person" (Mennell 2001: 37). However, for Foucault, the norms outlining the prescriptive social behavior are central to the construction of the normal and abnormal practices in society and set the contours of the disciplinary normalization. The norm depicts and ascribes a particular standard of behavior and conduct that establishes the contours of the normal and abnormal. Social, political, and legal norms tend to set the "dispositives, procedures, discourses and institutions, through which 'normalities' are produced and reproduced in modern societies" (Misztal 2015: 72).

Normalizing disciplinary techniques are enabled by the knowledge production on social conditions and the position of norms, which measures social behavior according to the standards and indicators of normalcy (see McWhorter 2014). Diana Taylor (2014: 4; Oksala 2011: 89) adds that "techniques of normalization enforce normality by reproducing particular social norms (and thereby reinforcing the idea of normality more generally) to the point that they come to be seen not as produced at all but simply as natural and necessary." When norms become sedimented to the point where they are uncritically accepted in this manner, they can be said to be "normalizing." As Foucault (2003: 50) argues, "the norm is not simply and not even a principle of intelligibility; it is an element on the basis of which a certain exercise of power is founded and legitimized." The norms ground the governance of others and self-governance through controlling the compliance of the others and the self in relation to the norm. A norm reaches the level of normalization when it is perceived as an inherent human behavior, "not only as natural but also as 'normal' and, therefore, as desirable" (Taylor 2013: 404). Thus, the power of normalization lies in its ability to decrease its external enforcement while legitimizing internal self-enforcement.

Ingrained in the process of normalization is gradeability, the characterization of an entity in terms of degrees along a scale. Hence, as Bear and Knobe (2016: 1) explain, "when people are trying to determine whether a given thing is normal or abnormal, they will take into account both information about whether it is statistically average and information about whether it is prescriptively ideal." The average is considered as the middle ground, the normal distribution, which is taken, in turn, as the ideal indicator prescribing normalcy. Normalization is about balancing between social extremes and perceived discrepancies. It is thus concomitant with the production of norms, standards for measurement and comparison, and rules of judgment (Ewald 1990: 148), as well as with pursuing typical social behaviors and seeking to preserve them (Garfinkel 1964: 188). Mary Beth Mader (2007: 6) similarly argues, "The uniqueness of normalization, as opposed to prior exclusive forms of power, is that it controls precisely by qualifying, but by qualifying bodies with quantifiable qualities. By endowing bodies with measurable features, it installs the conceptual basis for their control and management." Statistical measurements not only seek to describe a social reality—which is dependent on the onto-politics of concepts, approaches, and measurements devised to construct such a reality—but also ascribe corrective and prescribing power on social and political behavior, including disciplining subjects and pushing them into the conventional zones of normalcy. Normalizing practices seek to govern society through comparing between different units to differentiate social practices and to privilege specific practices while marginalizing others, setting, in the process, new power structures and societal hierarchies (see Young 1990).

For Foucault, disciplinary power is not necessarily repressive or prohibitive. Rather, it asserts influence through cultural, normative, and scientific discourses that determine the normal and abnormal state of affairs. Power "adapts and creates new strategies, tactics, and technologies to ensure its continued existence" (Havis 2014: 118). As Alan Sheridan (2005: 150) argues, discipline "makes" individuals (see also McGushin 2011: 133). Power is seldom triumphant and is, more accurately, "modest, suspicious, calculating" (Sheridan 2005: 150). The disciplinary process takes place through three distinct technologies of power. The first disciplinary technique is hierarchical observation, where the examiner surveys and tracks the conduct of the subject in relation to the norm. "Those who comply with the norm," notes Devonya N. Havis (2014: 114), "are rewarded and given a higher status within the hierarchy, whereas those who do not receive further training and discipline." The instruments of hierarchical observations entail redesigning the material properties of social activities as well as social tasks and roles in enforcing particular norms. Hierarchical observation consists of external surveillance and integrated self-monitoring of performance. As Karen Vintges (2011: 101) argues, "the idea that reason makes self-control possible leads to the application of disciplinary techniques not only by institutions, but also by individuals themselves, as a means of gaining such control." In this way, an internal "core self" is established, and the autonomous subject is born. For Foucault (1991: 177), this type of self-policing "enables the disciplinary power to be both absolutely indiscreet, since it is everywhere and always alert, since by its very principle it leaves no zone of shade and constantly supervises the very individuals who are entrusted with the task of supervising and absolutely 'discreet,' for it functions permanently and largely in silence."

The second disciplinary technique entails normalizing judgment, a process that seeks to use various putative and corrective measures to ensure conformity with the norm. It involves using judicial mechanisms as well as capacity-building and training institutions, to narrow the gap between the actual social conduct and the prescribed norm or perceived normal. In essence, the normalizing judgment combines both punishment and correction. For Foucault (1991: 180), "to punish is to exercise," and to exercise and be trained simultaneously is a form of punishment that requires social and material alternation. Judgment names and shames those who fail to reach the target, labels them as abnormal, and imposes additional disciplinary measures and conditions. In a normalizing society, all subjects are judges and law enforcers of one another. Central to normalizing judgment is comparison, a specific form of establishing what is normal through looking at the differences between subjects, practices, and relations. Richard Lynch (2016: 104) shows that normalization functions in two directions: "It pressures each individual to be just like everyone else—to be more like the norm—and it brings greater specificity and attention to each individual, by locating that individual within the grids of observation and evaluation." As part of normalizing judgment, gratification and reward are integral to the enforcement of the norm and the particular normalization order. The enforcement process leads to different hierarchies and distributes subjects in scalar fields. The actions of individuals are ranked on a scale that compares them to everyone else (Gutting 2005: 84). Through the continuous assessment of each individual, "discipline exercises a normalizing judgment" (Sheridan 2005: 152). That discipline does not necessarily have a negative implication, as the function of normalization is to increase the efficiency of subjects so that they become the performers and enforcers of the norms inscribed by the government and other societal structures. Taylor (2011b: 173) argues that "there are not emancipatory institutions and norms that enable us, on the one hand, and oppressive or normalizing institutions and norms that constrain us, on the other; rather, we are simultaneously enabled and constrained by the same institutions and norms." Yet Gutting (2005: 84) observes, "Normalizing judgment is a peculiarly pervasive means of control. There is no escaping it because, for virtually any level of achievement, the scale shows that there is an even higher level possible."

The third disciplinary technique in service of normalization is what Foucault calls the examination, which entails a ritualized process of visible observation of social practices, relations, and hierarchies, then making judgments and differentiations between them. Foucault (1991: 184) holds, "The examination combines the techniques of an observing hierarchy and those of a normalizing judgement. It is a normalizing gaze, a surveillance that makes it possible to qualify, to classify and to punish. It establishes over individuals a visibility through which one differentiates them and judges them." By nature, examination makes individuals, societies, and states into cases that are "described, judged, measured, compared with others," and, ultimately, "trained or corrected, classified, normalized, excluded" (Rabinow 1984a: 203). The product of the examination process is a specific type of knowledge describability, which functions as a mode of disciplinary normalization: "It is the examination which, by combining hierarchical surveillance and normalizing judgment, assures the great disciplinary functions of distribution and classification" (Rabinow 1984a: 204). According to Foucault, once a specific degree of normalcy is established, the supervision process takes place through a judicial, legal, and "scientific" process (Rabinow 1984a: 237). For Foucault, normalization works through the mechanisms of communication and interaction. Only through that iterative process, for instance, are certain types of knowledge accepted by others, internalized, and hence normalized on a wide societal scale. Knowledge dissemination and persuasion are crucial for adaptation and internalization of knowledge. For normalization to take place, the knowledge needs to be disseminated in a particular fashion accepted by the targeted subjects and almost seen to be coming from within their own social cast. The discourse of statistics serves as a regulatory mechanism that does not target specific individuals but addresses the wider population.

Foucault's three disciplinary techniques result in a circular normalizing order (Havis 2014: 113), sedimenting norms to the point that they become uncritically accepted and "normalized" (Taylor 2014: 4). While norms and disciplinary practices normalize subjects, the altered individuals can shape norms and shift the meaning and form of normalcy. That self-enforcement of normalcy, enabled by circularity, operates as follows: "the norm gener-ates the concept of the normal, which in turn generates techniques that, by way of promoting conformity with, reproducing, and thus presenting as ineluctable particular social norms, reasserts the significance of normality" (Taylor 2014: 4). Similarly, the concept of abnormality is facilitated by the circulation of power and the techniques of abnormalization, which seek to identify, define, categorize, observe, and render visible—in other words, to produce and enforce—particular agents, behaviors, and situations as abnor-mal (Taylor 2014: 5).

Perhaps the most important feature of normalization is how it results in the abnormalization of certain subjects, practices, and social behavior. Peter Cryle and Elizabeth Stephens (2017: 2) argue that normalization can have "a significant effect on the lives of those defined in contrast to it as abnormal, pathological, or deviant." Lennard J. Davis (1995: 29) explains that "with the concept of the norm comes the concept of deviations or extremes," which results in social differentiation and hierarchical organization among the nor-mal and abnormal subjects (see also Davis 2014). Deviance is then created through the making of rules against which infraction constitutes deviance (Becker 1963: 9). Thus, social labeling plays a central role in breaking the normal routines and inventing social abnormal actions. The normalization process often governs social relations by creating otherness and then putting pressure on social subjects to follow the institutional standards of normalcy, to avoid, for instance, what William Connolly (1991: 22) maintains as being put in the categories of "delinquency, irresponsibility, dependency, criminality, instability, abnormality, retardation, unemployability, incapacity, obsolescence, credit risk, security risk, perversity, evil, illness, or contagion." Yet, although normalizing societies tend to promote sameness, they allow difference in order to construct the normal in the first instance, as well as to justify the proliferation of a wide range of interventionary practices (Connolly 1995: 90).

For Foucault, the normal is determined through its opposite—the abnormal—whereby the differentiation between those two categories constitutes their distinctions. As Taylor (2014: 5) shows, "within the context of a normalizing society, abnormality can be understood in the most general sense as that which deviates from the norm." Taylor (2014: 5) further adds,

> In conveying to us what we do not want to be, and what we must try to avoid becoming, the concept of the abnormal effectively reasserts prevailing notions of normality not only by reinforcing prevailing social norms but also by challenging the limits of those norms and thus calling forth new fields of inquiry and producing new forms of knowledge, new institutions, and new state functions—in other words, by producing new norms. From a Foucauldian perspective, then, the abnormal, like the normal, is implicated in normalizing relations of power.

By focusing on the abnormal, Foucault (2003: 26) seeks to cast light on "the emergence of the power of normalization, the way in which it has been formed, the way in which it has established itself without ever resting on a single institution but by establishing interactions between different institutions, and the way in which it has extended sovereignty in our society." The practice of that distinction between normal and abnormal enables the delineation of identity and the production of power (see also Canguilhem 1978). Abnormality has historically evolved through the practice of "expert medico-legal opinion," which holds the power to determine the field of normal from the abnormal. To illustrate the historical meanings of abnormality, Foucault (2003: 55–59) presents three figures of abnormal individuals: the human "monster," who is the exception that contradicts the law to the furthest degree; the "incorrigible," who is regular in irregularities but whom the social institutions know how to discipline; and the "masturbator" (onanist), who appears to be a universal individual but, at the same time, is kept secret from everyone. Through the discussion of abnormality, Foucault (2003: 61) tried to explain the "technology of human abnormality," which, for him, "appears precisely when a regular network of knowledge and power has been established that brings the three figures together or, at any rate, invests them with the same system of regularities."

Foucault's conception of abnormality allows or justifies psychiatric and administrative interventions. Foucault argues that "normalizing regimes of power require the continued existence of a certain amount of abnormality or deviance both to give definite sense to norms in the first place and to justify continued imposition of discipline (that is, to support their maintenance and expansion)" (McWhorter 2014: 317). For Foucault (2003: 61), those three distinct domains of abnormalcy are subject to three different disciplinary technologies and regimes of power and normalization: "the monster falls under what in general terms could be called the framework of politico-judicial powers"; "the incorrigible will be defined, take shape, and be transformed and developed along with the reorganization of the functions of the family"; "the masturbator emerges and takes shape within a redistribution of the powers that surround the individual's body." The technology of normalization requires the creation and classification of anomalies and deviations, as well as the isolation or reformation of those abnormal individuals through coercive, corrective, or therapeutic interventions.

Foucault also argues that the imposition of a particular regime of normalcy and homogeneity goes hand in hand with the production and systematization of knowledge, which supports the normalization of social affairs. While "the power of normalization imposes homogeneity," it also "individualizes by making it possible to measure gaps, to determine levels, to fix specialties, and to render the differences useful by fitting them one to another" (Rabinow 1984a: 197–98). The normalization process associated "with disciplinary power do[es] not necessarily produce conformity or the monotonous regularity of identities often claimed in radical critiques. On the contrary, one of the prime effects of disciplinary power was to produce, precisely, individuality" (McHoul and Grace 1993: 72; see also Sheridan 2005: 152). Yet the hegemony of normalcy is the main trigger of resistance, which seeks to normalize another set of phenomena, perceived as being abnormal (Bigo 2008: 99). The anti-normalizing resistance often entails refusing regimes of normalization and developing reflective, temporal, and innovative methods for being, thinking about, and relating differently to others. Hence, for Foucault, questioning norms and unmasking their effects on power opens up many possibilities for preserving and expanding freedom (Taylor 2009: 46). Normalization can hardly be considered to contribute to the politics of empowerment simply because its very logic is situated on the binary between the forces that possess the knowledge and authority to normalize others and the devalued, discredited ones who are deviant and in need of treatment. Every practice of normalization results in a process of marginalization and exclusion of certain practices deemed abnormal. In this sense, Foucault's idea of normalization is closely related to Pierre Bourdieu's concept of internalization, which signifies the process by which certain practices become social structures and thus form the basis of a habitus that consists of pre-dispositions, of unconscious and taken-for-granted knowledge, norms, and habits, and of constraints and expectations. The politics of normalization and internalization represent aspects of symbolic violence as they enshrine a tendency for subordination by imposing the gradual internationalization and acceptance of certain discourses, ideas, and structures that, in turn, have a constraining and controlling function.

Normalcy is context-specific, fluid, and contingent on spatiotemporal entanglements. As Ian Hacking (1990: 160) shows, normalcy "is like determinism, both timeless and dated, an idea that in some sense has been with us always, but which can in a moment adopt a completely new form of life." What is normal is a result of what people consider as such; it is derivative of social interactions and discursive productions, as well as being prone to modification and transformation depending on shifting power relations, critical mass support, and the socio-ideological and material positionality of actors. What may be normal for one society and culture might be seen as highly abnormal for another (Horwitz 2016: 3), because "distinctions between normality and abnormality stem from value-laden constructions that vary from group to group and lack any objective natural foundation" (Horwitz 2016: 8). In fact, Sophists in ancient Greece considered normality and abnormality as "arbitrary social conventions that lacked any objective basis" (Horwitz 2016: 3). Although normalization seeks universalization of the particular, it remains socially and culturally specific and a relational process. For social interactionists such as George Hebert Mead, "what is pathological for one era, culture, or society is normal for another. There are no fixed boundaries between the normal and the pathological that have not been transgressed at some point in time in the history of societies" (Côté 2015: 48).

Foucault's critique of normalization tries to problematize and unsettle the fluid nature of power and its liquid and performative character embedded in norms and practices of external governance and self-discipline. In his later work, Foucault distinguished between normation and normalization, the former being the micro-techniques through which norms and the normal emerges, the latter the macro-power relations and societal trends that determine the norm (see Lynch 2016). In essence, the normal is "never static but changes from group to group, over time and from place to place" (Titchkosky 2015: 131). A norm simultaneously leads to individualization and collectivization of social agency. It lets the governed become the government and thus performs a fluid type of power. Havis (2014: 111) adds, "Disciplinary power, unlike sovereign power, relies heavily on rewards to induce correct behavior. And when individuals do not comply with the norm, the remedy is not simply punishment but more training and more discipline." François Ewald (1990: 141) elaborates,

> The norm is the principle that allows discipline to develop from a simple set of constraints into a mechanism; it serves as the matrix that transforms the negative restraints of the juridical into the more positive controls of normalization and helps to produce the generalization of discipline. The norm is also the means through which the disciplinary society communicates with itself.

The main purpose of shifting from enforcing the sovereign power through violent methods to a disciplinary power based on correction, transformation, and self-responsibilization primarily had to do with a more efficient way of governing societies and reducing resistance to rulers. In that context, normalization takes place through "homo juridicus"—through internalized and personalized self-policing and self-adjudication techniques that rely on statistical knowledge, metrics, and other forms of determining the average and "the normal." Disciplinary methods of ruling disguise the uneven power relations and techniques of governmentality behind the politics of social care, improvement, democratic process, and techno-political knowledge (see Harvis 2014: 112). As discussed by Foucault, normalization represents the highest form of intervention and, ultimately, the end of resistance. In liberal democracies, the discourse of normalization has been central in creating national identity, suppressing social difference, creating law-abiding and self-restrained subjects, and standardizing and legalizing social behavior. Jacob Segal (2003: 447) observes,

> Through normalization, liberal selves become "disciplined" selves. Normalization acts through the consciousness of the self. Normal and disciplined selves become their own judges and ceaselessly interrogate themselves as to whether they meet preferred norms. These

selves repress their own delinquent thoughts and feelings and force other wayward selves into the normal patterns of behavior.

The concept of normalization is closely related to the homogenization and heterogenization of society. Normalization processes entail the creation of homogeneous subjects that share common features, a process ultimately leading to the creation of differences associated with abnormal subjects. In that context, normalization is characterized as "a mode of observation, ordering, intervention, hierarchy, exclusion, and control that simultaneously homogenizes and individualizes its target populations by taking charge of individual behavior through forms of subtle authority" (Koro-Ljungberg et al. 2007: 1078). Normalization seeks to make exceptional and unusual practices into broadly accepted social conventions. That process of making the unconventional conventional pushes certain other norms and practices that were once conventional into becoming unconventional. For Cryle and Stephens (2017: 8), the purpose of normalization is not necessarily to make subjects "more normal" but to establish distance from the norm as a "distinguishing characteristic of individuals," so that measuring the distance between an individual and the norm "becomes a key figure of knowledge." The distinction between normal and abnormal relies on norms associated with the functional and the dysfunctional. The normal is then the ordinary and represents order, whereas the abnormal synonymizes disorder. As Peter Alexander (1973: 150) argues, "what is meant by being normal, in the sense of not needing treatment, is closely related to being able to function in some society, this being widely interpreted to mean being able to use one's capacities to the fullest possible extent."

For Foucault, imposing a particular regime of normality and homogeneity is the production and systematization of knowledge, which supports the normalization of social affairs (Bigo 2008: 99). Considering that norms should not be seen as given outside power relations and closed to critical analysis, he argues that by questioning norms and unmasking their effects of power, many possibilities open for preserving and expanding freedom (Taylor 2009: 46). In that regard, "the norm's function is not to exclude and reject. Rather, it is always linked to a positive technique of intervention and transformation, to a sort of normative project" (Foucault 2003: 50). As Taylor (2009: 47) shows, "normalizing norms encourage subjects to become highly efficient at performing a narrowly defined range of practices." Essentially, the production of norms is the production of power, which requires people to change their practices to ensure conformity with collective social norms (Taylor 2009: 52). For Foucault (2003: 50), the norm is an "element on the basis of which a certain exercise of power is founded and legitimized." Normalization does not work through the incursion of repressive power, ignorance, or enforcement. Rather, the logic of normalization works through different disciplinary mechanisms and formations of knowledge that are inventive, productive, and transformative (Foucault 2003: 52). Normalization is about exerting social control with the help of disciplinary power. It is an instrument of power, a productive approach for asserting influence without enforcement. Ultimately, self-governance of the subject is the goal of normalization that does not contest and question power dynamics and relations behind the construction and maintenance of the normal and abnormal in society. Such a governance of society operates through promoting the discourse of statistics and implanting such regularity interventions and mechanisms on people so that they regulate themselves in accordance with the norms and the perceived normal (see Golder 2015).

For most conventional sociologists, normalization is about the description of the present and the desired state of things. For Foucault, normalization refers to strategies of social control and disciplinary power. Foucault considers disciplinary normalization problematic because it is a mechanism of domination and sociopolitical enclosure, which ultimately results in legislating specific ways of being, thinking, and acting that perceive difference and the other as threats and potential targets for intervention to extend a normalizing regime. As Taylor (2009: 52) shows, the norm plays "a fundamental role in the emergence, legitimation, proliferation, and circulation of modern power." Normalization is also associated with privileged and dominant discourses, subjects, and social groups. Normalization results in social differentiation, which creates fictive hierarchies in terms of values and abilities. The hegemony of normalization results in an unjust distribution of power. Social techniques of normalization seek "to reduce the political to the judicial," turning struggles for justice and entitlements into rights-based frameworks and political obligations and responsibility (see Chambers and Carver 2008: 155). By nature, normalization weakens human agency and fosters "insecurity, self-doubt, anxiety, and resentment" (Heyes 2007: 116). As William E. Connolly (1991: 150) maintains, "a normalizing society is defined more by its proliferation of failures or near-failures and its tactical orientations to them than by its pristine examples of normality."

Problematic about practices of normalization is the embedded social Darwinism or social evolutionism, a belief that human subjects can evolve and progress through sociopolitical interventions. Normalization's process of social engineering posits social improvement through self-formation and self-governance and entails depoliticizing subjects by breaking away from collective identifications. Yet, in essence, social Darwinists "viewed normality and abnormality as rooted in biological differences among individuals, social classes, and races" (Horwitz 2016: 12). That meaning of normalization springs from the Western liberal ideology of progress and evolution, which considers social pressure, intervention, and modes of rationalization as crucial for moving toward a more perfect form of society. American pragmatists believed in social engineering, and "what precisely they hoped to achieve in their idealized humans and society . . . was the belief that it was a process that could and should be guided toward something normatively better" (Sterling-Folker and Charrette 2015: 84). For instance, by "applying the concept of natural selection to human societies," social Darwinists "unabashedly proclaimed the preeminence of White, Western, especially northern European, cultures and the inferiority of non-White, non-Western group" (Horwitz 2016: 12). Social categorization became an ideological tool to variously justify practices of Western colonialism, racism, Nazi atrocities, ethnic cleansing and war crimes after the Cold War, military interventions of a different nature, anti-Semitism, and, most recently, Islamophobia (Sterling-Folker and Charrette 2015: 83).

To conclude, Foucault's account of normalization helps us make sense of how certain states engage in international disciplinary and normalizing interventions both discursively and through affirmative actions. It highlights how various regimes of normalization embed tendencies and desires for domination (see Escobar 1984). Yet Foucault's account of normalization focuses predominantly on the genealogical formation of Western subjectivity, where power relations, authority, and compliance are regulated through norms that are widely self-enforced through repeated performances manifested in hierarchical observations, normalizing judgments, and various forms of examinations. So far, Foucault's work most examined in IR studies remains his conceptions of power, global governmentality, and biopolitics, which are widely used to make sense of contemporary state practices—mostly in Western societies, but also in external interventions (see Kiersey and Stokes 2011). Foucault's work on normalization is subdued by those major concepts, especially the regimes of governmentality and technologies of discipline. But as examined earlier in this chapter, Foucault's take on normalization is intricately related to his other dominant concepts. Although Foucault's conception of normalization focuses on its domestic manifestations, similar normalization discourses and practices are evident on the world stage. The remainder of this chapter maps out the conceptual features that underpin normalization discourses and practices in world politics.

MAPPING NORMALIZATION DISCOURSES AND PRACTICES IN WORLD POLITICS

While much has been written implicitly about normalcy and normalization in political and social theory, there is a lack of explicit studies that explore discourses and practices of normalization in the field of International Relations (IR). We argue that normalizing interventions are at the core of IR. While the international order is a by-product of never-ending wars, colonial exploitation, and a struggle between states for dominance and coexistence, the contemporary proliferation of the need for the normalization or transformation of societies and states emerges in relation to the dynamics of globalization, cosmopolitanism, socioeconomic transactions, transborder social interactions, and the development of the global commons. In global affairs, normalization discourses and practices are encoded within a wider web of formal and informal institutions, norms, rules, policies, and discourses that concern mainly peace, security, and development. As discussed earlier in this chapter, one of the main semantical invocations of normalcy in social and political theory is associated with order. The most important feature of order's lineup of things in different forms and shapes is norm enforcement, which includes interventionary practices for either building an orderly society, restoring an existing order, or accepting a particular order. When translated to international theory and world politics, order is a permanent quest in search of establishing, maintaining, and restoring normalcy between and within the society of states.

Looking at the normalizing interventions helps make sense of fluid, remote, overlapping forms of foreign interventions in world politics, which simultaneously combine forms of ad hoc military interventions with deep objectives for regime change, peacebuilding, statebuilding, and economic reconstruction in turbulent states. As Martha Finnemore (2003: 136) maintains, "intervention is thus becoming difficult (if not impossible) to separate from nation building in contemporary politics." In the contemporary normalizing order, threats are not dealt with through military intervention most of the time, as imposing norms through invasion, attack, and forcible regime change have proven to be unsuccessful and unacceptable. Instead, interventions take place through more sophisticated discursive practices. As Michael Barnett and Raymond Duvall (2005: 61) argue, "all practices of guiding and steering collective outcomes in global social life . . . derive from discourses that are productive of the social identities of the actors engaged in them." Framing the justification for intervention along the lines of normalization allows for respecting the norm of internal self-determination while engaging in internal interference. Multilateralist platforms are used by different states to pursue their agendas and provide political cover for their interventions. Normalizing interventions enable unilateralist interventions within multilateralist frameworks. Interventions for imposing, restoring, or accepting normalcy represent self-indulgent internationalism, in which everyone can do whatever they want as long as such interventions are framed for the purpose of normalization. In addition, looking at the existing international interventions from the perspective of normalization discourses and practices helps partially explain the externalization of modes through which Western societies govern themselves as collectivities and individual subjects—namely, exerting power and influence without always requiring the use of military force or violent enforcement techniques. It also helps explain how the efforts for democratizing, liberalizing, and empowering other states and societies function, first and foremost, to preserve the hierarchies of domination and differentiation and thus reproduce the discourses of normal self and abnormal other. As Finnemore (2003: 8) demonstrates, "states use their power and influence all the time to try to shape the actions of other states in a great variety of ways."

International normalizing order is (re)constituted by combining traditional understandings of power—as top-down, hierarchical, and repressive—with elements of soft power, which include symbolic and normative elements as well as other social forms of encouragement, affection, association, and entanglement. As Barnett and Duvall (2005: 68) maintain, "different forms of power have different domains of application to the extent that they illuminate different ways in which social relations affect and effect the ability of actors to control their fates." In that sense, international normalizing order is fluid and is reconfigured constantly through praxeological and discursive encounters and struggles. Most relevant for this study, we approach the international normalizing practices by exploring the uneven politics and international mechanisms for governing normalcy in world politics through imposing, restoring, and accepting a certain regime of normalcy in different societies and circumstances (see table 2). Embedded in the heart of

Table 2. Conceptual Framework

Foucault's figures of the abnormal	State figures	Categories of normalization	Techniques of normalization
Monster	Fragile states	Imposition	Liberal interventionism
Incorrigible	Disaster-affected states	Restoration	Disaster management
Onanist	Suppressive states	Acceptance	Confessionary practices

international normalizing society's will to govern and normalize others is an ideological optimization, often resembling liberalism and idealism and often appearing as realist and pragmatist in nature.

The international normalizing order functions based on the premise that normalcy is associated with stability, peace, and order, whereas abnormalcy is associated with war, violence, and disorder (see Clark 1989: 22–23). Normalcy is seen as a healthy condition for the world, whereas abnormalcy is analogous to disease. The progressive and interventionary character of the international normalizing society imposes a value judgment. Abnormalcy and the body politic on which it is inflicted are regarded as curable, with the possibility of returning to the previous or new condition of health. War and abnormalcy are considered unnatural and subject to intervention and cure. The cure involves diagnosing and undertaking remedial action to restore or achieve normalcy again. In most cases, Western states that are normalized through disciplinary technologies are intolerant to difference, and the perceived other are often associated with the abnormal. Deeply enshrined within the politics of self-care is the notion that normalized societies "care" for the "other" as well. Care for others is part of disciplinary mechanisms for widening the zones of normality—of sameness—and thus reducing risks of uncertainty and threats coming from other forms of thinking, being, and acting. That complex intolerance foregrounds the will to normalize others. In most cases, normalizing interventions are about imposing those specific meanings of normalcy. States that are prone to intervene abroad tend to use their own sense of normalcy as a normative and justificatory basis for intervention. They seek global control through extending democracy, human rights, and liberal economy and converting them from region-specific regimes into universally applicable ones.

In international normalizing interventions, there is a congruence of techniques of normalization and domains of knowledge, between the measures designed for imposing, restoring, and accepting normalcy. All states that are subject to different modes of normalization are exposed to different disciplinary technologies. They are subject to hierarchical and external observation and examination through different technologies of measurement and to the normalizing judgment manifested through different instruments, and they are constrained by the norms, rules, and institutions that form the international normalizing order. Hence, exploring techniques of normalization requires problematizing the discourse of normalization and the process of knowledge production, as well as deconstructing practices, performances, and actions undertaken to maintain, enforce, or impose normalcy. Hierarchical observation tends to use international or regional organizations as intervening structures and relies on codified international norms and practices, as well as on knowledge assembled particularly as a justificatory base for intervention. Those international structures provide the socio-material foundation for surveillance, judgment, and alternation of targeted societies. In the international normalizing society, UN agencies, regional organizations, and nongovernmental organizations and think tanks serve the purpose of identification, classification, and intervention of societies that are deemed either normal or abnormal. By that very action, they set the criteria of normalcy in world politics. There is growing consensus that "only multilateral bodies can carry out these tasks in ways that have the appearance of serving the community's interests as opposed to the particularistic interests of self-seeking states" (Finnemore 2003: 137). International institutions and, by extension, international missions in conflict and disaster-affected societies often operate based on the logic of a panopticon. Basing their operations on a complex political technology of practices that encourage self-policing and mutual enforcement, they govern through various regimes of supervision, regulation, accountability, and transparency, as well as through diffuse power among member states of international organizations, global civil society, media, and other social movements. They also provide a disguise that seeks to dissociate normalizing interventions with colonialism and civilizing missions. While anticolonialism and antiracism discourses on the global stage have precluded labeling states as savages and barbarians, it is deemed acceptable nowadays to label states as failed, collapsed, rogue, or vulnerable. The former labeling contains cultural derogatory references, while the latter is based on the stateness capacity.

State Figures

Central to the discourses and practices of normalization in world politics is a process of labeling and differentiation of states. International normalizing society operates through a complex scheme of intelligible norms, apparatuses of conditionality, and modes of interacting with turbulent societies. That scheme includes categorizing states according to a wide range of criteria of state capacity, peacefulness, and normative conditions, as well as economic and security situations. Such analysis produces hierarchies that determine states' international statuses, resulting in the distinction and categorization of states. Disciplining of states takes place through identifying, diagnosing, examining, prescribing, administering, and monitoring the conduct of states.

Normalization goes through several stages, from knowledge production, policy advocacy by norm entrepreneurs, and internationalization of discursive frames, to implementation through rewarding and sanctioning techniques, such as alliance-building and socialization efforts and economic and political conditionality, as well as other noncoercive and coercive measures. External regulation sets certain targets and accordingly judges states' behavior, labels and categorizes states, and enables intervention in internal affairs without local resistance, making normalizing interventions distinct forms of interference in internal affairs of states without formally breaching state sovereignty. In that context, normalization works through positing first a model of the ideal state, which, in the current constellation, resembles the Western state. Its operationalization consists of trying—through peaceful, diplomatic, and sometimes coercive methods—to force other states and societies to conform to the Western state model, whereby normal states are those that internalize it, while fragile, failing, and deviant states are those incapable or unwilling to conform to the externally imposed norms. The prescriptive character of norms plays a major role in the determination and identification of what is normal and abnormal in a society. The origins of policy prescriptions are located on the knowledge–power nexus that dominates contemporary international interventions. Often, though, the origins of prescriptive norms have their roots in the description of difference and the "other" as abnormal, which gives rise to disciplinary technologies for homogenizing it.

The process of normalization is nurtured by a transformation of political discourses into scientific data and objects of measurement that produce both implicit and explicit hierarchies of knowledge and make certain practices subject to interventionary practices. Gradeability is centered around the production of knowledge about conflict, peace, and security. Indexes, rankings, and diagnoses of conflict or the state of peace are all complicit in normalizing certain societies, cultures, and practices while excluding and abnormalizing others. State labeling and grading is based on a number of global benchmarks, which set "a comprehensive normative vision regarding what various types of transnational actors should look like, what they should value, and how they should behave." Benchmarks are "translated into numerical representations through simplification and extrapolation, commensuration, reification, and symbolic judgements" (Broome and Quirk 2015: 819). Jonathan Joseph (2012: 137) argues, "The benchmarking process and use of indicators help in constructing a particular reality to which states must conform. This renders states as calculative agencies, in constant reflection on their performance and driven by global standards of conduct." The benchmarking process is "a means of regulating state behavior through compiling statistics, monitoring performance and using these to make normalizing judgments about states and their forms of governance" (Joseph 2012: 72).

Based on that logic, states are often categorized according to political ideology, wealth and power, religion and identity, and status, such as liberal/democratic versus authoritarian states, stable versus fragile states, stable and powerful versus weak and fragile states, recognized versus unrecognized states, and Western versus non-Western states. All those dyadic state labels are characterized by an underlying value where one labeled state is normal while the other is abnormal. Some of those varieties of state labeling in world politics correspond well to Foucault's genealogical discussion of the three figures of the abnormal, discussed earlier in this chapter. In international policy discourse, some societies are labeled as monstrous and unable to self-normalize and are thus subject to external intervention, particularly fragile states that have experienced protracted and violent conflicts. Other states are labeled as incorrigible and captured by misfortunes and as worthy of light intervention to restore previous conditions of normalcy and to build resilience for future self-sufficiency. That label particularly falls to states affected by chronic and episodic disasters caused by nature or human conflict. Finally, a strand of states are accepted as normal regardless of their deviant behavior or persistence of abnormal conduct and are thus spared external intervention. Generally, those states can stand up for themselves or are protected by their allies and thus project the powers of a classic sovereign state.

State labeling reveals the process of normalization and abnormalization and highlights the power of discursive knowledge and its regulatory and exclusionary character. Labeling contributes to reproducing normalcy in world politics, while also sanctioning how we should think and act toward deviant actors and societies. Labels that affirm normalcy or abnormalcy of a state and society condition what set of interventionary mechanisms are deployed, how local subjects should be treated (especially with regard to respecting their human rights and needs), and what expectations to have from those interactions. As Rebecca Adler-Nissen (2017: 202) maintains, stigmatization, as a form of labeling, "plays a crucial function in international relations by shaming states, displaying normality and clarifying the boundaries of acceptable behavior." Those semantics of statehood play a profound role in constituting global affairs and, most important, in creating stratificatory and hierarchical orders, where some states deemed more normal enjoy greater status and benefits in world politics compared to those that are deemed fragile, deviant, and abnormal. As Judith Kelley (2017: 7) argues, "grading countries' performance is becoming an increasingly common way to try to exert influence." That such semantic differentiation has become a structuring principle for categorizing and labeling states has far-reaching implications, because it tends to elevate different interventionary practices to either accept, restore, or impose a specific regime of normalcy. Certain degrees of turbulence are tolerated, while serious departure from the conventional conception of states results in the labeling of fragile, deviant, pariah, or rogue states. In that regard, international normalizing society creates "abnormal" states by making and reproducing the rules of global normality (as an attempt to universalize particularism) and labeling outliers to the norms. State labeling increases the likelihood of maintaining interventionary practices and of unevenly and subjectively imposing certain regimes of normalization for certain states and societies deemed normal and acceptable by other states and societies. Moreover, as a precursory stage of normalizing interventions, stigmatization leads to discriminatory practices and reduces the status of states and societies in world politics.

Categories and Techniques of Normalization

The labeling of states as normal and abnormal becomes an organizing principle that conditions the position of states in the international system. It produces an ontological indeterminacy that forces affected states to constantly struggle to achieve normalcy and be accepted as normal by other states. It even forces a state to compromise on foundational matters, such as sharing sovereignty with foreign entities (both state and international organizations) and accepting impositions for transforming and restoring its status into a normal state and society. By default, the quest for normalization through various metrics and measurements reproduces stratification and inequality among states, ranking some states higher than others and thus permitting various forms of intervention in the name of normalization. As Mathias Albert (2016: 65) maintains, "there is no empire without stratification." Looking at the normalization in world politics, we can clearly see that sovereign equality and noninterference among states are fading metaphors, with sovereign equality "undermined and accompanied by institutionalized forms of stratificatory differentiation between states" (Albert, Buzan, and Zürn 2013: 18). A stratificatory order, where states are labeled into normative categories and accordingly subjugated to different regimes of normalization, is more prevalent than is often recognized.

States that are subject to normalization are asked to act responsibly toward their subjects and the wider international community by accepting external intervention in internal affairs. They are deemed responsible by the fact that they are recognized states and members of the society of states. In comparison, states that are powerful and in a dominant material position are exempted from such a view of responsibility. They vest themselves and expect others to recognize their special responsibilities. Specifically, the justification of great powers for deploying normalization interventions abroad derives from the principle of differentiated status, which is "rooted on material inequality" to "enhance the efficient working of international order" (Bukovansky et al. 2012: 7–8). Normalizing interventions empower certain states with the authority to police the behavior of other states and to ensure that they act in accordance with a set of mutually agreed norms. There is a semantical and ontological differentiation between states that are deemed normal and those deemed abnormal and thus subject to different modes and techniques of normalization interventions. Thus, taking up the guiding principle of degree and scope of intervention, we categorize the normalization interventions into those with the intention to impose, restore, or accept normalcy.

The first category of normalizing interventions covers those that seek to impose new regimes of normalcy over states and societies that are affected by violent conflict and labeled as fragile. Societies subject to imposed normalcy are perceived as monstrous and as a threat to international peace and security. We use Foucault's conceptual underpinnings of monstrosity and the judicial-political techniques of normalization as a guiding framework for identifying and problematizing the discourses and practices for imposing normalcy over fragile states that are seen as monstrous anomalies in the international system. State fragility and failure, representing the most extreme form of abnormalcy in world politics, is disciplined and controlled through judicial-political methods, including military interventions, deployment of peacekeeping, international administration, and other assistance and reconstruction missions. As the monster is associated with criminality, the punishment for states falling under that category is submission to external intervention and acceptance of disciplinary measures that ultimately weaken the affected subjects and empower external forces. Regimes are enabled to impose normalcy, as Foucault (2003: 73) stipulates, because of a shift in understanding of monstrosity, from monstrosity of nature to monstrosity of conduct. In other words, abnormalcy is seen as a social feature that can be controlled through disciplinary technology. Abnormal societies are conceptualized as in dire need of normalization through the imposition of external blueprints of normalcy, in the form of norms, rules, standards, and practices in distinct areas of governance, institutions, economy, social relations, and culture.

In the context of conflict-affected and fragile societies, the normalization process is guided by a conglomeration of politico-judicial powers, vested on a group of states backed by international organizations and other nongovernmental groups of interest, which impose particular norms on a state and society through ad hoc international missions and other discussed forms of interventions, such as democratic assistance, statebuilding, peacebuilding, and stabilization efforts. The main body of knowledge and domain of interventionary practices that demonstrates the technology of imposing normalcy is liberal interventionism implemented through a peacebuilding and statebuilding framework. Peacebuilding and statebuilding are comprised of a wide range of interventionary components, such as imposing and incentivizing rules, norms, and conditions to govern post-conflict transitions in the areas of elections, institution building, security sector reform, economic reconstruction, the promotion of civil society, the rule of law and justice, reconciliation, and transitional justice (Richmond and Visoka 2021). Interventions to impose an externally devised normalcy occur both at the individual level and in the societal environment. They seek improvement (rather than punishment) of society, as a pragmatic attempt to reduce risks and uncertainties emanating from such political, economic, and sociocultural differences. Thus, international normalizing society has both states and their populations as targets of intervention and discipline. Often, they surpass the state and work directly with local populations, through civil society, media, and other non-state actors. In other cases, they pursue top-down, elite-level engagement only. Bottom-up engagement with actors seeks to delegitimize state authority and thus disciplines a targeted society's conduct in accordance with externally imposed norms of good and responsible governance. Imposed normalcy thus represents some of the most intrusive forms of disciplining political subjectivities and creating new political orders in conflict-affected societies.

The second category of normalizing interventions covers those that seek to restore a society to its previous condition of normalcy, a condition deemed normal and acceptable for international and local actors after experiencing a particular difficulty that required external assistance. Subject to that form of intervention are states and societies that relapse to crises determined by unexpected and reoccurring disasters. Due to their geographical location and other historical and sociocultural factors, those disaster-prone societies are seen as incorrigibles that, at best, should be assisted to the restoration of a previously acceptable or good enough state of normalcy. That category of states fits well with Foucault's depiction of incorrigible individuals who expose partial anomalies controllable through interventions that seek to reorganize and cure anomalies through various functional changes. In the context of disaster-affected states, such reorganization signifies structural, institutional, and political adjustments within the state and society, to enhance resilience, transformation, and social change. It signifies the establishment of complex governance and self-reliance systems for societies to use in correcting themselves, without needing constant external assistance and support. The logic of interventions for restoring normalcy combines both reactionary and preventive aspects. It is reactionary and imposing in the sense of focusing on controlling and curing a perceived abnormality, and it is preventive in the sense of trying to address the underlying causes and symptoms of abnormality by building resilience in coping with disaster-caused anomalies. When there is desire to restore normalcy, we often see that the previous condition deemed normal is promoted and justified as a desired state of affairs. That promotion and justification takes place through norm redefinition and reinterpretation that are assisted by various measures intended to reinstate and restore the previous normalcy.

The discourse of restoring normalcy can be found not only in the disaster relief literature—where it is associated with recovery efforts, defined as the protracted process of recuperating pre-event norms—but also in stabilization discourses and in debates on resilience building. In that cluster of social practices, normalcy can be understood in two separate ways. On the one hand, it is a willingness to return to pre-conflict or pre-disaster social, political, and economic conditions—a status quo ante—while being linked to local and international perceptions of what constitutes "stability" or the pre-event normalcy in that context. On the other hand, restoring normalcy can entail striving for a new normal state—"bouncing forward" rather than "bouncing back"—and achieving a new stable, more resilient equilibrium. Despite the marked difference between those two understandings of restoring normalcy (most notably, their ambitions and perceived end goals), much more unites than separates them. Both approaches entail coming to terms with a permanent state of crisis and instability made of contingency, adaptability, and vulnerability. The normalization of emergencies makes resilience a coping mechanism to deal with anticipated and permanent crises. In that framework, instability is not necessarily viewed as abnormal, and conflicts and disasters can be viewed not necessarily "as deviations of the normal state of affairs" but as inherently constitutive of the reality that many developing countries face on a day-to-day basis. Despite policy differences between the two streams of restoring normalcy, the discussion of "building back better" or striving for a new, more resilient normalcy points to the fact that "new normal conditions" tend to oddly resemble the old, imperfect normalcy. The narrative of resilience is gradually becoming a withdrawal symptom from the liberal aspirational politics of global progress and positive transformation of the human condition, which is tied to a renewed interest in containment.

The international normalizing order is deeply subjective in determining what is normal in one context and abnormal in another. The third category of normalizing interventions covers those interventions seeking to accept as normal a range of suppressive states that engage in serious human rights abuses and other violations. The category of suppressive states resembles Foucault's third category of the abnormal, that of the onanist who performs practices that are widely prohibited by social norms. In the instance of states with accepted normalcy, the resembling metaphor of onanist practices are human rights abuses that are common but widely denied in many countries. The process of accepting the normalcy of a particular state entails also contesting and defusing norms deemed global and universal in other instances. Such efforts are often made to justify the state of affairs in domestic instances but are also nurtured and supported by foreign allies, lobby groups, and other regime advocates. Thus, accepting normalcy of suppressive states— regardless of the abnormalcies—is closely linked to the politics of alliances and strategic relationships. We assume that the closer the ties between states are, the higher the likelihood of acceptance will be. In the context of accepting normalcy, the discursive frameworks are intentionally constructed to tolerate and accept that a specific order of (ab)normalcy is sustained by justifying and creating a regime of expectations, shared ideas, and beliefs about the appropriateness and exceptionality of circumstances in those states and societies. In the instance of accepting normalcy of suppressive states, there is a selective tolerance of norm-breaking behaviors and continuation of granting recognition and unhindered international access despite domestic conditions. Whereas dominant states tend to invoke cultural relativism and political pluralism when handling suppressive states deemed strategic allies, the latter invoke the narrative of sovereign equality and nonintervention to force their normalcy, escape interventionism, and retain international acceptance and legitimacy.

Foucault shows that the figure of the onanist is handled through noncoercive, self-helping, and transformative measures and redistribution of powers at the level of the individual without affecting the entire society. It is a matter handled within a family or trusted community. In the international context, we can observe state acceptance through two major examples. The first concerns state confession. Foucault shows that confessionary practices are central to self-controlling onanist practices while ensuring social continuity and acceptance. Similarly, suppressive states tend to engage in complex confessionary practices through multilateral platforms to justify their state actions and generate international acceptance. The second example, often derivative of the first, concerns lite forms of international engagement undertaken to observe and monitor suppressive states through ad hoc commissions of inquiry or fact-finding missions. Those (com)missions tend to take a pastoral role to identify specific anomalies in the conduct of state affairs and offer nonbinding recommendations for individual responsibility for misconduct or ad hoc disciplinary measures against private and public subjects, including the military and police, state officials, and others. State confession and lite modes of interventionism are often seen as sufficient to address concerns in suppressive states without needing to invoke more radical methods of intervention or exclusion from the international community.

Methodological Aspects

Methodologically, this book is grounded in Foucauldian discourse analysis, shedding light on how representations of normalcy become institutionalized and "normalized" over time, becoming sets of statements and practices (see Foucault 1972; Arribas-Ayllon and Walerdine 2008). We are interested in capturing discourse as both text and social practice and with tracing the intersubjective and co-constitutive features of discourse that enable optimized normalization interventions (Neumann 2008). We have selected and analyzed what appeared to us as the canonical texts (both academic and/

or policy-oriented) that have come to structure the discourse on normalcy, becoming "events" and referenced as such. In doing so, we have tried to engage with as much as possible from as many genres as possible, loosely following Foucault's insistence that one should "read everything, study everything." At the textual level, we have explored discursive content and forms of expression to understand how content is organized in particular forms and how different contents imply different textual forms. In particular, we have traced the different invocations of the concepts of normal, normalcy, and normalization in theory and practice, to capture the key discursive formations invoked by the proponents of normalization interventions, most of them currently residing in or associated with the West (see Foucault 1972). That tracing took us on a highly enriching journey through literatures on imperialism, resilience, liberal interventionism, New Urbanism, disaster management, and stabilization, among others. Similarly, this book does not focus on a few selected cases but tries to connect the experience of multiple case studies together, allowing them to act more as vignettes than as in-depth case studies. The purpose here is to trace representative and illustrative discursive practices across a wide range of cases and spatial formations. As processes related to the production and consumption of text, discourse practices and technologies mediate the relationship between texts and social practice and can be seen in a hegemonic struggle to transform the order and power relations of discourse (Jørgensen and Phillips 2002).

To make sense of normalization discourses and practices in world politics, we look at a wide range of case studies and deconstruct multiple policy discourses where international organizations and dominant states have imposed, restored, or accepted a context-specific meaning of normalcy. State labeling constitutes a discursive formation that is supplemented by different technologies of intervention, which we categorize on a spectrum ranging from imposition to restoration and acceptance (see table 2). In other words, the main criteria we used to categorize certain discourses as imposition, restoration, and acceptance has been the type of interventionary technologies and the scope and scale of abnormalization discourses invoked to justify different responses and engagement with targeted states and societies. Discourse and practice are deeply intermingled, and only by combining and looking at both of them simultaneously can we make sense of normalization interventions in world politics.

In particular, we approach the study of normalization in world politics through the method of problematization. As a method, problematization features prominently in Foucault's quest to question and challenge social and political discourses and practices. As Foucault (1985: 9) points out, problematization is an "endeavour to know how and to what extent it might be possible to think differently; instead of legitimising what is already known." Problematization entails questioning what is given and deemed normal, and it is central for understanding how normalcy is constructed and unevenly applied across different states and societies. Central to problematization is taking as a point of reference and object of inquiry an examination of the logics and underlying assumptions behind selective meaning and the application of normalcy and uneven application in practices through different normalization techniques. As Mats Alvesson and Jorgen Sandberg (2013: 52) argue, the method of problematization requires, first, "the opening up of subject matter for critical inquiry by scrutinizing the ways they have emerged historically and on what assumptions and conditions they rest" and, second, generating "new areas of inquiries, potentially leading to new ways of being, doing, and thinking." Problematization is suitable as a method precisely because it not only enables seeking answers about the discursive and praxiological conditions normalizing and abnormalizing certain subject matter but also helps to explain the paradoxes and discrepancies underlying such knowledge and practices. It is a quest for explaining some of the mysterious operations of international interventions.

The method of problematization contains the description of forms of normalization and traces the contingent emergence, application, and transformation of discourse and practices of normalcy in world politics. As Colin Koopman (2013: 48) argues, "problematization functions to open up our problems in their full contingency and complexity in a way that makes them available for critical investigation." The method thus cherishes contingency and complexity over solidity and simplicity. Moreover, problematizing normalization interventions materializes the thought and action needed to evaluate the possibilities and impossibilities of state transformation through disciplinary techniques as well as the reconstitution of power dynamics and hierarchies in world politics. In a nutshell, we problematize how normalcy is problematized in the discourse and practice of international interventions.

In the remainder of this book, we examine the problem of normalcy in world politics through the problematization of dominant discourses and practices underpinning the normalization of states. We try to provide a coherent account of the uneven and problematic nature of international interventions. We explore the politics and paradoxes of normalization in world politics by tracing dominant practices for imposing, restoring, and accepting normalcy across different states and societies affected by nature and human-made conflicts, disasters, and sociopolitical turbulences. By looking at concrete normalization practices—such as actions, events, decisions, and conduct—we are able to identify discursive features and sociopolitical determinants that make and unmake normalcy. They jointly form discursive formations and practices that contribute to the demarcation of fields of normalcy and abnormalcy, which enables and legitimizes the application of different strategies of intervention and nonintervention in world politics. In problematizing discourses and practices of normalization, we look at a broad range of historical and contemporary countries and international mechanisms. We look at the dominant discourses as well as illustrative examples for each mode of normalization, while also accounting for the epistemic origins and praxiological transformation of state normalcy in world politics.

CONCLUSION

Mapping out how normalcy is understood across different social and political theories, this chapter offered a conceptual framework for studying normalization in world politics. Since the concept of normalcy is underresearched in the field of IR, we looked at the invocation of the concept across different sociological debates, to identify the contribution and limits of such debates. Our analysis revealed a lacuna of different perspectives, with mostly an affirmative and unproblematic view of the normal and normalization in a symbolic interactionist perspective. The first section of this chapter focused on the work of Foucault, whose critical reading of disciplinary normalization and the categorization of the abnormal offers valuable insights for exploring normalization discourses and practices in world politics. The chapter's second section outlined a new framework for studying normalization in world politics, inspired by Foucault's critical scholarship. There, we laid out the mirroring figures, interventionary categories, and discursive techniques that guide the study of normalization in world politics in the remainder of this book.

This chapter's discussion highlights the importance of approaching contemporary international interventions from the prism of normalization. First and foremost, our proposed framework of analysis enables looking at the international aspects of disciplinary normalization—namely, the global governmentality regimes—and how disciplinary practices unfold across different states and societies through different hierarchical observations, normalizing techniques, and examinations. In particular, we are able to map out how labeling states as fragile or disaster-prone, coupled with different discursive frameworks, enables different interventions aiming at imposing, restoring, and accepting normalcy. The justificatory basis for normalization in world politics relies on different ethical repertoires. Imposing normalcy operates on the ethics of humanistic universalism, according to which the human quest for development, empowerment, and emancipation is universal in nature, regardless of geographical location and cultural features. Restoring normalcy operates on situational and emergent ethics that allow fluid measures in an attempt to return disaster-affected societies to a previous condition of normalcy, which often ends up creating a new normalcy without admitting it. Accepting normalcy operates on the ethics of cultural relativism, which pragmatically accepts varieties of normalcy across different states.

Second, our proposed framework enables us to take a more holistic view of international interventions, bringing together a broad variety of discourses, interventionary techniques, and societies that are often studied separately as part of distinct disciplines and research programs. Normalizing interventions in world politics are more than simply imposing, restoring, or accepting normalcy of other states and societies. The very process of normalization of turbulent societies reinforces and creates hierarchical relationships and uneven power dynamics between states and societies. The quest for normalization generates special and differentiated responsibilities among states, constituting differential material and social power that can be exemplified by a state's enhanced international status as normal, responsible, and capable. In such hierarchical relations, states labeled as fragile, disaster-prone, or suppressive are obliged to obey external orders, whereas states labeled as normal and capable are elevated to a special status with higher international privileges and entitlements. That differential among states generates ontological insecurity in some and promotes self-confidence and expansionist ambitions in others.

3 ✦ Imposing Normalcy

In this chapter, we explore dominant discourses and practices mobilized for justifying interventions imposing normalcy in societies that are labeled as fragile states emerging from violent conflicts. The normal is associated with a peaceful state, making the word *normal* an antonym to conflict. Conversely, normalization is invoked as a discursive practice and technique for peacebuilding in conflict-affected states. This chapter problematizes how the international community has attempted to contain and transform violent conflicts in recent decades by characterizing them as anomalies to a rule-based international order governed by democratic norms and global institutions. In the chapter's first section, we connect the abnormalization of failed states to the figure of the monster, constituting a lens through which we can apprehend world politics, revealing, in its own ways, standards of normalcy. Failed states are understood as prototypical monsters, defying the laws of nature and politics but also constituting the "principle of intelligibility of all the forms that circulate as the small change of abnormality" (Foucault 2003: 56). We also explore how the pathologization of failed states operates through the use of scientific language, especially through diagnostic medical analogies. We find that labeling states as fragile and failed entities is connected to the doctrines of imperialism, especially as the latter were structured around a distinct ordering of world politics, with one specific system for "developed" or "civilized" states and with another system for the world to be colonized. We look at the transformation of the colonialism discourse to fit the failed state agenda, connecting therapeutic governance to international trusteeship of failed states. Ultimately, the pathologization of those societies—namely, through narratives of deviancy and abnormality—opens up the space for intervention and for the imposition of a specific understanding of normalcy and a normal life.

In the chapter's second section, we analyze how liberal internationalism, or what has been dubbed the "liberal peace," is mobilized to impose normalcy through international administration of conflict-affected societies. We argue that intervention becomes a mechanism for normalizing and abnormalizing states deemed as fragile, failing, or collapsed. We focus on how liberal interventionism is constructed as a remedy for maintaining international peace security and as a cure for fixing fragile states. In the work of Michel Foucault, the theme of liberal governmentality is conceived of as a specific collusion of power and knowledge techniques aimed at the administration of life, as opposed to the juridical sovereign kind of power that threatens death. The onto-politics of liberal interventionism rely on the assumption that the Western state should serve as the yardstick by which to measure and hierarchically surpass all other forms of statehood in world politics. The justificatory framework for liberal interventionism—namely, the will to normalize failed states—takes place through a thin line of respecting and breaching well-defined principles and norms of international society. No longer measured in terms of noninterference, state sovereignty is conceived in terms of openness to external examination and self-discipline. State weakness is utilized not only as an opportunity for foreign intervention and thus exploitation, imposition, and subordination but as a responsibility for the betterment, transformation, and empowerment of fragile states. The "cure" for fragile states is conditioned on the extent to which they evade cultural and political difference and adhere to a universalized model of Western statehood. This chapter's second section outlines the emergence of international governance mechanisms as an enforcement component of liberal interventionism, which contains elements of international protection and liberation, as well as echoes of occupation. The discourse of fragile states, coupled with the technology of international governance, has rendered acceptable externally imposed political, economic, and sociocultural regimes of normalcy.

The third section of this chapter delves into the practices of imposing normalcy on fragile and conflict-affected states through international peacebuilding and statebuilding activities. We look at the key features of peacebuilding and statebuilding interventions as techniques for imposing normalcy over a number of conflict-affected societies that have hosted UN and other international transitional administrations. In particular, we explore how a new order of normalcy is envisaged through a range of top-down and bottom-up techniques. Imposed normalcy practices operate through seeking to engineer a new political, institutional, and security system that, in the long run, both remains dependent to external forces and serves as an enforcer of local normalization. To ensure rapid social transformation and reconstruction of social order, normalcy is imposed from the bottom-up through civil society groups and other grassroots movements operating at the local and everyday aspects of life. A new order of normalcy in fragile and post-conflict societies—trying to replicate the liberal state model and prioritize democracy, human rights, justice, and development—should not necessarily be seen as a negative phenomenon. Local elites often call for international intervention and are open to transformation through external examination and supervision. Matters become problematic when there is a gap between good intentions for normalizing fragile states and the subsequent actions and outcomes that proceed. Although areas of interventions (such as security sector reform, the rule of law, and institutional reforms) may appear as technocratic processes, they serve as important segments for imposing a complex order of normalcy, which may overcome fragility in conflict-affected societies but may also introduce new modes of dependency on external assistance.

We argue that the imposition of a new order of normalcy through total political and social reengineering is unlikely to reach its desired goals. Contrary to the general assumption, failure of normalization efforts becomes a rationale for justifying protracted interventions and displacing the responsibility for failure to the local context. Those dynamics cast doubt about whether the will to normalize in fragile states is nothing but a will to intervene and advance power-ridden interests in world politics. As Jonathan Joseph (2009: 413) shows, "the aim of international organizations might be less the regulation of populations as the application of governmentality to states." Discorded governmentality, rather than normalization, seems to be the optimal outcome of interventions in fragile states.

FAILED STATES AS MONSTERS IN WORLD POLITICS

The figure of the monster and monstrosity traditionally features as the most extreme form of abnormalcy. The figure of the monster is the embodiment of difference, a breaker of category, and a resistant Other. As a construct and a projection, the *monstrum* is etymologically and simultaneously "that which reveals" (*monstrare*) and "that which warns" (*monere*) (Cohen 1996: 4). The concept of the monster seeks to depict "an action or a person or a thing [that] can't be processed by our rationality" (Asma 2009: 10). As unreasonable and unpredictable conduct, monstrosity permits undertaking extraordinary measures to tame such behavior or subjects. Stephen Asma (2009: 283) shows that, throughout history, monsters have been perceived as those with whom we cannot reason, who are unnatural and ugly, and who are powerful, evil, and inspire terror. The figure of the monster is not the only being invoked as a figure of the Other. A similar othering process can be understood through "abnormal" figures such as the witch, who could be understood as a "feminist monster," or through the figure of the barbarian, structuring the boundaries between civilization and "the rest" (Salter 2002). That structuring goes back to the general process of othering. For instance, considerations about normalcy appear preeminently in Edward Said's (2003: 40) work, where "the Oriental is irrational, depraved, child-like, different, thus the European is rational, mature, virtuous, 'normal.'" However, we argue, along with Foucault, that there is something specific about the figure of the monster: it is coupled with a specific pathologization process. If the monster is *contra naturam* (against nature), the concept of the barbarian does not necessarily entail a "condemned category," despite the common trope of the barbarian as representing a violent threat to the civilized inside (Salter 2002: 4). In ancient Greece, the barbarian is one who is difficult to understand but toward whom the Greeks do not show a particular form of animosity, especially since they believe they can learn something from the barbarian from time to time. The ancient Greeks fought between themselves as much as (if not more than) against barbarians (Ramel 2009: 684). The barbarian is not inherently abnormal; he is strange since he does not speak Greek, is less modern and sophisticated, but is nevertheless part of the wide international community, even as an imperfect member with less rights. In imperial doctrines of the sixteenth century, the barbarian ignores Christian truth and is deemed less civilized but nevertheless has rights of dominion; at least, that is an element of debate within, for instance, the Spanish doctrines of Francisco de Vitoria, Juan Ginés de Sepúlveda, or Bartolomé de Las Casas (Bain 2003: 15–16).

By contrast, the figure of the monster refers to an individual or a collective that is simply out of the realm of the natural, hence sitting outside the community and even outside nature. It is the figure of the monster on the Lenox Globe (1504) and the famous *hic sunt dracones*, with the monstrous figures occupying "the edges of unknowing, simultaneously forbidding and enticing would-be adventurers to draw near" (Beal 2001). From Niccolò Machiavelli's centaur to Thomas Hobbes's leviathan and behemoth, monsters have persistently lurked at the fringes of the political world (Devetak 2005: 631). The monster is also a cultural and political category defined by opposition to the "norm" of humanity and civility (Kappler 1980), which is revealed through the existence of the figure of the monster; the monster becomes the "fragmented assemblages of deviance deployed to reinforce and perpetuate existing social norms" (Laliberté 2013: 878). We agree with Dona Haraway (1991: 180) that "monsters have always defined the limits of community in Western imaginations," which is how the figure of the monster differs from similar semantic categories. Another useful figure to explore in that regard and in discussion on corrective disciplining is the figure of the terrorist in the post-9/11 world as a "person to be corrected," who is, in a certain way, the "monster's cousin" (Puar and Rai 2002: 119). The figure of the terrorist differs from the monster's figure in that the former "needs to be protected from her/himself so as not to become a monster because there's still the possibility for rehabilitation for the monster's cousin"; in contrast, "the monster is, by definition, beyond hope" (Laliberté 2013: 878).

The figure of the monster features as a major concept in Foucault's work on the process of abnormalization and the politico-judicial mechanisms of normalization. Foucault (2003: 56) explains,

> The monster is, so to speak, the spontaneous, brutal, but consequently natural form of the unnatural. It is the magnifying model, the form of every possible little irregularity exhibited by the games of nature. In this sense we can say that the monster is the major model of every little deviation. It is the principle of intelligibility of all the forms that circulate as the small change of abnormality.

For Foucault (2003: 56), the monster is perceived as violating the laws of both state and nature, thus becoming a "juridico-biological" problem. The monster is hence something between an animal and a human (Foucault 2003: 63). As the monster contradicts the law and falls in the domain of criminality, it must be handled through judicial measures. Those who challenged the sovereign and its laws were labeled as criminals and thus became subject to the political-judicial techniques of suppressing monstrous conduct. By default, acts of resistance and bottom-up agency were criminalized and thus subject to punishment, which was meant to correspond to the crime and often surpassed it to set a disciplinary example for the rest.

Punishment of crimes entailed reproducing monstrous conduct but was justified as a legitimate use of force and entitlement vested on the king or the state. In that process, prisons emerged as mechanisms of punitive power to govern monstrosity and discipline populations. The codification of penal measures resulted in the categorization of the crimes and the emergence of acceptable norms of behavior. Acting in accordance with a fundamental social pact started to be associated with the normalization process. The despot was a legal monster, whereas other individuals were accidental or occasional monsters. Foucault's analysis of the monster shows that at the heart of such abnormalization was a power struggle, a will to control social behavior that was deemed unacceptable and that was defined as such by the sovereign powers.

When seen as a biological problem, the monster requires medical attention and isolation from society. As a figure of social irregularity, the monster is handled through psychiatric institutions and medico-judicial actions. As Foucault (2003: 116) shows, "the law cannot be applied if the subject is not rational." That problem led to the creation of medical knowledge as a form of power that was vested with the institutional responsibility of distinguishing the normal from the abnormal. The essence of medical knowledge was to diagnose a condition or degeneration that provides the rationale and explanation for abnormalcy. Foucault (2003: 213) maintains that "the individual who suffers from a condition, who has a condition, is not a normal individual." The cure for that condition determined the domain of medical interventionism for controlling and, if possible, curing abnormalcy. That type of knowledge codified deviation from the norm, and by addressing social behaviors that were not covered by the codified laws, psychiatry served as a sovereign power to ensure that all aspects of social life are governed and regulated, in one form or another (see also Foucault 2002).

Foucault's analysis of the monster points out that the origins of monstrosity can be found in the struggle of the sovereign powers to control resistance and disobedience by labeling and criminalizing such behavior through punitive power. That process led to the criminalization of unacceptable behavior, which, by default, led to the codification of normal behavior, intended to have a normalizing effect on the wider population. As all acts of criminality were unable to be controlled through punitive powers, the categorization of monstrous behavior as abnormal opens up the space for the treatment of such cases through psychiatric institutions and medico-judicial knowledge. That new form of power ensured state control over all social affairs and, by determining conditions of abnormalcy, ultimately determined the conditions of normalcy and vice versa. Foucault's analysis of the monster is mostly limited, however, to offering a genealogical account of that figure of abnormalcy in the context of France and Western Europe.

The concept of the monster not only depicts an individual but has been invoked as a derogatory term to describe collective groups, cultures, and states (see Haraway 1991; Devetak 2005; Capasso 2001). Most of the time, the blame for monstrosity is collectivized and attributed to systems, ideologies, and collective identities. Monstrous states are blamed for promoting war crimes, genocide, terrorism, torture, and other forms of physical and structural violence. In the international context, the concept of the monster has been widely present in colonial discourse. Labeling non-European peoples as monsters, barbarians, and savages features in the work of early Western scholars such as Hugo Grotius, Emer de Vattel, and John Stuart Mill (see Piirimäe 2019). In some official policy and legal discourse, colonial subjects and non-Western states are labeled as savages, and uncivilized subjects are excluded from the society of civilized nations (Asma 2009: 243). In the discourse of colonialism, the monster is associated with madness, barbarism, and anti-modernity. Colonialism is then justified as a regime for converting monsters into reasonable, progressive, and modern subjects. During colonialism, the figure of the monster is transformed into a political device both to distinguish the colonizers from the colonized and to justify morally and normatively questionable exploitative practices toward colonial subjects (see Ashcroft, Griffiths, and Tiffin 2000). In the liberal theory of John Rawls (1999), states that are not liberal, well-ordered, and decent in their conduct of political and social affairs are labeled as outlaw states. For Rawls (1999: 81), "outlaw states are aggressive and dangerous; all peoples are safer and more secure if such states change, or are forced to change, their ways."

The distinction between civilized and noncivilized nations is clearly made with the purpose to legitimize imperial relations from the former toward the latter. As Michael Hardt and Antonio Negri (2009: 97) show, "the monstrousness and savagery of the native . . . legitimates the rule of the European in the name of modernity." During colonial times, as Sebastian Conrad and Marion Strange (2011: 46) illustrate, "colonial regimes always attempted to create the impression that their interventions were done for the benefit of those ruled." In essence, colonial discourse functions only if it promotes "the inferiority of the colonized, the primitive nature of other races, the barbaric depravity of colonized societies, and therefore the duty of the imperial power to reproduce itself in the colonial society, and to advance the civilization of the colony through trade, administration, cultural and moral improvement"

(Ashcroft, Griffiths, and Tiffin 2000: 38). However, the civilization missions were not about civilizing and normalizing colonial subjects and enhancing their socioeconomic emancipation and empowerment. Rather, colonial subjects were transformed into weak and fragile societies, ethnically divided and economically impoverished, precisely to enable the colonial powers to retain their supremacy and continue exploitation. Delegating governance powers to the natives was merely a technique to tame local resistance and divert the blame for failure. There are many definitions for the concept of imperialism, but it usually captures the "process by which peoples or nations conquer, subdue, and then dominate other peoples or nations" (Snyder 1962: 13).

In international relations, the figure of the "monster" has been analyzed sparsely (with the exception of Devetak 2005). That figure's relabeling and association with failed states caught in internal wars for secession or regime change represents a shift from colonial language of monstrosity and severity to more technocratic language of fragility, incapacity, and failure. As contemporary monsters in politics, failed states come to be seen as inherently contradicting simultaneously the "laws of nature" and the "laws of nations," through which normal states are considered to perform functions necessary to meet citizens' basic needs and expectations. As Kalevi J. Holsti (2004: 167) argues, "war has been characterized as a crime, a disease, a tragedy, a great mistake." Hence, through its very existence, the monster of the failed state simultaneously violates the laws of both nature and society. Scholars such as Francis Fukuyama (2004: 92) maintain that "since the end of the Cold War, weak and failing states have arguably become the single-most important problem for international order." Fragile states are seen as a serious international threat because they permit "high levels of corruption and weak rule of law; safe havens for illicit activity; poor border and customs control; lack of licit economic alternatives; and unique criminal opportunities provided by violent conflict and its immediate aftermath" (Patrick 2011: 12–13). The *SIPRI Yearbook 2001* observed that "the main threat to the security of the international community is the weakness of states owing to a lack of democratic structures and an inability to manage and combat such phenomena as organized crime, international and domestic terrorism, corruption, lack of political liberties, human rights abuses, religious and ethnic conflicts, and aggressive nationalism" (Rotfeld 2001: 3). The United States considers fragile states as "ungoverned, under-governed, misgoverned, or contested physical areas (remote, urban, maritime) or exploitable non-physical areas (virtual) where illicit actors can organize, plan, raise funds, communicate, recruit, train, and operate in relative security" (Clunan 2010: 7). In particular, post-conflict states are often distinguished from or compared to normal states, indicating an overarching assumption that conflict-affected states are less normal or are abnormal (see Del Castillo 2008). Conflict is described as a "collapse of the normal order" (Holmqvist 2014: 129).

The pathologization of states operates through the use of scientific language, especially through diagnostic medical analogies, in which state failures are seen as an illness that needs to be cured, "sick patients that can be revived" (Kraxberger 2007: 1055), or a "degenerative disease" (Lyons and Samatar 1995: 1). For example, the medical analogy is central in a seminal article by Gerald Helman and Steven Ratner, which has contributed to cementing the policy agenda on "failed states." The authors portray failed states as entities affected by a serious illness or as helpless persons who suffered from a bad turn of fate. The medical analogy directly informs their prescription: "Forms of guardianship or trusteeship are a common response to broken families, serious mental or physical illness, or economic destitution. . . . It is time that the United Nations consider such a response to the plight of failed states" (Helman and Ratner 1992–93: 12). Drawing on the medical definition of abnormality as something "outside the expected norm," such political analysts define the normal state as a set of criteria that all functioning states ought to display: ability to control a given territory, to deliver public goods to the population, and to enforce the rule of law.

Labeling failed states opens up new possibilities of normalization and transformation. As noted by Mary Manjikian (2008: 335), "just as sick people have less autonomy than those who are well, sick states have less sovereignty than healthy ones." In the Parsonian sense, being sick is defined as "being in need of medical help to return to 'normality,'" as "the sick must put themselves into the hands of medical practitioners to help them get well again" (Lupton 1994: 7). That definition suggests "a potentially unending disciplinary intervention, similarly awarding power to the professional to define the limits of normality and to impose therapeutic regimes" (Hughes and Pupavac 2005: 880). Not all interventions will inherently "cure" failed states; for some, "state building is more likely to resemble psychiatry: long and frustrating treatment bringing only incremental change" (Mandelbaum 1994: 12). In an essay on failed states in Africa, Stephen Ellis (2005: 136) similarly argues, "Dysfunctional governments are more like sick people. Like humans, states fall ill in a variety of ways, can continue to function (after a fashion) even when sick, and do not all respond to treatment the same way." The "therapeutic security paradigm" (or "therapeutic governance" approach) developed by Vanessa Pupavac (2002) helps capture the essence of the dialectic between pathologization and intervention: the pathologization of populations problematizes their right to self-government and encourages the development of a new mode of international therapeutic governance entailing new parameters of external intervention. The process of normalization "constructs all war-affected populations as traumatized and subject to psychosocial dysfunctionalism" (Pupavac 2002: 489–90; see also Hughes and Pupavac 2005), denying any agency to the local population and seeing them as colonial subjects—"half-devil and half-child," to use Rudyard Kipling's turn of phrase—or as patients (Thornton 1965: 6).

No other "failed state" has struck international imagination as vividly as Somalia following the coup against Siad Barre in 1991—in many regards, the ultimate "African apocalypse" (Harper 2012). Somalia's internal battle between factions has made the country one of the most durable cases of state collapse in the modern era, even if lack of government does not mean that it is without governance (Menkhaus 2008: 188). It has been called "a truly ungoverned area, with no functioning central government, no single entity in control of most of the country, and widespread localized contests for control over small areas of territory" (Lamb 2008: 17). Robert Rotberg (2004: 9) refers to Somalia as the sole example of a protracted "collapsed state," a "rare and extreme version of a failed state," and "a mere geographical expression, a black hole into which a failed polity has fallen." A UN report depicted the country as having "degenerated into a 'black hole' of anarchy" (UN 1999: para. 62). That metaphor shows how Somalia is perceived as a monster both defying the laws of nature (black hole behavior is known to defy the laws of astrophysics) and challenging the laws of society. Somalia also has been called a "hell on earth" (Abdul-Ahad 2009). That metaphor, again a reminder of the fact that failed states sit outside the community (according to traditional Christian theology, hell follows a sentence imposed in the last Judgment), is an evocative way of presenting the travails of the failed state as the burning of an eternal fire, a never-ending conflict and pervasive lawlessness. Traditionally defined by what it is not, hell is the absence of God. That the idea of absence is present in most of the popular depictions of hell, from C. S. Lewis ("Black Hole") to Dante ("cone-shaped pit"), ties together the metaphors of "hell" and "black hole." As "hell on earth" or a "black hole," Somalia can be understood by not so much what it displays as what it is not—as the complete absence of all the functions of the state (see UN 1999: 63). It is an area of "limited statehood," completely missing any domestic sovereignty (Brozus 2011: 264). It is "an absence of governance" in "ungoverned spaces" (Clunan 2010: 4), understood as including "under-governed, misgoverned, contested, and exploitable areas as well as ungoverned areas" (Lamb 2008: 6; see also US Department of State 2018a: 225).

In an effort to sideline the association of the discourse of fragile states with colonial jargon, there is now a tendency to move the debate toward more technocratic or ideologically neutral notions, such as "limited statehood," which seeks to categorize states along their degree of statehood rather than along biased dichotomies (see Risse 2015). Nonetheless, the ontological position of that new label is still embedded in the Western ideal of a sovereign state that has full authority throughout the territory, is able to exercise the legitimate use of force under the rule of law, and is capable of implementing policies (see Herbst 2004). As Lars Brozus (2011: 263–64) shows, "areas of limited statehood consist of territorial, social, and functional spaces lacking certain features of 'modern' forms of governance that characterize the political process in the developed or OECD world." The discourse goes as far as considering states with limited statehood "more of a source of insecurity than security" (Risse and Stollenwerk 2018: 107). Regarding efforts for statebuilding as counterproductive because they risk creating predatory states, it suggests a much deeper form of intervention: a shift from statebuilding to governance building. The latter entails a deep form of normalization, where the only way to create stability is for local subjects to accept external intervention and grant interveners a license for total intervention in the name of service provision. The key to generating local social legitimacy is to subject all social and identity groups to the process of normalization. In addition, the discourse of limited statehood expands the scope of Western states to intervene in societies that do not experience civil war. It permits intervention not only in fragile, failing, or failed states but in other states with different degrees of statehood as defined by the Eurocentric and Western epistemic community. By default, the concept of limited statehood has expanded the scope of Western states to include states such as Brazil and China in the category of states with limited statehood, which expands the opportunity for judging the status of states in world politics. Thomas Risse and Eric Stollenwerk (2018: 106) argue, "The vast majority of states in the contemporary international system . . . display areas of limited statehood to different degrees. More than 70% of all countries in the world contain significant areas of limited statehood."

The discourse of monstrosity in international relations has a performative and generative function. As collective subjects and as "departures from normality," monsters permit a wide range of interventionary measures (Asma 2009: 159). The discourse normalizes and empowers the status of states associated with law, peace, order, and goodness and reduces those labeled as monsters to unlawful and dangerous subjects that should be punished and tamed. In particular, indexes and ranking of states in accordance with their fragility or peacefulness tend to play a role in institutionalizing the prevailing assumptions and hierarchies of the worthiness of states in the international system, which, in turn, enables various forms of intervention. The comparison between state capacities in international relations intends to establish a hierarchical order organized around consolidated states and failing and failed states that have limited statehood and are captured by internal wars and chronic insecurities (see Risse 2011). As Gerry Simpson (2004: xi) argues, outlaw states represent "a figure whose estrangement from the community of nations and demonization by that community," seen as "mad, bad or dangerous" and "incapable of forming the correct attitude towards the international legal order." Most of the states labeled as outlaws tend to be implicated in serious domestic human rights abuses and aggressive actions against other states: "A state is outlaw not because it is undemocratic or internally illiberal but because it is illiberal in its dealings with other states or because it is a gross violator of human rights" (Simpson 2004: 296). Often, misrecognition of states tends to be a political and strategic construct intended to devalue and undermine the international standing of states that might have different affirmation (see Murray 2019).

Once a state is designated as outlaw, criminal, or failed, it is deprived of the norms of sovereign equality and nonintervention in internal affairs. It may be subject to sanctions, exclusion from international organizations, and military intervention. No other recent interventionary cases exemplify that logic better than the 2003 intervention in Iraq. The otherization process started with the depiction of Saddam Hussein as "a monster"—as "the embodiment of evil, depravity and darkness" (Devetak 2005: 634). The Iraqi government was demonized based on unverified claims that it possessed chemical and biological weapons. The demonization of the Hussein regime mostly drew on the analogies and experiences of the early 1990s invasion of Kuwait and brutal campaign against the Iraqi Kurds (Davidson 2011). The 2003 invasion of Iraq without the authorization of the UN Security Council violated international law and was categorized as a war of aggression. Yet the discourse argued that the invasion was key to pursuing world order: "By reconnecting Iraq to the world, we are not just rehabilitating a longtime pariah, we are stepping up to the role of Gap Leviathan" (T. Barnett 2004: 155). In that discourse, the destruction of monsters becomes the purpose of the international community and reinforces existing international hierarchies and structures. Labeling states as monstrous gives other states—dominant, middle range, or small—the chance to gain a position of authority and to police the international order "from a position of assumed cultural, material and legal superiority" (Simpson 2004: 5). It reproduces the international order along a spectrum from democratic and liberal, decent states to failed and outlaw states. In particular, as Simpson (2004: 6) shows, "the Great Powers often identify or define the norms that place certain states in a separate normative universe," and "there is an identifiable connection between the propensity of the Great Powers to intervene on behalf of the international community and the labeling as outlaws some of those states subject to intervention." In turn, the monstrous acts committed by great powers in the name of normalization tend to be overlooked and justified as being either in self-defense or for the defense of the international norms and order. The use of force and intervention supersedes the norm of territorial integrity and political independence of outlaw states.

The internalization of causes and dynamics of conflict results in purifying the role of external intervention as the only savior for the perennial crisis caused by internal political, economic, and sociocultural factors. As Adam Branch (2011: 28) shows, people in conflict-affected societies are portrayed as "trapped in vicious cycles of violence and breakdown that they are incapable of getting out of," and "the initial agency for transformation must come from the outside, through external intervention." As Susan Woodward (2017: 3) shows, "the concept of failed states is not just a label but an ideology." At the heart of that ideology is the shared belief that post-conflict, failed, or failing states are abnormal, a belief established through comparative narratives, metaphors, and evidence of the condition of states, order, and stability in the Western world. Bob Jessop's (2016: 221) adds, "All states fail in certain respects, and normal politics is an important mechanism for learning from, and adapting to, failure. In contrast, 'failed states' lack the capacity to reinvent or reorient their activities in the face of recurrent state failure in order to maintain 'normal political service' in domestic policies." Normalization interventions become explicitly about steering fragile states "towards modern, liberal norms, which are supposed to replace the traditional, illiberal, and thus conflict-prone individuals, societies, economies, and cultures" (Branch 2011: 29). Interventions thus adopt a Western model of the state and society as a curative ideology for failed states, the "conscious or unconscious process by which Europe and European cultural assumptions are constructed as, or assumed to be, the normal, the natural or the universal" (Ashcroft, Griffiths, and Tiffin 2000: 84). State performance becomes the yardstick of normalcy, with Western states instituted as models of governance. Such modeling is the "road to Denmark," the "imagined society that is prosperous, democratic, secure, and well governed, and experiences low levels of corruption" (Fukuyama 2015: 25). In the process, normalcy is defined jointly as a fairly specific set of functions that every state is supposed to perform (see Lemay-Hébert 2019). Normalcy can be understood through a technocratic or institutionalist lens, focused on what requirements the state should meet, or through a normative lens, as a set of ideals with which actors and institutions have to conform and of methods by which the state should meet its normative requirements. Those lenses are not exclusive: it is possible to rank states according to their performance and identify the "core of monstrosity behind little abnormalities" (Foucault 2003: 56). The "average," typical, fragile state thus becomes "the everyday monster," the "pale monster" (Foucault 2003: 57), colored on a fragility map not in bright, crimson red but using the full spectrum of pale light reds.

LIBERAL INTERVENTIONISM AS NORMALIZATION IDEOLOGY

The normalization ideology of liberal interventionism is embedded in two moral imperatives: self-interest and cosmopolitanism. Self-interest consists of advancing the stability and protection of the geopolitical interests of dominant states, "in terms of containing or controlling contemporary security risks, supposedly emanating from the so-called 'fragile' or 'failed' states" (Sahin 2015: 17). For instance, Rawls (1999: 90–91) argues that "well-ordered peoples, both liberal and decent, do not initiate war against one another; they go to war only when they sincerely and reasonably believe that their safety and security are seriously endangered by the expansionist policies of outlaw states." Rawls's concept of "burdened" peoples, understood as "societies unable to create well-ordered regimes due to unfavourable historical, economic, or social circumstances" (Rawls 1999: 90), directly echoes the concept of noncivilized peoples in imperial doctrines, with the aim of bringing such societies into the society of well-ordered peoples. In Rawlsian philosophy, there is a duty of assistance for "burdened peoples," and "in the long run it may well involve changing the political culture and institutions of burdened societies," which can be achieved through military interventions or "regime change" (Wilkins 2007: 166). Conversely, Rawls defends the principle of nonintervention in the affairs of peoples who are free, independent, and equal and who respect human rights. The imperative for imposing normalcy lies in the assumption that all human societies deserve the same treatment and that if humans are treated differently abroad, they threaten the way of life at home (see Gheciu and Welsh 2009: 127). The logic of liberal interventionism is that "war can not only be used to create order, but indeed a specific type of order, a liberal democratic order, in target states" (Holmqvist 2014: 130). The political regime of democracy is seen as "the 'normal' form of government to which any nation is entitled— whether in Europe, America, Asia, or Africa" (Sen 1999: 4).

The cosmopolitan aspects highlight "an appeal to common humanity and a responsibility to assist the vulnerable" (Gheciu and Welsh 2009: 126). In particular, the imposition of normalcy by foreign occupying forces is more likely to succeed if there is "a sustained and serious commitment by the occupying power to build democratic institutions" (Gunitsky 2017: 16). As Adam Branch (2011: 31) shows, interventions are framed as necessary to alleviate suffering and promote the right to aid, health, shelter, and, ultimately, life; to promote human rights, justice, and democracy; and to promote the right to peace. In other words, liberal interventionism sees a duty of assistance for troubled and burdened peoples, which "in the long run . . . may well involve changing the political culture and institutions of burdened societies," which could be achieved through military interventions or regime change (Wilkins 2007: 166). Moreover, liberal interventionism after violent conflict is justified on the basis of postbellum justice and responsibility to "improve the prospects that aggression will not be repeated" (Doyle 2015: 157). As Rawls (1999: 111) argues, "the duty of assistance . . . aim[s] to help burdened societies to be able to manage their own affairs reasonably and rationally and eventually to become members of the Society of well-ordered Peoples."

In particular, since military occupations are no longer deemed acceptable and legal under international law, interventions are justified with post-conflict reconstruction, statebuilding, and peacebuilding. The mechanisms that enable external interventions without being labeled as occupation are international territorial administrations, which are mostly run via the UN and other regional organizations. As Carsten Stahn (2008: 25) argues, "state occupations often carry a pejorative stigma that is less directly associated with UN peace operations, namely the image of unilateralism and coercion." The contemporary law of armed conflict does not include the international administration of territory by the UN as a form of occupation (Stirk 2009: 33). While military occupations are imposed by force or threat from outside powers, international administrations use force and threat more covertly, justifying them on the grounds of defending the mandate of the intervening power. International administrations also tend to be more acceptable, as a degree of grudging consent by the parties in conflict is usually present. As Peter Stirk (2009: 49) shows, the literature has "suggested that military occupation and United Nations' 'governance' follow distinct logics, in that the former 'presumes a pre-existing fully functioning state' and seeks the restoration of the status quo whereas the latter presumes some form of state failure and is oriented toward reconstruction." In principle, military occupation is not supposed to transform the political structure and the regime of the occupied society. Although military occupations such as those in Germany and Japan imposed a new constitutional order, the degree of imposition undertaken by international administrations goes further than previous forms of interventions. International administrations seek not only to impose a new constitutional order but to engage in regime change and economic, societal, and cultural transformation among the norms, rules, and culture of the intervening forces. International transitional administrations are seen as "a potential means to fulfil the requirements of the natural duty of justice in response to the suffering caused by severely unjust social and political conditions" (Jacob 2014: 1). Thus, international administrations may be benevolent and externally imposed occupations that make them difficult to distinguish from liberations and revolutions (see Arato 2009: 11). In addition, Western think tanks, such as International Crisis Group (ICG), have played a significant role in examining, monitoring, and observing fragile and conflict-affected states and have exerted "influence on agenda setting, policy making and policy implementation" (de Guevara 2014: 546). In particular, as Sonja Grigat (2014: 655) shows, ICG and similar groups have tried to "discursively discipline their audience through practices and procedures characteristic of liberal governance into this specific form of social action and corresponding mind-sets, thus perpetuating liberalism as the global 'regime of power.'"

In the age of liberal interventionism, the combination of the norms of human rights and peremptory self-defense against the perceived risks coming from fragile states tends to surpass other competing international norms of noninterference in the internal affairs of other sovereign states. The principle of nonintervention is overridden by humanitarian considerations in the case of fragile states. Fragile situations are seen as abnormal and thus subject to the deployment of exceptional powers for imposing normalcy. The label "failed state" enables all forms of intervention—from drone strikes to military adventurism. One of the most intriguing aspects of liberal peace is the justification of interventionism and the challenging of strong and weak states that have adapted non-liberal regimes to create liberal societies and promote economic development. Michael Doyle (1983) explains how liberal societies pursue a two-track policy: a peace-prone policy toward other liberal societies and a war-prone one toward the powerful and weak non-liberal societies. He maintains that liberal foreign policy has resulted in exacerbating interventionism against weak non-liberal societies and hostility toward powerful non-liberal societies. Largely perceiving non-liberal governments as aggressor regimes, liberal societies cultivate an enmity culture toward them. The logic of exceptionalism has a normalizing effect for other states, signaling that if sovereignty, equality, and noninterference in international affairs is to be enjoyed, states must self-normalize along the prevailing international norms and rules that, in essence, mostly are driven by and originate from Western states (see Doyle 2015). As Holsti (2004: 67) maintains, the ultimate purpose of international rescue efforts is not to "replace states, but ultimately to strengthen them."

Using normalization as a discursive framework for justifying interventions is not entirely motivated by a desire to expand liberal peace in the world. Rather, it is symptomatic of how the international order is structured. There is an expectation that states at the top of the pecking order and dominant hierarchies hold specific responsibilities and should intervene abroad to preserve the balance of power, contain and limit wars, and enforce international norms (see Macmillan 2013: 1045). It is thus unclear if liberal interventionism is a reaction to the "breakdown or collapse of the normal order" or if the "surge of optimism about the prospects for a new, liberal, international order made possible by the end of the Cold War" explains the quest for normalization in fragile states (Holmqvist 2014: 129). By the very process of abnormalizing other states, Western states reenforce their ontological security, and the existing order is legitimized as being effective, democratic, and prosperous. Through the discourse of the responsibilization of states, international interveners further normalize their hierarchically dominant roles and reproduce their international status, power, and self-conferred privileges. The need to normalize other states gives meaning to the international community and multilateral frameworks, as spaces for exercising power and controlling conduct in world politics. Imposing normalcy over conflict-affected societies is also aimed at local consumption; it indirectly serves the purpose of reproducing normalized orders in Western societies by reminding Western citizens of the benefits of living in peaceful and rules-based social and political orders.

Moreover, the "normalized" West seeks to expand the same experience and process of normalization to the rest of the world in order to justify and reproduce its own mode of normalization and avoid being seen as exceptional or even abnormal by the rest of the world community. The international administrators vest in themselves moral and epistemic authority—as the embodiment of universal principles and values of human rights, democracy, and the rule of law—and the possession of necessary expertise and capacity to transfer those norms and standards to the local subjects. By preaching human rights, democracy, and the rule of law and by possessing the enforcement capacity through military and police personnel as well as financial resources, international actors are able to project not only symbolic but political and sovereign powers. The international administration of conflict-affected territories is often conceived as "a technique to help states to live up to their obligations under international law in situations of conflict and transition" (Stahn 2008: 31). To project such benevolent power, international administrators reduce local actors to unknowledgeable subjects who have to be trained and socialized with international norms. Imposing normalcy operations occurs through the logic of empowerment, where transplanting external norms, rules, and codes of social and civic behavior is effective only if it is voluntarily accepted by the local subjects. To enable the localization of external visions of normalcy, technocratic approaches have been used to build local capacities. International administrations operate on the assumption that local subjects have "the capacity to transcend their anti-liberal, violent modes of thought and action, and to evolve into self-disciplined liberal subjects" (Gheciu 2005: 128).

In the early 1990s, the so-called new wars were increasingly perceived as serious threats to international peace and security. Of particular relevance, the breakup of Yugoslavia and the Soviet Union triggered violent regional ethnic conflicts with devastating domestic and international implications, generating a new international consensus for engaging proactively in halting the violence and restoring peace and stability in those societies. After the Cold War, new violent conflicts emerged around the time when interventions occurred to spread democracy and the market economy to non-Western societies, which were widely labeled as fragile and failed states. State failure and violent conflicts became the main threat to dominant states and international institutions, transcending the classical interstate conflict as the dominant form of instability among nations (Rotberg 2004). The portrayal of failed states as monsters and threats to international peace justifies interventions aimed at imposing specific conceptions of normalcy. As already noted, "the concept of failed states is not just a label but an ideology" (Woodward 2017: 3), which, we argue, acts as a window into the logics for imposing normalcy. Thus, imposing normalcy entails promoting a discourse that the previous and existing conditions that led to violent conflict are abnormal and should be changed. For example, Gregory H. Fox (2008: 42) depicts "the civil wars that precipitated UN involvement" as "signals of social dysfunction, if not outright collapse, in the host states," labeling local protagonists as "rebel groups" that "had simply opted out of normal politics." The concept and idea of fragile and failed states entails the notion that something is broken and needs to be fixed, rebuilt, and reformed by outsiders. Associating post-conflict states with weak governance structures, lack of economic freedom, and social backwardness categorizes and treats them as "special cases of transformation societies that are transitioning from authoritarian rule to democracy" (Schneckener 2011: 237). The prevalent discourse of failed and conflict-affected states as anomalies to international order that need to be contained, managed, and eventually transformed has become the dominant justification for international interventions in world politics. The remedy for fixing failed states was founded on the predicaments of liberalism. In particular, the liberal peace is seen as an optimal solution, where states establish domestic and interstate peace based on a shared democratic system, human rights protection, and economic connectivity and interdependence (Doyle 2012). It is an extension of the democratic peace theory holding that democracies do not go to war with each other. The liberal peace agenda enshrined the will to normalize fragile states through international missions ambitiously designed "to reverse as much . . . institutional collapse as possible" through "monitoring elections, securing human rights, reinvigorating criminal justice systems and demobilizing combatants," in the hope of engineering "cohesive political communities that reflected the principles of pluralism and tolerance" (Fox 2008: 42).

Early efforts to globalize the liberal peace took place after the Second World War, with the occupation and normalization of Germany and Japan. The American occupation of Germany showed that "defeated populations can sometimes be more cooperative and *malleable* than anticipated" (Dobbins et al. 2003: 20; emphasis added). Japanese occupation showed that "democracy can be transferred to non-Western societies" (Dobbins et al. 2003: 51). The "demilitarization and democratization" agendas—which took different forms in both cases—were hence seen as a success that could be used in other conflict-affected societies. During the Cold War decades, international interventions were mostly related to ideological rivalry between the United States and the Soviet Union, which exploited local conflicts and regime change to expand their geopolitical influence. A limited number of UN peacekeeping missions were deployed in zones where the status quo and frozen conflicts suited great powers. Since the early 1990s, a new era of interventionism emerged, coupled with the enhancement of doctrinal thinking. One of the most impactful examples of policy adaptation of the liberal peace was the "Agenda for Peace" in which UN Secretary-General Boutros Boutros-Ghali observed, "There is an obvious connection between democratic practices—such as the rule of law and transparency in decision-making—and the achievement of true peace and security in any new and stable political order. These elements of good governance need to be promoted at all levels of international and national political communities." Since then, UN peacebuilding has been understood as providing "support for the transformation of deficient national structures and capabilities, and for the strengthening of new democratic institutions," resting on "the consensus that social peace is as important as strategic or political peace" (UN Secretary-General 1992: para. 59). Liberal interventionism was later reinforced by former British Prime Minister Tony Blair, whose 1999 doctrine of international community recommends that international leaders "establish and spread the values of liberty, the rule of law, human rights and an open society" in which "we are all internationalists now." US President George W. Bush advocated a highly interventionist military doctrine of "pre-emption," alongside the pursuit of liberty and freedom, in his National Security Strategy of 2002 (Dunne and MacDonald 2013: 8).

IMPOSING NORMALCY THROUGH STATEBUILDING AND PEACEBUILDING

The discourse of failed states posits two anomalies in conflict-affected societies: the incapacity of the state to govern and the broken social relations among the groups in conflict. As a remedy, statebuilding and peacebuilding took hold as a discourse and policy of intervention, becoming central to the work of the UN and other international organizations as well as a foreign policy priority of many Western states. By nature, interventions seek to reconfigure local identities, norms, institutions, and practices and to "bring about outcomes that would otherwise not have occurred" (Reus-Smit 2013: 1065). Through peacebuilding and statebuilding activities, the international community seeks to create the institutionalized and legal conditions for governing, disciplining, and normalizing local populations (Richmond and Visoka 2021). Ultimately, the adoption of international norms, materialized through legal enactment and implementation of norms, is seen as the main objective of peacebuilding and statebuilding interventions (Groß 2015: 315).

In policy discourse, normalizing fragile and conflict-affected societies features prominently in most international peacebuilding and statebuilding interventions. For example, the United Nations Mission of Observers in Tajikistan explicitly linked its mandate to the "restoration of peace and normalcy in the country" (UN Security Council 1994). The focus of the United Nations Special Mission to Afghanistan was to "bring about the restoration of peace, normalcy and national reconciliation and the reconstruction and rehabilitation of war-stricken Afghanistan" (UN General Assembly 1995: 2). Later, the UN's emergency assistance for Afghanistan, prior to the US-led intervention in 2001, was framed around the close interrelationship between peace, normalcy, and reconstruction (UN General Assembly 1998). The UN Interim Administration Mission in Kosovo explicitly endeavored "to create conditions of normalcy in Kosovo under which all peoples can enjoy the benefits of democracy and self-governance" (UN Security Council 1999: 23). Later still, the efforts of the European Union (EU) at peacemaking between Kosovo and Serbia was explicitly about the normalization and improvement of the everyday lives of people (Visoka 2017b). The purpose of the UN Integrated Mission in Timor-Leste was to assist the country to "return to normalcy" and achieve "full institutional normalization" through "security-sector reform, strengthening of the rule of law, democratic governance and socio-economic development" (UN Security Council 2009a). In Iraq, one of the main functions of the Coalition Provisional Authority (2003) was "to ensure the wellbeing of the Iraqi people and to enable the social functions and normal transactions of everyday life." In the conflict-affected region of Bangsamoro in the Philippines, normalization was a central feature of the 2014 peace agreement, signifying "a process where communities can achieve their desired quality of life within a peaceful and deliberative society" (President of the Philippines 2019: 2). To that goal, multifaceted normalization programs were envisaged to cover "the aspects of security, socio-economic development, sustainable livelihood, political participation, confidence-building, and transitional justice and reconciliation" (President of the Philippines 2019: 2).

If statebuilding and peacebuilding feature prominently in those missions' objectives, statebuilding is understood as an antidote to rebuilding and fixing failed states, focused on "strengthening state structures and institutions as well as the capacities for the state apparatus to govern" (Schneckener 2011: 235). Statebuilding has emerged as "a disciplinary, bureaucratic and problem solving process" devised to maintain "the neoliberal state, current patterns of resource distribution, the liberal normative claim of superiority, global governance, externality and conditionality as well as the framework of rights, intervention and moderated forms of sovereignty" (Richmond 2014: 9). However, as Woodward (2017: 7) observes, states that are labeled as failed are not necessarily "failed or even failing" but "lack the specific capacities and qualities that these various intervening actors need to accomplish . . . their own organizational mandates and goals." Similarly, peacebuilding becomes a platform for the pacification and normalization of conflict-affected societies through a new normalcy. Peacebuilding entails addressing the root causes of conflict and developing structures for preventing the recurrence of violent conflict. It aims at dealing with the past by dealing with justice, dealing with the present by offering services and development, and dealing with the future by engineering state and societal transformation. It has come to be understood by the UN as the sum of all "efforts to create the foundations for sustained peace after conflict" (UN Secretary-General 2014: 2). As argued by Roland Paris (1997: 56), "peacebuilding is in effect an enormous experiment in social engineering—an experiment that involves transplanting Western models of social, political, and economic organization into war-shattered states in order to control civil conflict: in other words, pacification through political and economic liberalization." Such discourse is also prevalent in scholarly debates. Richard Caplan (2005: 65) defines "normality" as "a stable peace and the establishment of effective mechanisms of domestic democratic governance." For Mary Kaldor (2012: 65), normality is a synonym for "long-term peace." Those who support normality are considered "local advocates of cosmopolitanism," whereas others are labeled as "nationalists" (Kaldor 2012: 128).

Imposing normalcy through statebuilding requires constructing governance structures that are not only capable of shaping a local population's conduct through different institutions, procedures, and policies but can also grant a disciplining, monitoring, and examining role for the international civilian and military presence (see Joseph 2009). To create "normal" societies, international interveners first need to construct a capable state. As Timothy Edmunds and Ana Juncos (2020: 5) illustrate, seeking to build a capable state represents a "form of governance insofar as it aspires to constitute particular kinds of subjects through dominant discourses and imaginations about what a 'capable state' is or should be." Thus, capacity building is linked directly with the political project of imposing on local societies what a normal state should look like and how it should act. Particularly promoted is the Weberian form of statehood, concentrating on security provision through a focus on the exclusive monopoly over the use of force and other institutional capacity-building objectives (Edmunds and Juncos 2020: 9; Lottholz and Lemay-Hébert 2016). In the Weberian model, capacity building takes the form of enhancing liberal subjects with knowledge, skills, and normative values to carry on the implementation and enforcement of liberal norms at the local level, enabling further responsibilization and self-normalization. The primary techniques for creating responsible subjects consist of deploying administrative and supervisory mechanisms. Capacity building often involves training local public servants and politicians on policymaking, implementation, and evaluation. Those particular types of knowledge and skill are seen as crucial for developing a capable state that responds to the demands of the wider population. Capacity building reduces the agency of local actors, though, on the assumption that they lack knowledge and that they should receive incentives for becoming normal and functioning agents. As Edmunds and Juncos (2020: 17) show, "the recipients of capacity building are problematized as 'incapable states,' weak in institutions, lacking power and agency in the face of the challenges they face, and in need of external assistance and expertise." Doyle (2015: 181) confirms that characterization when positing that "international capacity offsets local incapacity and can launch a process of peacebuilding that restores order, builds new institutions, and launches economic development." Simultaneously, the very attempt to build capacities for local subjects results in "building their own capacity for statebuilding and related interventions" (Woodward 2017: 76), a process that perpetuates and reproduces hierarchies of power and dominance. Accordingly, Woodward (2017: 124) holds that "state-building has become ever more institutionalized, but not in the countries where they intend to intervene but rather for and among these intervening actors."

Relevant examples of how statebuilding operations superseded local agency can be found in Afghanistan, Bosnia, Kosovo, or Timor-Leste. The UN's main goal in the latter three countries was to build new state institutions and impose new constitutions, norms, rules, and practices by populating those post-conflict societies with a large number of international experts who would set an example and promote Western and democratic norms (Gheciu 2005; Arato 2009). Creating capable states requires constant diagnosis and examinations that take place through externally designed knowledge production, which determines the degree of normalization as well as the duration of the international presence. In imposing a new order of normalcy, the UN constantly engaged in monitoring and reviewing the performance of national authorities. As a strategy for statebuilding, the 2006 Afghanistan Compact was described as an effort to nurture the country's transition to "normalcy." The strategy, aimed at rebuilding Afghanistan by mirroring Western state structures, aspired to build "an effective, accountable state in Afghanistan, with targets for improvements in security, governance, and development, including measures for reducing the narcotics economy and promoting regional cooperation" (Rubin 2006: 1). Democratic governance and the protection of human rights was considered a cornerstone for political progress in Afghanistan. The liberal state in Afghanistan was envisaged to "rapidly expand its capacity to provide basic services to the population throughout the country," through recruiting "competent and credible professionals to public service on the basis of merit"; to "establish a more effective, accountable and transparent administration at all levels of Government"; and to "implement measurable improvements in fighting corruption, upholding justice and the rule of law and promoting respect for the human rights of all Afghans" (London Conference on Afghanistan 2006: 3). Such statebuilding strategies and contracts were intended to ensure that national actors internalized liberal norms and values and demonstrated their learning and capacity for self-government of their own population. That process intended not only to implant new codes of institutional and social conduct but also to maintain international authority and supremacy over the national actors.

Prior to a full-scale normalization process, the establishment of security infrastructure was considered fundamental for ensuring the consolidation of state institutions as well as social and economic recovery. Security sector reform is defined by the UN as "a process of assessment, review and implementation as well as monitoring and evaluation led by national authorities that has as its goal the enhancement of effective and accountable security for the State and its peoples without discrimination and with full respect for human rights and the rule of law" (UN Secretary-General 2008: 6). Security sector reform is usually linked to effective disarmament, demilitarization, and reintegration of former combatants and is seen as critical to ensure a statebuilding process operating on the basis of the rule of law, civilian control, and democratic accountability.

As part of security sector reform, the UN and other international organizations undertake activities to establish new security forces, reform the police and intelligence sector, train border and prison guards, and develop other necessary providers of public security. Building an effective local police force is seen as crucial for building normalcy in the aftermath of violent conflict. In Timor-Leste, for example, the UN's main mechanism to build the capacity of local police forces consisted of short basic trainings on conflict management, human rights, and domestic violence, as well as the dissemination of leaflets and learning materials (UN Security Council 2002b: 4). To ensure that local police forces internalize external norms, UN missions may retain certain policing responsibilities (executive policing) and supervise local counterparts. While police reform is perceived as immediately necessary to restore order and enforce the law, it is also seen as a rare opportunity to install a culture of democratic policing, embedded in a Western style of policing consisting of effectiveness, efficiency, accountability, and transparency (Neild 2001: 22). The United Nations International Police Task Force (UNIPTF) defines democratic policing as "concerned strictly with the preservation of safe communities and the application of criminal law equally to all people, without fear or favor" (see Stone and Ward 2000: 4). As part of that democratic policing agenda, it includes civilian oversight of police structures, adherence to human rights standards, depolitization, inclusiveness toward minorities and women, and community-oriented policing (Stone and Ward 2000: 11).

An important feature of international interventions and stabilization missions is their monitoring function. In the Foucauldian reading, monitoring represents a complex technology of normalization that entails a dose of disciplinary power but mostly performs power through hierarchical observation and judgmental presence. In short, monitoring ensures that the targeted subjects are encouraged to normalize themselves while being supervised by an external body. Normalization-building through monitoring missions has taken a prominent meaning in the EU's external actions. For instance, the explicit mandate of the European Union Monitoring Mission (EUMM) in Georgia was to "monitor, analyse and report on the situation pertaining to the normalisation process of civil governance, focusing on rule of law, effective law enforcement structures and adequate public order" (Council of the European Union 2008: 27). Normalization was listed as the intermediary phase between stabilization and confidence building, while "contributing to informing European policy in support of a durable political solution for Georgia" (Council of the European Union 2008: 27). In that instance, the function of monitoring was "conferring a sense of normality to these border areas" (Raquel Freire, Duarte Lopes and Nascimento 2015: 191). When the mandate of the EUMM was renewed in 2019, the meaning of normalization building subtly evolved to include "the resumption of a safe and normal life for the local communities living on both sides of the Administrative Boundary Lines (ABL) with Abkhazia and South Ossetia." While the scope of normalization in Georgia is primarily about returning to the previous conditions of local normalcy, it seeks, in essence, to impose new norms and practices, such as addressing normative and societal issues that previously were deemed normal but that the new regime of normalization building rebrands as abnormal and hence as obstacles to normalization.

While security sector reform in conflict-affected societies is seen as crucial to establishing a sense of normalcy, the promotion of the rule of law also features prominently as a core technique of imposing normalcy. The discourse in Afghanistan was framed along the lines that "security cannot be provided by military means alone. It requires good governance, justice and the rule of law, reinforced by reconstruction and development" (London Conference on Afghanistan 2006: 2). As Mark Fathi Massoud (2019: 10) stipulates, "law becomes part of the technology they [elite actors] use to create stability and sow legitimacy in those areas where and among those populations over whom they seek control." The rule of law is an essential part of liberal peacebuilding. According to the United Nations (2004: 4), the rule of law is "a principle of governance in which all persons, institutions and entities, public and private, including the State itself, are accountable to laws that are publicly promulgated, equally enforced and independently adjudicated, and which are consistent with international human rights norms and standards." In the UN discourse, promoting justice and the rule of law is part of UN "efforts to maintain international peace and security and to rebuild shattered societies," and "without credible machinery to enforce the law and resolve disputes, people resorted to violent or illegal means" (United Nations 2004: 59). The rule of law is considered a distinct normative value of modern liberal democratic states and an instrumental principle to achieve political and social order as a precondition for post-war stability, peace, and justice (C. Bull 2008: 44).

As a field of intervention, the rule of law aims to achieve the maximum effect of normalization. By seeking legal coherence and fair and impartial enforcement of the law, interventions make sure that everyone in a society is subject to normalization. In other words, the principles of equality before the law, accountability, fairness, legal certainty, and transparency function to develop homogeneous social conduct and equalize power relations, ensuring that everyone who behaves in accordance with the law avoids putative measures and enjoys freedom. The law is proclaimed to be the sovereign that determines what is normal and abnormal. By default, a society governed by democratic laws can counter "recalcitrant and repressive authority," and "end corruption, instability, and tyranny" (Massoud 2019: 2–3). The rule of law retains the disciplinary and sovereign powers of the state while also seeking to discipline and constrain the conduct of the general population. As "a vehicle of disciplinary power," the rule of law "is the means through which a uniformity of objectives and norms is efficiently normalized and transmitted" (Humphreys 2010: 105).

Following the international intervention in Bosnia and Herzegovina (BiH) in the early 1990s, the UN prioritized reforming the police service and reestablishing the rule of law. Toward that achievement, the UNIPTF was charged with "light" authority to monitor, observe, advise, train, facilitate, and assess the policing dynamics in Bosnia. Mainly driving the focus of those goals were contextual factors evident after the war in BiH. The strategy of international community was to use vetting and screening of local police to filter and reconstruct those forces, remove the deviant and spoiler elements, and ensure compliance with international policing standards (Vejnovic and Lalic 2005). The UNIPTF provided short training courses that consisted of information about police reconstruction, human dignity, and community policing (Day 2000: 157–60). The United Nations Mission in Bosnia and Herzegovina (UNMIBH) established two police academies in Bosnia, to train police and new cadets, including minority police officers. UNMIBH's police restructuring involved creating institutional and organizational structures, reducing political interference in police work, establishing independent police commissioners, and deploying minority police officers to different regions of BiH. Parallel activities included strengthening police components within the criminal justice system (which entailed creating various institutional mechanisms to foster cooperation between police and judicial bodies in Bosnia) and consolidating effective state law enforcement institutions and inter-police cooperation mechanisms, such as the integrated State Border Service, which manages the land and airspace borders for the whole territory of Bosnia (UN Security Council 2002a). Following the inability of the UNIPTF to reform successful police forces and establish solid structures for democratic policing in Bosnia, the EU launched its first police mission abroad, in 2003, to address that issue. The European Union Police Mission (EUPM) in Bosnia and Herzegovina aimed at "mentoring, monitoring and inspecting, to establish in Bosnia a sustainable, professional and multiethnic police service operating in accordance with best European and international standards" (Council of the European Union 2005). The

EUPM's activities consisted of improving the capacities of local police forces and the institutional framework of the police, as well as monitoring political control over the police. While the main preoccupation of the EUPM was police reform, its efforts to fight organized crime were limited to providing institutional support to Bosnian police authorities. The EUPM engaged in soft approaches, by trying to coordinate all local and international actors, networking and exchanging information, and promoting partnership with civil society.

In Kosovo in 2008, the EU deployed its first and largest rule of law mission abroad, the mandate of which was to "assist the Kosovo institutions, judicial authorities and law enforcement agencies in their progress towards sustainability and accountability and in further developing and strengthening an independent multi-ethnic justice system and multi-ethnic police and customs service, ensuring that these institutions are free from political interference and adhering to internationally recognized standards and European best practices" (Council of the European Union 2008: 2). That mandate entailed enforcing an external agenda on the rule of law through the EU's own special police force as well as through judges and prosecutors who administered international or hybrid trials. In addition, the European Union Rule of Law Mission in Kosovo tried to impose the norm of the rule of law by monitoring Kosovar law enforcement agencies and courts, passing on new skills and knowledge, and advising on how to internalize and perform rule of law norms while retaining some executive and correctional powers to enforce disciplinary power. Isabelle Ioannides and Gemma Collantes-Celador (2011: 417) explain, "this approach of strong control over the police/rule of law reform process tries to combine—even within a single mission—an international presence whereby limited executive and oversight competences (executive mandate) can co-exist with monitoring, mentoring and advisory roles towards the local administration (non-executive functions)."

International administrations impose normalcy not only from the top down, through statebuilding, but from the bottom up, through peacebuilding and social reconstruction. That approach is enabled by extending the discourse on failed states to also include disintegrated and broken societies. In other words, the discourse of failed states is concerned not only with the failure of state institutions to provide order and security but with social relations and its conditions in the aftermath of war. A remedy for a broken society is its reconstruction. Social reconstruction has emerged as a "crucial component of peacebuilding and peace maintenance in states and societies that have been disrupted to the point of collapse as a result of civil conflict and intercommunal violence" (Elliott 2003: 257). Social reconstruction is seen as "reactive, restorative and preventive" and as "directed towards individuals, towards the rehabilitation of communities and towards the rebuilding of civil society" (Elliott 2003: 259). Reconstructing a society entails seeking to impose a new set of norms and values that would form the new social fabric. Social reconstruction aims at "constructing a cosmopolitan sensibility" (Kaldor 1996: 513). The normative target is for the wider population to achieve a "level of tolerance and peaceful co-existence;" so that it "gains social cohesion through acceptance of a national identity that transcends individual, sectarian, and communal differences" (United States Institute of Peace, n.d.). Tolerance is seen as a remedy to overcome anger and prejudice, resolve disputes peacefully, and practice mutual respect. It is seen as crucial for restoring social relations and achieving reconciliation. The process of social transformation and intergroup reconciliation takes part within the framework of the rule of law and through new state institutions. The capacity of societies to internalize norms is cherished as an enhancement of social capital, aimed to ensure that individuals and communities comply with the rules and norms and, when necessary, police and discipline themselves through social intervention.

The main technology for imposing normalcy from the bottom up and through everyday normalization is the development of an active civil society encompassing nongovernmental organizations, media, and other think tanks guided by Western values and dependent on donor funding. Liberal peacebuilding prioritizes the development of civil society as a way to improve the chance of succeeding in post-conflict transformation through widening local participation, improving socioeconomic conditions, and maintaining public order and stability. As part of a peacebuilding agenda, civil society is expected to help create spaces and opportunities for dialogue and reconciliation, to prevent and mitigate local violence, to resolve conflicts by applying features of a traditional justice system and customary values and norms, to provide space where former combatants can transform and contribute to peace, and to facilitate engagement between subaltern communities and state institutions. The international community uses civil society to "foster the principles of good governance" and "ensure respect for human rights and the rule of law, as well as promote the peaceful resolution of conflicts within societies" (Paffenholz 2013: 348–49). For instance, the rule of law is seen as more likely to be successful when local communities are involved in the process of making and enforcing laws and where the potential conflict spoilers and moderate political parties and civil society groups are consulted in the process of appropriate adjustment of the rule of law and justice institutions. The role of civil society groups is to work with local communities and educate them with liberal norms (see Carey 2012). That task involves establishing numerous educational programs, such as summer camps to promote democracy, human rights, and peaceful coexistence between communities. Media campaigns, intended to reach out and discipline the wide population with new norms and values that should guide societal conduct, are aimed at the mass society and seek to abnormalize local norms and to privilege new international norms and codes of conduct. International actors tend to support civil society only as long as they mediate the normalization process and serve as a local proxy. When local civil society groups are associated with critical social movements, donor support is withdrawn (Hellmüller 2013; Vogel 2016).

For example, in Kosovo, Western donors have used civil society groups and think tanks as instruments for imposing norms on the rule of law through examination, reporting, and monitoring of the performance of the government and compliance of the wider society. The focus of the rule of law in Kosovo has been developing government policies and legislation as well as enhancing the capacity and effectiveness of courts and law enforcement agencies to fight corruption and organized crime and to reduce political interference in the judiciary. For example, since 2015, the Group for Political and Legal Studies has run the Rule of Law Performance Index in Kosovo, which serves as "a monitoring mechanism designed to assess the performance of institutions, with a particular focus on the justice system in Kosovo" (Group for Political and Legal Studies 2020: 5). That initiative and others undertaken by media and civil society groups (such as the Balkan Investigative Reporting Network) represent bottom-up interventions that seek to pressure the government and public institutions to internalize and comply with rule of law norms. Such comprehensive forms of examination through monitoring, consulting, and assessment of judicial institutions enable the formation of knowledge that ranks the process of normalization as well as identifies areas for further intervention. The function of court monitoring not only serves to discipline judges, prosecutors, and defense lawyers but also is intended to have a wider societal impact by demonstrating the putative measures that could happen for those who breach the law. Such bottom-up interventions turn civil society into citizen police who observe and report on the compliance of the norms related to the rule of law. By using media reporting charged with naming and shaming discourse, bottom-up interventions may be more effective in demonstrating the normalizing function of the law and its putative measures and thus enhancing the strategic interests of foreign interveners than are other top-down measures undertaken by donors and foreign interveners.

The locus of interventions not only encompasses state institutions and civil society groups but also reaches out to the everyday life of ordinary people. The everyday is "discovered" as a space where "ordinariness, normality and routine are performed, existing in places but transcending all physical spaces at the same time" (Brewer et al. 2018: 16). Normalization interventions are seen as plausible only when they are intermingled with the everyday practices and routines. As Roger Mac Ginty (2014: 550) shows, "the everyday is regarded as the normal habitus for individuals and groups, even if what passed as 'normal' in a conflict-affected society would be abnormal elsewhere." It allows a deep form of social engineering, where subjects are expected to overcome and replace ethnic anger, hate speech, intolerance, and violence with a new culture of peace and civility. Everyday peacebuilding has emerged as the most intimate form of normalization. Its process places the burden and responsibility for transformation on citizens themselves and holds them accountable for any violent conduct. Everyday peacebuilding seeks to target different social groups, but youth are considered most often as crucial for implanting a new generation of peacebuilders. Brewer et al. (2018: 251) submit, "Children need to be socialized into everyday practices of peace building, [to] develop socially learned behavior which they inherit from their parents, extended family, teachers and church leaders. Everyday life peacebuilding practices are thus future oriented and can address positive peace and social transformation." The everyday approach is a form of peacebuilding that seeks to change the mundane ways in which citizens think about conflict and other fellow citizens.

Central to promoting everyday peace is the process of generating data for measuring and thus examining and judging it. Everyday normalization goes as deep as utilizing indigenous technical knowledge as a means through which local abnormalities are identified through hybrid and participatory methods and then distilled into policy-relevant knowledge guiding new modes of intervention (see Visoka 2020). Roger Mac Ginty and Pamina Firchow have proposed everyday peace indicators as a qualitative measurement of knowing the everyday peace. Those indicators seek to use local indicators that define the context-specific meaning of peace, rather than donor-imposed frameworks of determining local normalcy. Using everyday peace indicators seeks to involve local communities to "establish their own priorities, contribute to their own projects and determine their own outcomes," as well as to "be actively involved in the design, monitoring and evaluation of any external interventions" (Firchow 2018: 152). While that approach may appeal as inclusive and emancipatory, the foremost aim of everyday peace indicators is to seek to add legitimacy to international interventions and to make them more effective. They intend to expose grassroots areas that need to be normalized, and they ultimately silence critical voices that long have highlighted the methodological and epistemological limitations of Euro-centric knowledge of post-conflict societies. As Firchow (2018: 155) admits, "using community generated indicators to identify community priorities is helpful to interveners designing participatory interventions."

Despite efforts to impose normalcy through peacebuilding and state-building measures, the experience of the past three decades has shown that international interventions do not tend to have a definitive and clear-cut ending. The exit of foreign intervening powers is often conditioned on the capacity of local institutions to continue on the "right path" and generate legitimacy. Although the end goal of contemporary interventions is normal-ization, the fluidity of that condition leads to never-ending interventions, always blaming the local subject for failing to achieve the externally imposed standard of normalcy. In other words, if local authorities want foreign forces out of their country as soon as possible, they have to fulfill the external conditions at what is more often than not an unrealistic pace. In itself, the discourse of normalization of conflict-affected societies normalizes the per-manence of conflict and the impossibility of achieving a desired normalcy (Holmqvist 2014). Thus, contemporary efforts for imposing normalcy are prone to and driven by failure. Often, to maintain political agency and avoid responsibility, peacebuilding organizations tend to ascribe their failures to the unintended consequences caused by multiple agencies (Visoka 2016). Embracing failure as an enabling force for international intervention makes success and performative effectiveness an unattractive and irrelevant crite-rion for justifying and legitimating governmentality over post-conflict and troubled societies. When policymakers fail at imposing normalcy, they tend to blame local actors or the local context for such failures, otherizing the failures in the process. There is an interesting parallel to be made here with the story of Mary Shelley's *Frankenstein*. Through a contemporary reading of Shelley's book, Bruno Latour notes, "We have failed to care for *our own* creations. We blame the monster, not the creator" (Latour 2011: 20).

Consequently, genuine efforts for peacebuilding and reconciliation disappear in an endless struggle of priority diffusion, mission reconfiguration, and adaptation to changing local circumstances. The ontological politics of ignoring the consequences of peacebuilding are related to the desire to preserve the authority and legitimacy of peacebuilding organizations, to maintain dominant hierarchies of order, and to achieve externally constructed intentions at the expense of distorted local peace. Contrary to what we often know, the exit of peacebuilding operations does not represent the end of international intervention in the societies involved. As noted by Doyle (2015: 186), "the age of intervention is far from over," and "the record of interventions is far from consistent." Thus, failure of liberal interventionism has a productive and generative function. As Branch (2011: 30) argues, "intervention becomes highly self-referential and self-justifying." Failure triggers more intervention, intervention necessitates more intervention, and more intervention means more dependence, more fragility, more resistance, and, ultimately, more open and covert conflict (Visoka 2017b). Existing global normative and political conditions permit both intervention and nonintervention regardless of the inability to succeed in achieving the desired outcomes, while causing harmful consequences. In that constellation, the modes of interventionism become more hidden and fluid in nature, and it is difficult to distinguish intervention from nonintervention, normalcy from abnormalcy.

CONCLUSION

At the heart of contemporary interventions is the desire to universalize particular conceptions of normality, especially in relation to failed states. Western states are most known to launch wars and interventions abroad in the name of spreading and defending liberal values, democracy, and human rights. The target of normalization always shifts away, making intervention a never-ending process rather than a limited endeavor. Entry into fragile states is framed as being about addressing human rights abuses, whereas exit is conditioned on turning them into functioning and responsible states. In the name of those liberal values, Western states constantly search for places that are deemed illiberal and thus abnormal in relation to the Western lifestyle. Difference is abnormalized on the pretext that liberal values are universal and resonate with all humans, and liberal democracy is obliged to defend those values abroad. In that context, normalization becomes a practice in pursuit of human betterment, progress, and happiness. Essentially, the liberal has recently taken the connotation of the global. The allusion to global values is actually to particular Western values and norms normalized on the global stage. Waging wars and imposing normalcy through peacebuilding and statebuilding interventions are seen as necessary practices for creating order, to be directed against monstrous enemies who have captured fragile states and become a risk to the normal international order.

Thus, the prevailing assumption that international interventions intend to rebuild states and societies that reflect Western norms and states could be misleading. Although the narrative of international interventions in conflict-affected societies is about rebuilding peace and stability or reconstructing state institutions, the scope of normalization is not about returning to the past order of normalcy or about establishing a new normalcy that resembles many political, economic, and cultural features of Western states. It is about the creation of zones for intervening actors to perform their power and realize their interests. In that regard, as technologies for implementing the ideology of liberal interventionism, peacebuilding and statebuilding are not necessarily interested in spreading international norms; rather, they seek to implant contextual regimes of governmentality as well as to retain hierarchies of inequality and imbalance between states in the international system. The prevailing logic in international interventions is not that of reflection but that of diffraction—namely, the constant displacement and redirection of purpose and outcomes of intervention. In other words, international interventions do not simply want to build states and societies that perfectly mirror the Western model of statehood; they want to build hybrid and ambivalent states that are derivate of Western states but that are never as authentic and able as the idealized Western state. That effort is enabled by invoking fluid meanings of normalcy and accepting the dynamics of hybridization with local norms and practices. Constant in the endeavor, though, is a quest to ensure that states and societies subject to intervention are never good enough and as normal as the Western states and that they are constantly subject to hierarchical examination and political judgment. It seems, then, that the project of imposing normalcy is a project for normalizing international governmentality, where fragile states provide a suitable discursive space to exercise that governance.

4 ✦ Restoring Normalcy

In this chapter, we attend to dominant discourses and practices for restoring normalcy in disaster-affected countries. Normalcy-restoring practices have been alternatively justified as aiming to facilitate the return to "conditions before the intervention" (Kratochwil 2010: 198), a status quo ante, or as interventions aimed at establishing a new normalcy—more stable and resilient than a past situation. In that broad cluster of practices, normalcy is understood as a willingness for conflict- or disaster-affected societies to return to pre-event social, political, and economic conditions, through local and international perceptions of what constitutes "stability" or the previous normal state in this context or through the establishment of a new normal configuration. This chapter reviews the wide range of discourses and practices for restoring normalcy, focusing particularly on the strands of resilience building and disaster management. The first strand looks at the restoration of preexisting conditions—at "bouncing back" and stabilization as supporting the establishment of a semblance of normalcy. The second strand understands restoring normalcy in a more proactive sense, with references to "bouncing forward" and "building back better" as well as normalization through structural or societal stability, with the aim of creating a more stable "new normal"—stable enough in its dysfunctions to self-manage and avoid disturbing the established order. Both strands begin from the same premise of mapping out the wide array of abnormal behaviors in the international system and the limited capacity of international actors to transform "turbulent societies" into fully accepted (normal) actors in the international arena.

This chapter is divided into three main sections, highlighting the separate discourses and practices of restoring normalcy. The first section looks at the normative common ground between those discourses and practices, that is, the recognition that we are operating in a complex environment and the understanding of restoring normalcy as a way to deal with the normalization of instability. That understanding generally fits well with the Foucauldian figure of the incorrigible. We argue that conflicts and violence are increasingly normalized, along with emergencies and disasters, which constitute a stepping-stone for discourses and practices of restoring normalcy. Echoing Foucault is the portrayal of "difficult" or "turbulent" states as normal in their abnormality, harboring violence as a constitutive trait, and normalizing instability to the extent that what constitutes an "emergency" becomes the new normal. Analyzing the general turn toward complexity theory as buttressing the framework of restoring normalcy, we contrast that framework with the modernistic one associated with imposing normalcy practices, discussed in chapter 3. Operating in a complex environment does not mean the end of intervention; actually, the complexity framework enables new forms of interventions, moving away from international liberalism and toward alternative practices of interventions. Coexisting in the literature are two competing understandings, "simple complexity" and "general complexity," both associated with a specific understanding of restored normalcy. Simple complexity theory helps us understand practices aimed at restoring a semblance of normalcy. A disaster is seen as destabilizing the status quo, and actors aim at reverting back, or "bouncing back," to a previous equilibrium, the status quo ante. General complexity theory presents an alternative discourse for understanding complex social systems that have emerged under the label of "nonequilibrium approaches," or punctuated equilibrium theory, where disasters or conflicts produce large-scale departures from the past, leading to radical change. That understanding of complexity is closely associated with discussions about aiming for new normalcy, or, in general, "bouncing forward" to a new, more sustainable equilibrium, rather than "bouncing back" to an old, imperfect one.

The second section of this chapter analyzes the two strands of discourses and practices of normalcy restoration: restoring normalcy as a return to a preexisting state and restoring normalcy as striving for a new, more sustainable normal state. We specifically trace discourses and practices in the fields of resilience building and disaster management. In the third section, we look at three case studies that, combined together, give us a perspective about normalcy-restoring practices and different understandings of normalcy. First, we analyze the reconstruction in the Philippines after Typhoon Haiyan and the concept of "building back better," which is specifically tied to the discussion on new normalcy. "Building back better" has particularly emerged in the disaster management literature as a slogan for disaster recovery and reconstruction, especially since the Indian Ocean tsunami in 2004. Second, we look at the reconstruction of New Orleans after Hurricane Katrina, which exposes both a pre-disaster normal to which nobody wanted to return and intrinsically political and racialized efforts to build a new normalcy. We connect that discussion with the literature of New Urbanism, which details how plans and designs for glorious new urban communities have met with local resistance or simply failed to deliver on promises. Third, we look at Haiti after the 2010 earthquake, connecting "dreams of normalcy" in Haiti with the constant abnormalization of the country since its independence. Since the earthquake, the concept of the "refoundation of the state" has particularly emerged as a leitmotif for avoiding reverting back to the state of "bad normalcy" that prevailed as a status quo ante. So far, however, the "refoundation of the state" has not yielded the expected results, which has not stopped Haitians from dreaming of a normalcy that would be more sustainable and inclusive. Finally, we conclude this chapter with thoughts about the new containment strategies through which the world's politicians aim to deal with on-the-ground complexity. It appears that most projects aiming at building "new normalcy" end up re-creating a semblance of "old normalcy"—a distorted image of the status quo ante, embedded in the prevailing and preexisting sociopolitical structures.

THE INCORRIGIBILITY OF DISASTER-AFFECTED STATES

The discourse of restored normalcy sits well with the discussion of the incorrigible figure in Michel Foucault's typology of "abnormals," as discussed in chapter 2, even if that figure is less developed than the other two in Foucault's work. For Foucault, the incorrigible is "the individual who cannot be integrated within the normative system of education" (Foucault 2003: 291) but, at same time, is "caught in the apparatus of rectification" (Foucault 2003: 328). If the monster is, by definition, the exception (the quintessential "failed state" that calls for practices imposing normalcy, as discussed in chapter 3), the "individual to be corrected" is an everyday phenomenon (Foucault 2003: 58). According to Foucault (2003: 299), there is an imbalance of the whole, a sort of bad setup in the structures that ensures that the instinct, or a certain number of them, is made to function "normally" in terms of their own regime, but "abnormally" in the sense that the regime is not controlled by levels whose function is precisely to take charge of the instincts, put them in their place, and delimit their action.

We argue that Foucault's discussion finds echoes in the portrayal of "difficult" or "turbulent" states as normal in their abnormality, harboring violence as a constitutive trait, and normalizing instability to the extent that what constitutes an "emergency" becomes the new normal. What becomes abnormal in such a context is a relative period of calm and sustainable growth uninterrupted by crises, political protests, and spikes of violence. Globally, 90 percent of casualties during disasters over a twenty-year period (1996–2015) occurred in low- or middle-income countries (CRED and UNISDR 2016), and 90 percent of road deaths happen in low- and middle-income countries. In turbulent societies, disasters and death seem to be features of normal life. They become normalized forms of abnormalities. That normalization leads scholars such as Robert Kaplan (1994) to normalize conflicts in the Global South, where "criminal anarchy emerges as the real 'strategic' danger." The solution to such danger does not rest, however, with transforming abnormal countries into well-behaved members of the international community. Kaplan observes, "We are entering a bifurcated world. Part of the globe is inhabited by Hegel's and Fukuyama's Last Man, healthy, well fed, and pampered by technology. The other, larger, part is inhabited by Hobbes's First Man, condemned to a life that is 'poor, nasty, brutish, and short'" (1994; see also R. Kaplan 2014). Those states are stuck in a "pre-modern" world, without possible avenues. As Robert Cooper (2004: 17) explains, "Nobody wants to pay the costs of saving distant countries from ruin. The pre-modern world belongs, as it were, in a different time zone: here, as in the ancient world, the choice is again between empire or chaos. And today, because none of us [in the liberal, postmodern West] sees the point of empires, we have often chosen chaos." Since, as posited by Kaplan and Cooper, the West cannot really sort out the "chaos," Edward Luttwak (1999: 44) advises policy elites to actively resist the emotional impulse to intervene in other peoples' wars. In the last twenty years, multiple authors have reiterated that type of otherization, broadly associated with a thesis dubbed the "new barbarism" (Duffield 1996; Richards 1996; Salter 2002: 150–53; Tuastad 2003). It has also appeared in other forms, notably in seminal works in the discipline, through a conceptualization of "primal anarchy" (Buzan, Wæver, and de Wilde 1998: 50, 52, 70), a framing recently and rightfully questioned by other authors (Howell and Richter-Montpetit 2019: 5–9). According to Michael Ignatieff (1999: 98), one of the most prominent liberal interventionist scholars, the real-life implications that the "new barbarism" thesis has for policymakers include "eroding the ethics of engagement."

Beyond the "new barbarism" thesis, the discourse of restoring normalcy is associated with the recognition of the various little abnormalities that make up the abnormal figure of the incorrigible. As discussed above, incorrigibles function "'normally' in terms of their own regime, but 'abnormally' in the sense that this regime is not controlled by levels whose function is precisely to take charge of the instincts, put them in their place, and delimit their action" (Foucault 2003: 299). We find such functioning clearly in the discourse about building resilience in fragile states, "where violence may have come to be accepted as 'normal'" (OECD 2016: 58). Normalizing violence becomes a natural trait for "abnormal" countries in which "the population witnessed, and many of them participated directly in, the civil war's violence, thus normalizing violence" (USAID 2015: 13; see also FAO et al. 2017: 50). Departing from the Hobbesian approach of civil violence as the antithesis of "normal" social process (Rule 1992: 91), the resilience-building approach connects with the definition of structural violence as "the normal, unexceptional, anonymous, and often unscrutinized violence woven into the routine workings of prevailing power structures" (Soron 2007: 2), or, in general, with political theories of civil violence (Rule 1992: 170). Slavoj Žižek (2009: 2) calls that violence "objective violence"—the violence inherent in the normal state of things.

The normalization of armed conflicts and violence is not a new phenomenon. As Mark Duffield (1999: 20) noted more than twenty years ago, "there are about fifty conflicts which are considered as normal," and "in order to draw international attention, a local crisis has to reach record-breaking levels of barbarity." In a similar fashion, the United Nations Office for the Coordination of Humanitarian Affairs (2015: 3), referring to the longevity of humanitarian crises and highlighting the international reluctance to end protracted crises, argues that "protracted is the new normal." It notes that 89 percent of humanitarian funding from members of the Development Assistance Committee of the Organisation for Economic Co-operation and Development (OECD) goes toward protracted crises with the average duration of displacement being seventeen years and growing. For Human Rights Watch's Philippe Bolopion (2019), "atrocities the world had promised to end are the new normal." There is nothing exceptional about the international dimension of such normalization; similar everyday normalization of violence also takes place on the domestic level, with gender, race, ethnicity, or religious dimensions to the process. Gendered or racialized violence in the United States and many other developed states needs to meet a similarly exceptional threshold to make the news.

In parallel with the normalization of violence, emergencies have also increasingly become "normal" events. The United Nations Development Program (UNDP 2004: i) deplores that "the development community generally continues to view disasters as exceptional natural events that interrupt normal development and that can be managed through humanitarian actions." Although emergencies are traditionally defined as urgent situations created by an abnormal event, mounting attacks on this understanding beckon us to approach disasters as no longer exceptional and extraordinary events. In the "dominant view" in disaster studies in the past, categorizing an event as a "disaster" implied "a discontinuity with normal, routine events" (Hewitt 1983: 10), while categorizing it as a "catastrophe" indicated the termination of a "normal state." To recover from disaster then means to restore a sense of normal time, to bring back a routine order, and to provide social stability and functioning (Phillips and Fordham 2010: 8). That understanding is tied to the fact that it has become increasingly difficult to separate a disaster situation from "normal" conditions of poverty, something that can be more aptly described as "permanent disasters" (Khondker 2002: 335–36). Hence, some argue that "for the greater part of humanity, hazard and disaster are simply just accepted aspects of their lives. So normal, in fact, that their cultures are partly the product of adaptation to those phenomena" (Bankoff 2002: 3). As Peter Walker (2007: 5) argues, "we call it a chronic crisis; they call it normality." Hence, he explains further, "outside of some truly abnormal events—we can think of hurricane Katrina hitting New Orleans or the tsunami hitting Indonesia—there are few exclusively humanitarian crises. There are extremes of normality." The normalization of humanitarian crises is also characterized by the growing acceptance of higher levels of vulnerability, malnutrition, and morbidity (Bradbury 1998: 330). The "difficult places," the wide array of fragile states that do not conform to the civilized norm of advanced countries, are hence understood as "countries where crises are the norm" and "where what are often considered the prerequisites for 'normal' development are absent" (Levine and Mosel 2014: 1).

In that context, resilience building is understood as restoring some notion of normalcy, and coping refers to what people do "in the short term in abnormal circumstances" (Levine and Mosel 2014: 3; UNDP 2004: 135). It means enhancing the capacity of individuals and communities "to absorb, adapt and transform to the shocks and risks that they should normally be expected to deal with" (OECD 2013: 1). Hence, coping becomes adapting to the normalcy of abnormality. Resilience is then seen as the ability to accommodate abnormal or periodic threats and disruptive events (Haigh and Amaratunga 2011: 6).

Discussing the concept of the "emergency imaginary," Craig Calhoun (2008: 87) suggests, "Today we see not one large emergency dismissed as an exception, but innumerable smaller ones still treated as exceptions to an imaginary norm but repeated so frequently as to be normalized." Even disaster sociologists, whose literature is reviewed below, have come to terms with that normalization. One key figure in that literature, E. L. Quarantelli (2006), notes that "far more 'social' facilities and activities need to be restored to 'normal' functioning after a catastrophe than after a disaster." The sociology approach moves toward a "vulnerability framework" where normal daily life becomes difficult to distinguish from disaster (Wisner et al. 2003: 10). A "social vulnerability approach" to disasters entails viewing them not as exceptional events but as the product of normal or usual processes. For Kenneth Hewitt (1983: 25), most disasters "are *characteristic* rather than accidental features of the places and societies where they occur." Hence, it is crucial to recognize how the roots of disaster management depend on the way "normal everyday life turns out to have become abnormal, in a way that affects us all" (Bertolt Brecht, cited in Hewitt 1983: 29).

The normalization of emergencies creates new apparatuses for managing populations at risk and posing risk—for instance, the refugee camp infrastructure, whose main function, according to Michel Agier (2011), is to "manage the undesirables." The normalization of emergencies also makes resilience a coping mechanism to deal with anticipated and permanent crises. In that framework, instability is not viewed as necessarily abnormal, and conflicts and disasters are seen not "as deviations of the normal state of affairs" but as inherently constitutive of the reality many countries face on the everyday level. Interventions are not confined to exceptional situations but acknowledge the continuities and discontinuities between crisis and normalcy (Duijsens and Faling 2014: 172). In that context, resilience, or "efficient recovery," entails coming to terms with a permanent state of affairs made of contingency, adaptability, vulnerability, and instability. In their critical account of resilience, Brad Evans and Julian Reid (2014: 3) convincingly argue that "instability and insecurity are the new normal as we become increasingly attuned to living in complex and dynamic systems which offer no prospect of control." Resilience is thus about adaptability and recovery and seeks to normalize instability through a succession of various forms of intervention—the "normalization of the sense of perpetual, background instability that so often acts as the affective background for resilience-based policies and programs" (B. Anderson 2015: 62).

Policymakers' capitulation in the face of that complexity again echoes Foucault's discussion of the figure of the incorrigible, who requires correction because all the usual techniques, procedures, and attempts at training within the family have failed. Nineteenth-century psychiatry attempted "correction" through the "infantilization" of the figure and its acts. The incorrigible calls up around him a number of specific interventions, a new technology of rectification, and needs to be restrained but fails to be completely transformed. In normalcy-restoring practices, we see a similarly paternalistic discourse, treating difficult states as countries that simply cannot be transformed. Either there has never been a "road to Denmark" for those states (Fukuyama 2015: 25), or that road has long being closed and quarantined. There is simply a possibility to mitigate, to a certain extent, the effects of their abnormality on the world stage—in other words, to normalize the abnormality. Their internal structure is normally violent and prone to episodes of turbulence, and they function normally in terms of their own regime; however, the effects of that specific setup need to be checked and managed. In that context, resilience-building practices and disaster management discourse act as a new technology of normalization, managing the repercussions of those turbulent states on world affairs rather than attempting to fully transform them into liberal states.

If the normalization of emergencies and crises constitutes one of the normative foundations for discourses and practices of restoring normalcy, the second normative foundation can be found in complexity theory and its logical extension, the governance of complexity. Restoring normalcy is grounded in the general conversation about complexity, and understanding the different iterations of that concept sheds light on the different understandings of restoring normalcy. The governance of complexity is closely linked to complexity theory in its diverse iterations—whether, to use the typology of Edgar Morin (2007) or Paul Cilliers (1998), through "simple complexity" (also known as "restricted complexity") or a more "extended understanding of complexity" (or "general complexity"). In the former framework, the object of intervention is constructed in terms of complexity; in the latter, the divide between the subject and the object of intervention is effaced through an understanding of the embeddedness of the relationship (Chandler 2014: 26; Byrne and Callaghan 2014: 39–56). As discussed in the following sections of this chapter, restricted complexity is associated with restoring normalcy as bouncing back to a state of normalcy, whereas general complexity is associated with restoring normalcy as bouncing forward to a new, more stable equilibrium.

The association between complexity theory and the literature on resilience makes that understanding more explicit. The concept of resilience, which was developed within systems ecology in the 1970s, was connected with the neoliberal laissez-faire theories of Friedrich Hayek (Walker and Cooper 2011: 143–44; Chandler and Reid 2016: 34–39) and has since flourished in various subfields, including international relations. Resilience is understood there as a "discursive field through which we negotiate the emerging problem of governing complexity" (Chandler 2014: 13). The governance of complexity, which is loosely based on a spontaneous order and social evolution close to Hayek's theories (Walker and Cooper 2011: 148–50; Chandler 2014: 23), presupposes that complex life is beyond the planning, control, or comprehension of any individual. Reductionist theories, such as those that have buttressed modern liberal interventionist approaches, have therefore failed to grasp the interactive nature of complexity (Chandler 2014: 21). To a certain extent, both understandings of complexity (restricted or general) rely on overcoming universal linear assumptions—the presupposition that one can trace specific outcomes of interventions to a single cause. Through the recognition of our limited ability to manage the sheer complexity of social systems, disasters came to be seen as normal features of international relations. The "normal accident" theory, for instance, says that disasters are to be expected because of interactive complexity and tight coupling (Perrow 1999). In that context, nonlinearity and complex causation do not necessarily mean the end of interventions, as some would assume; to the contrary, complexity enables new forms of interventions, moving away from international liberalism and toward practices of restoring normalcy.

Niklas Luhmann's well-known system theory provides an example of complexity theory (albeit one generally depicted as belonging to the category of "restricted complexity") and of its connection with normalcy. For Luhmann (1990: 180), a complex social system "feeds upon deviations from normal reproduction"; it thrives on disruptions to its own state of equilibrium. System trust rests on the appearance that everything is normal. The point of departure for Luhmann is the shift in the current norm toward disorder, nonlinear complexity, and unpredictability. Following Erving Goffman (see chapter 2), Luhmann calls the appearance of normalcy the "presentational" base of system trust (Lewis and Weigert 1985: 463)—a way of reducing complexity or a general mechanism or attitude that makes our everyday life manageable. The improbability of social order explains its normality (Luhmann 1995: 116). Thus, Luhmann's theory aims at cutting through the appearance of normality and looking to explain the "normal as improbable" or "the other side of the normal form" (Luhmann 1993: 114, viii). That explanation seems closely aligned with the characterization of the Foucauldian figure of the "incorrigible," "typically regular in its irregularities" (Foucault 2003: 58).

A SENSE OF NORMALCY OR BUILDING A NEW NORMAL? FROM BOUNCING BACK TO BOUNCING FORWARD

This section sets out to analyze and distinguish the two specific strands of discourses and practices of normalcy restoration: restoring normalcy as a return to a preexisting state and restoring normalcy as striving for a new, more sustainable normal state. The first understanding of restoring normalcy is associated with restoring a semblance or a sense of normalcy by aiming to revert to the situation that prevailed before an event occurred, be it a "natural disaster" or a conflict. That specific understanding of restoring normalcy is directly connected with the "simple complexity" paradigm, as discussed previously. Indeed, most definitions of resilience connect with the return to a preexisting state, the status quo ante. As argued by Thomas Koslowski and Patricia Longstaff (2015: 7), "probably the most comprehensive development of the idea of resilience frames the concept as a return to normalcy"; hence, as noted by Brenda Phillips (2009: 21), "one of the most common desires heard after a disaster is to 'return to normalcy.'" The general meaning of the word *recovery* is to regain a normal position or condition, which connects with the Latin root of the word *resilience, resilire*, meaning "to spring or jump back." As a team of researchers from the Public Entity Risk Institute notes, recovery has typically come to mean a return to a status quo ante (Alesch et al. 2001: 14).

The view of restoring normalcy as a return to a preexisting state is generally connected with the concept of "engineering resilience," understood as the ability of a system to return to an equilibrium after a disturbance (Holling 1973: 17). The faster the system bounces back, the more resilient it is (Pimm 1984). Since the 1970s, the resilience concept has also been used in ecology literature, to describe systems that undergo stress and have the ability to recover and return to their original state (Klein, Nicholls, and Thomalla 2003: 35). Resilience is viewed there as a buffer for conserving what you have and recovering to what you were (Folke et al. 2010), as "being able to bounce back from being battered or wounded" (Timmerman 1981: 32). The concept also has roots in the psychology and psychiatry of the 1950s, the term *resilience* having emerged from a longitudinal study of children born into poverty (Johnson and Wiechelt 2004: 658). In that perspective, resilience is seen as the "capacity to cope with unanticipated dangers after they have become manifest, learning to bounce back" (Wildavsky 1988: 77).

The equilibristic view of resilience has been very influential, especially in policymaking circles and in the everyday usage of the word *resilience*, with an emphasis on the ability to "bounce back" to normalcy after the occurrence of a disaster (Davoudi 2012: 300–301; McEntire et al. 2002: 269). That emphasis is also present in urban studies: "many scholars of urban and regional phenomena—perhaps following on the example set by disaster studies—hew closely to a single-equilibrium or 'bounce-back' version of resilience" (Pendall, Foster, and Cowell 2010: 73). Examples abound of such an understanding of restoring normalcy, along with multiple concepts gravitating around the understanding of resilience and recovery as "bouncing back." David Omand (2005: 14), former UK security and intelligence coordinator and permanent secretary at the Cabinet Office, defines resilience as "the capacity to absorb shocks and to bounce back into functioning shape, or at the least sufficient resilience to prevent stress fractures or even system collapse." Similarly, the Interagency Group—composed of six major nongovernmental organizations (NGOs)—understands resilience as recovering or "bouncing back" after an event (Twigg 2009: 8). The OECD (2011: 15) defines social resilience as "the capacity of a community (or organization) to adapt under adverse conditions and restore a sense of normalcy from an external shock," and along with the US Department of Homeland Security, the OECD defines rapid recovery as "the ability to return to and/or reconstitute normal operations as quickly and efficiently as possible after a disruption" (OECD 2014: 25). Similarly, "efficient recovery" is defined by the World Bank (2014: 98) as "steadying lives and livelihoods back to normalcy, and rapidly restoring critical social, physical and productive infrastructure and service delivery." Historically, similar concepts, such as restoration, also implied getting back to normal.

In that context, local businesses can be seen as playing a large role in restoring "some form of normalcy" in a post-conflict setting while being instrumental in promoting "pockets of normalcy" during conflict (Sweetman 2009: 57). Investment in the private sector can create jobs, drive infra-structure development, and "strengthen the sense of normalcy and peace" (UNDP et al. 2016: 5). The same can be said of traditional, non-state leaders who have been identified as crucial actors in "restoring some semblance of normalcy and security" in Darfur (Tubiana, Tanner, and Abdul-Jalil 2012: 102) or Somalia (Jeng 2012: 272). Efficient service provision can also help restore a sense of normalcy: "regular functioning of the school system signals stability and a return to normalcy and builds the foundation for peace and investment in the future" (UNDP et al. 2016: 8). The return of refugees is usually one of the signs hinting at restoring a semblance of normalcy on the ground. For instance, a few months after the American interven-tion in Afghanistan, a spokesperson for the UN High Commissioner for Refugees highlighted that there were "some signs of stability and normalcy returning to parts of Afghanistan, including the return of more than 14,000 people to various parts of the country over the past week alone" (UNHCR 2001). In the context of post-conflict Sierra Leone, normalization has been understood as infra-politics, with people conducting their routine business through low-level activities that cumulatively buttress a sense of stability (Hills 2011; Martin 2016).

In considering the iteration of normalcy-restoring practices that empha-size bouncing back, it is important to underscore the difference between the general objective and the actual practice by actors. Most practices of restored normalcy do not lead to a return to a mythical "previous condi-tion," or "pre-event norms." Conflicts and disasters transform societies in multiple ways, making it impossible to return to pre-event social configura-tion. Instead, normalcy-restoring practices create new features of normalcy. Their distorted mirror image of the status quo ante does not exactly match the original image of normalcy. Hence, in that context, one could say that most actors are primarily concerned with the creation of a "semblance of normalcy" (Tamer-Chammas 2012: 218) rather than with genuinely return-ing to pre-event norms.

The second understanding of restoring normalcy aims at "bouncing for-ward" to a new normalcy, understood as being more stable and sustainable than the previous order. Partially in response to the limits of the approach that emphasizes "bouncing back" and returning to a former, single equilib-rium, an alternative discourse to help understand complex social systems emerged under the label "nonequilibrium approaches," or punctuated equi-librium theory. That discourse is associated with the previously discussed "general complexity" paradigm, where disasters or conflicts are understood to produce large-scale departures from the past, leading to radical change. Nonequilibrium approaches range from multiple equilibria systems— understanding how social systems adapt in times of change, leading to new equilibria—to evolutionary resilience (Davoudi 2012: 302), complex adaptive systems analysis (Pendall, Foster, and Cowell 2010), or social-ecological resilience (Folke et al. 2010), directly challenging the idea of equilibrium. The semantics used in those approaches is more proactive, with practices of restored normalcy seen as producing a "new normal" by "bouncing forward" (Manyena et al. 2011) after a disaster and "building back better."

According to the first iteration, in which a system may "bounce forth" to a new equilibrium (Davoudi 2012: 301), destabilizing events change the "normal" process of equilibrium and status quo, leading to the establishment of a new equilibrium (Baumgartner, Jones, and Mortensen 2017: 56–57). While "minor accidents recede in the normal operations of everyday life," a "major catastrophe explodes the map and brings a new resolution to systemic networks of power, revealed as fundamentally disaster-ridden" (Larabee 2000: 4). That strand of the discourse of restoring normalcy recognizes that "the hope or confidence that things would soon get back to normal belies the reality of the post-disaster dynamics" (Alesch et al. 2001: 75). Simply restoring infrastructure will not bring "things back to normal"; the social systems comprising the local communities have been changed forever. Beatrice Pouligny (2014: 5) similarly notes,

> Discourses too often refer to the idea of "restoring" or "returning to" something associated with the status quo before the violent conflict, or even "repairing" what has been broken or destroyed. But violence transforms as much as it destroys. It creates new realities and forms of relationships, particularly when it has lasted for decades. International aid programs themselves induce additional transformations. These nonlinear evolutions need to be fully considered when thinking in terms of resilience.

Another good example of the same type of thinking is encapsulated in President George W. Bush's State of the Union address four months after 9/11: "The last time I spoke here, I expressed the hope that life would return to normal. In some ways, it has. In others, it never will" (Bush 2002). Bush's statement reflects an understanding of the magnitude of the change brought about by the 9/11 terror attacks. According to Froma Walsh (2002: 34),

Resilience is commonly thought of as "bouncing back," like a spring, to our pre-crisis norm. However, when events of this magnitude occur, we can not return to "normal" life as we knew it before September 11. Our world has changed and we must change with it. There is no going back. A more apt metaphor for resilience might be "bouncing forward," to face an uncertain future. This involves constructing a new sense of normality as we recalibrate our lives to face unanticipated challenges ahead.

"Bouncing forward" entails grasping the opportunity to do better. As Walsh (2002: 35) notes, the Chinese pictogram's symbol for crisis represents both danger and opportunity. It means, in other words, embracing disaster's true potential. Disaster can lead to the creation of a "therapeutic community," increasing the social bonding and group culture, but soon after a disaster, the ordinary ways of thinking and interacting creep back in, and life goes back to normal. In some cases, the "therapeutic community" is replaced by a "corrosive community," wherein existing inequalities are exacerbated, different agendas and perceptions emerge, blame is assigned, and groups fight for resources (Nigg and Tierney 1993: 16; Passerini 2010: 313; Picou, Marshall, and Gill 2004). Attempts to fix blame for disaster losses are a common occurrence and can lead to protracted conflicts between social groups.

For a specific strand of the literature—broadly understood as the sociology of disaster—"the central meaning of disaster is social disruption" (Rodríguez, Quarantelli, and Dynes 2007: xiii). That strand is generally associated with the broad church of functionalism in organizational theory, providing its scholars with a model of society under normal conditions and a way of thinking about disasters as systemic disruptions (Webb 2007). In that tradition, disaster "seriously disrupts normal activities" (Cisin and Clark 1962: 30); hence, "disaster is interpreted as a rupture in the 'normal' human–nature relationship, as a break with the understanding of nature as maternal and life-giving, and the irruption of the monstrous and the aberrant" (Hoffman 2002: 126–27; Munro 2015: 510–11).

Social disruption, that irruption of the aberrant, can lead to positive change *in fine*. The long history of scholarship on disasters as moments of opportunity for social change can be traced back to the 1920s (Lovekamp 2010: 369; Nigg and Tierney 1993: 1; Pacholok 2013: 24), to an analysis of a munitions ship explosion in 1917 in Halifax, Canada (Prince 1920). Samuel Prince argued that because catastrophes interfered with the equilibrium of the social institutions within a given society, they are critical to social change: "Halifax has been galvanized into life through the testing experience of a great catastrophe. She has undergone a civic transformation, such as could hardly otherwise have happened in fifty years" (Prince 1920: 139). Similar examples include the Three Mile Island nuclear accident. After that disaster, the local power structure in a small town in Pennsylvania became more pluralistic, and community politics became more "cosmopolitan" (Behler 1987). Those cases are part of an established nexus of work on how disasters can lead to social change, with actors vying to reestablish the former equilibrium and with other social groupings vying for a different ordering of society (Sjoberg 1962: 356; Sorokin 1942).

Traditionally, such analysis starts with the notion that in a disaster context, "the population is not in, and will never quite return to, its normal predisaster state" (Killian 1956: 4). Within a society, a disaster can create channels for mobility and demographic shifts that might not exist in "normal" times, or a disaster may bring to light structural changes that were already in motion prior to the catastrophe (Lovekamp 2010: 370). For instance, Form et al. (1956: 181) discuss how a "disaster system arises spontaneously to meet the human problems created and to restore a social equilibrium," so that as new systems emerge, continuity is found between the old and the emergent social systems. Disasters hence produce "a window of opportunity" (Olsson et al. 2006), opening up new alternative systems of configuration. According to that logic, seizing emerging windows of opportunity is considered to be the mandate of the Office of Transition Initiatives of the United States Agency for International Development (USAID 2020). Such windows are the "resilience dividend" that Judith Rodin (2015), former president of the Rockefeller Foundation, sees as enabling populations to create and take advantage of new economic and social opportunities after catastrophes. For Ulrich Beck (2015), disaster-produced opportunity is the "emancipatory catastrophism" that enables the analysis of the "positive effects of bads."

That understanding makes some researchers following a Schumpeterian logic of creative destruction, such as Kamila Borsekova and Peter Nijkamp, argue that disasters are a blessing in disguise: "Apparently, an environmental disaster may lead to a better and more sustainable outcome for an ecosystem in the long term. Similar positive findings may be recorded on external shocks in human-made or social systems" (Borsekova and Nijkamp 2019: 2; see also Nigg and Tierney 1993: 6–8). After discussing how countries in a war may sometimes be better off in the long run compared to countries at peace, Borsekova and Nijkamp (2019: 2) argue that "in human history it appears that disasters may create challenges or threats which may be turned into new opportunities," even though there are ample examples about how, as Michal Lyons (2009: 385) explains, "reconstruction usually reproduces vulnerabilities, failing to take forward, or even recover development." Interestingly, that strand of work is based on nonlinear dynamics in complex spaces, with strong roots in complexity theory, as discussed earlier. If disaster management is usually geared toward achieving the original equilibrium situation (Borsekova and Nijkamp 2019: 3), communities also have the possibility to strive for a new, more optimal equilibrium.

BUILDING BACK BETTER

One particular example of the new normalcy discussion is the semantics that has emerged around the concept "build back better" in disaster management literature. "Build back better" has become a slogan for disaster recovery and reconstruction since the Indian Ocean tsunami in 2004 (Mannakkara, Wilkinson, and Francis 2014), with the UN Secretary-General's special envoy for tsunami recovery, Bill Clinton, endorsing the concept in his recommendations. Clinton (2006: 6) explicitly connected the concept with the social change approach discussed above, noting that "while a disaster can actually create opportunities to shift development patterns—to build back better—recovery can also perpetuate preexisting patterns of vulnerability and disadvantage." In the literature, building back better is directly connected to practices of restored normalcy, especially as an alternative to the limitations of approaches promoting a return to the status quo ante. Even before 2004, building back better was seen, in its first iteration, as "opportunities to rebuild in a better way, instead of succumbing to the natural desire to put things back the way they were as soon as possible" (Monday 2002: 4). In discussing post-recovery Sri Lanka, Sarah Khasalamwa (2009: 73) noted that "post-crisis recovery should not be merely a return to the status quo ante but an attainment of a 'new normalcy,'" Similarly, following the private sector summit on post-tsunami reconstruction, James Lee Witt Associates (2005: 19) wrote, "The primary goal for reconstruction is beyond returning communities to their previous sense of normalcy. It is, instead, building back better." Mannakkara, Wilkinson, and Francis (2014: 1) retraced the provenance of the concept of building back better.

> As a result of witnessing the ongoing impacts of disasters on communities, a concept started to emerge where post-disaster reconstruction

was to be taken as an opportunity to not only reconstruct what was damaged and return the community to its pre-disaster state but to also seize the opportunity to improve its physical, social, environmental, and economic conditions to create a new state of normalcy that is more "resilient." This concept was termed "Build Back Better," suggesting that successful recovery of communities following disasters needs to amalgamate the rehabilitation and enhancement of the built environment along with the psychological, social, and economic climates in a holistic manner to improve overall community resilience.

The concept of building back better came to be particularly salient following Typhoon Haiyan in the Philippines, partly because the Philippine administration used such semantics. The language of the planning document for reconstruction after Typhoon Haiyan (or Yolanda, as the storm was known in the Philippines), entitled "Building Back Better," percolated into regional and local disaster recovery and reconstruction plans and led a wide array of international NGOs (including ActionAid, Islamic Relief, and Plan International) to use the same semantics (see Islamic Relief Worldwide, n.d.; Yates 2014). Interestingly, while most actors understand that building back better incorporates a process drastically different from returning to a pre-event norm, the plan sets out that "the objective . . . is to restore the economic and social conditions of these areas at the very least to their pre-typhoon levels and to a higher level of disaster resilience" (National Economic and Development Authority 2013: 1).

Typhoon Haiyan killed more than sixty-three hundred people when it hit the Philippines in November 2013, displacing four million people and broadly affecting over sixteen million across forty-four provinces. At the same time, with more than twenty typhoons hitting the country on a yearly basis, the natural state of emergency came to be normalized by local politicians and international actors. The undersecretary of the national civil defense agency, Alexander Pama, stated, "We live in a new normal now and it can be hard for people to understand that things are different now" (Milman 2015). Greg Bankoff (2002: 178) pointed out that in the Philippines, disasters are "a frequent life experience" that "has been normalised as an integral part of culture." That "new normal" is internalized by the Disaster Risk Reduction Framework adopted by leaders of the Asia-Pacific Economic Cooperation in 2015. The framework "facilitates collective efforts to build adaptive and disaster-resilient economies in the face of a 'new normal' of increasing disaster risks due to social and environmental changes such as climate change and rapid urbanization" (APEC 2018: 6). Climate change variability for the Philippines is also seen as "the new normal" for which leaders must plan accordingly (Australian Volunteers for International Development 2015: 16), even if a poll conducted in 2015 showed that "only 17.6 percent of the population feels that life has returned to 'normal'" (Tanyag 2018: 565).

Following Typhoon Haiyan, the Sendai Framework for Disaster Risk Reduction, which the UN adopted during the World Conference on Disaster Risk Reduction in 2015, promoted the idea of building back better as a key priority for disaster reconstruction, understanding it in a resilience fashion, as "integrating disaster risk reduction into development measures, making nations and communities resilient to disasters" (United Nations 2015: 21). The UNDP (2010: 19) also presents its recovery efforts as focusing largely on "restoring normalcy following a crisis, transitioning effectively from crisis to development, and using recovery work as an opportunity to 'build back better.'" Like all concepts, however, building back better is prone to manipulation by actors. It comes as no surprise that local NGOs in the Philippines "could not press the elected leaders to explain the concepts of 'building back better'" (Mangada, Tan, and dela Cruz 2016: 24). Others noted that projects for building back better in Sri Lanka and Aceh experienced limited results amid the polysemy of the word *better* (Kennedy et al. 2008; Lyons 2009). The relative easiness of reverting practices back to the status quo ante meant that "many initial intentions to Build Back Better following disasters are quickly overtaken by a need to rapidly get back to a perception of economic and social normality" (UNISDR 2017: 36). That conclusion was shared by the Philippine Working Group, which noted that "many stakeholders have come to think of disaster resilience as 'bouncing back.' Indeed, previous disaster experiences in the Philippines have shown that communities do 'bounce back,' from these events. Communities return to 'normal,' to 'business as usual' and often, this means a return to situations of risk and exposure where they remain vulnerable to the next hazard or disaster event" (ESSC 2016).

As discussed previously, there is an explicit criticism of the "bounce back" approach in the "bouncing forward" discussion. Some have criticized that in the former, "the emphasis is on the return to 'normal' without questioning what normality entails" (Pendall, Foster, and Cowell 2010). In line with the work of Goffman (1959: 21–22), Hendrik Vollmer (2013: 39) has noted that "participants, just like sociological observers of their involvement, will generally tend to refer to *any* order associated with a frame of activity prior to a disruption as having been normal," so long as nobody complains. Good examples of the potential undesirability of the "normal" pre-disaster condition can be found in New Orleans before the onset of Hurricane Katrina and in Port-au-Prince, Haiti, before the 2010 earthquake.

Hurricane Katrina struck New Orleans on August 25, 2005, killing 1,800 people, impacting 2.5 million residences, and displacing between 700,000 and 1.2 million people. The total economic impact to Louisiana and Mississippi is estimated to exceed US$150 billion. Katrina not only destroyed the physical fabric of New Orleans and multiple cities along the coast but also revealed social processes that many people started contesting—a pre-disaster normal to which nobody wanted to return. In other words, "it revealed a set of 'normal' conditions many observers found unacceptable as a recovery target" (Pendall, Foster, and Cowell 2010: 74). A "new normal" was aspired to in social, economic, and political terms (Enarson 2006; Pendall, Foster, and Cowell 2010: 74). Indeed, why would people want to return to "normal" when what had come to be normalized was so obviously and profoundly dysfunctional? As D. E. Apter (2008: 771) explains, "'normalcy' as a social condition may of course hide all kinds of festering sores which, redefined as injustices at a later time can become politically significant." Katrina peeled away the surfaces of the American social order: "[It] was a horrifying act of nature, but one which simultaneously, as a global media event, involuntarily and unexpectedly developed an enlightenment function which broke all resistance. . . . America and the world were confronted by the repressed other America, the largely racialized face of poverty" (Beck 2006: 338–39). In its own way, Hurricane Katrina laid bare, for the world to see, that America, too, had its own castes (Fair 2009: 36).

In line with the premises of the sociology of disasters, Hurricane Katrina was perceived by local government officials and urban planners as a space-clearing moment when the city could be transformed through the application of expert plans, policies, and practices conceived on the premises of neoliberal governance (Barrios 2016: 148; Klein 2007: 513–34). In line with the discourse of new normality, Hurricane Katrina was seen as "open[ing] a window of opportunity for creating more resilient communities" (Berke and Campanella 2006: 193). One of the wealthiest developers in New Orleans, Joseph Canizaro, known as "the local Donald Trump," encapsulated that sentiment by saying, "I think we have a clean sheet to start again. And with that clean sheet we have some very big opportunities" (Rivlin 2005). Even the apostle of laissez-faire economics, Milton Friedman (2005), called the disaster "an opportunity." However, that new beginning had a highly racialized, political nature for many. Richard Baker, a Republican congressman from the city, observed, "We finally cleaned up public housing in New Orleans. We couldn't do it, but God did" (Klein 2007: 4). A white political activist said, "It was impossible not to pick up on this sentiment that this was our chance to take back control of the city. There was virtually a near consensus among whites that authorities should not do anything to make it easy for poor African-Americans to come back" (Rivlin 2015: 56). Talking about a "smaller, safer city" or a "small, taller city" became coded language for a redefinition of the social fabric of New Orleans.

The rebuilding vision after Hurricane Katrina took form through a contingent of New Urbanists, who came to Mississippi and Louisiana to help plan the process and take advantage of the "terrible opportunity" (Dellinger 2006) or "disastrous opportunity" (Lewis 2006). The *New York Times* called New Urbanism's vision for human-scaled urban design, meant to counteract the rise of suburbia, "the most important collective architectural movement in the United States in the past fifty years" (see http://sustainable-transportationsc.org/beyea/), even though the movement has been attacked for resting "on wishful thinking and the arrogance of social engineers who override individual preferences" (Ward 2002: 43). Internal debates in the field of urban planning aside, the rebuilding plan designed by John Beckman for Wallace Roberts & Todd was selected by New Orleans mayor Ray Nagin and the Bring Back New Orleans Commission. It was "a kind of New Urbanism pipe dream" (Rivlin 2015: 210), made of an archipelago of connected neighborhoods. A different yet complementary New Urbanist vision for New Orleans, appropriately dubbed "Operation Rebirth," was put forward by New Orleans real estate developer Pres Kabacoff, who planned to turn "New Orleans into a city like Paris" (Price 2005). Those plans met with local outrage when people realized that they entailed abandoning the more flood-prone neighborhoods of the city to be converted into green space—in effect, turning "black people's neighborhoods into white people's parks" (Rivlin 2015: 214)—and the plan by Wallace Roberts & Todd was later withdrawn by the administration. The rebuilding plans for communities along the Mississippi coast, put together by the Governor's Commission for Recovery, Rebuilding and Renewal in partnership with the Congress for the New Urbanism, largely met the same fate. As pointed out by Eric Owen Moss, director of the Southern California Institute of Architecture and a critic of New Urbanism, the plans for the Mississippi coastline would appeal "to a kind of anachronistic Mississippi that yearns for the good old days of the Old South as slow and balanced and pleasing and breezy, and each person knew his or her role" (Kamin 2005). In most cases, the "communities felt dissatisfied with their design-based plans because they were not appropriate for the time and place of post-Katrina Mississippi" (Evans-Cowley and Zimmerman Gough 2009: 439). Other, approved New Urbanist plans "may be legitimately critiqued as simply perpetuating an old social order" (Tallen 2008: 290). New Urbanist ideas have been "appropriated to justify the demolition of much of the city's public-housing stocks which had been under threat before the storm, and which, contrary to some claims, weathered Katrina remarkably well" (Hartnell 2017: 11). Nevertheless, Beckman's project was selected as part of the US entry at the 2006 Venice Biennial, "a nice compensation for the rough treatment it received in the Big Easy earlier this year" (Saffron 2006).

Quite tellingly, the founding member and leading spokesperson of the Congress of the New Urbanism, Andrés Duany (2009), argues that "looking through the lens of the Caribbean, New Orleans is not among the most haphazard, poorest or misgoverned American cities, but rather the most organized, wealthiest, cleanest, and competently governed of the Caribbean cities." In a sense, the abnormality of New Orleans when compared with other major American cities becomes suddenly normal once otherized from the country and incorporated into an abnormal region. That perspective connects with the wider fact that New Orleans is considered exemplary of national trends (in terms of racial inequalities, for instance) but "foreign" in the national imaginary (Hartnell 2015: 50). The "otherization" of New Orleans led politicians and media commentators to adopt the term *refugee* to describe Katrina evacuees from New Orleans, in a racist denial of American citizenship (Hartnell 2015: 53). At the same time, again in line with the restoration of a new normal semantics, the disaster is understood to offer "the rare opportunity to start over from scratch, potentially with quick results." Duany explains, "For a city to become a city that's planned, it has to destroy itself; the city literally has to molt. Usually this takes 20 years, but after a hurricane, it takes five years. The people can see the future in their own lifetime" (quoted in Pogrebin 2006). Quoting the Stanford economist Paul Romer, who said that "a crisis is a terrible thing to waste," Kenneth Foster and Robert Giegengack (2006: 57) stated, "We must not waste the opportunity that the current crisis in New Orleans represents."

In a sense, the new normal resembles the old normal more than any utopian dream sold to local inhabitants. Even the iconic "Katrina Cottage," which was the shining star of the New Urbanist work on the Gulf Coast after the storm and was supposed to revolutionize emergency housing, ended up as a failed experiment. While it was once seen as bringing "a revolution, where small, efficient and affordable houses on narrow lots in walkable neighbourhoods will be the new normal and the new hot commodity," people preferred their settled ways (Alter 2015). The cottage design, by New Urbanist Marianne Cusato, won a National Design Award from the Cooper-Hewitt Smithsonian Design Museum in 2006. However, though arguably an improvement over the trailers provided by the Federal Emergency Management Agency to serve as temporary housing solutions after disasters, the cottages always had one fundamental problem according to one of the lead designers: as long as they resembled mobile homes, they were susceptible to the strong rejection of mobile homes that most communities exhibit. There was also the issue of the name. One resident pointed out to an architect responsible for the second version of the Katrina Cottage ("Katrina Kernel Cottage II"), "Steve, you made a huge mistake. 'Katrina Cottages' are 'Losing Everything I Ever Owned Cottages,' or 'The End of My Life as I Knew It Cottages.' How could you guys possibly name them that?" (Mouzon 2015). The similar initiative of the "Mississippi Cottage," based on the original design of the Katrina Cottage, received US$280 million through the Alternative Housing Pilot Program, to build 2,666 units along the coast of Mississippi; ten years later, only 100 units could be spotted by New Urbanist Ben Brown. Most have been sold at auction, often at deep discounts, and are hidden in backyards or used as hunting cabins. For New Urbanists, the assessment is clear: people did not want a "new normal," "they wanted to get things back to the way they were as quickly as possible" (Brown 2015).

After Hurricane Katrina, the New Urbanists' bright ideas, although exciting and inspirational, housed only a handful of people (Jacobs 2010). Brad Pitt's foundation Make It Right and its post-Katrina housing project, part of the Katrina Cottage movement, is a representation of the failed experimentation. Once thought of as a project that would recast the possible for the next generation of architects and developers (Curtis 2009), it employed such architectural legends as Shigeru Ban, Thom Mayne, David Adjaye, Kieran Timberlake, and Frank Gehry. But it ended up building houses that are collapsing, rotting, and caving in, and the foundation is now facing a multitude of lawsuits. The ambition of the project was not to return to normality. An architecture journalist pointed out with exuberance in 2008 that "no one could look at these houses and think life here had returned to normal," and the foundation's director said, "The citizens of the Lower Ninth Ward have been accustomed to getting less than regular, so this is an opportunity *to go beyond the normal*" (Blum 2008; emphasis added). What did that opportunity to go "beyond normality" entail? Of the one hundred or so houses built by the foundation, many are now abandoned, and other residents have found themselves with mortgages they cannot afford to break (Bendix 2019). The death knell of those utopian visions was also encapsulated in the launch of a plan called "Resilient New Orleans," which maintained that the constant state of disaster simply needed to be embraced, rather than transformed through grand projects of new normality: "Our adaptation must be both physical and behavioral. Rather than resist water, we must learn to embrace it" (City of New Orleans 2015: 4).

That perspective brings researchers to focus on the concept of continuity (rather than social change) as an analytical device, which was the starting premise of the sociology of disasters. In the context of New Orleans, that concept entails "continuity of social order but also of the conditions of inequality; resumption of a mundane life routine but also endurance of a stratified social structure" (Henry 2011: 221). In a sense, the resilience of the social order is the dominating feature of the restored normalcy after Katrina. As pointed out by Nathanael Rich (2015), "New Orleans has always been a place where utopian fantasies and dystopian realities mingle harmoniously." The follow-up to the disaster mirrored the idea that the new normal is oddly similar to the old normal: "African American hurricane victims in New Orleans were characterized as rampaging thugs, shoot-to-kill orders were issued in response to (erroneous) claims of rampant lawlessness, and New Orleans residents seeking refuge in nearby communities were turned back at gunpoint" (Tierney 2007: 512). The "windows of opportunity" that disasters open connect more with specific interests that can exploit for their advantage than with utopian plans to transcend unjust social systems grounded in sociopolitical history. As such, Duany and Pitt's plans for New Orleans are "illustrative of this tendency to fasten a socially liberal rhetoric of community empowerment to private sector development" (Johnson 2011: 199). New Urbanism is increasingly challenged on the basis that it builds communities for the rich (Dellinger 2006), but after being met with local resistance in New Orleans, even its projects have not been able to redesign the social fabric of the city.

New Urbanism was not only prevalent in New Orleans. The same school of thought extended to Haiti following the 2010 earthquake, bringing similar debates about what kind of normalcy local and international actors aimed to restore. It is first useful to stress the incorrigible nature of Haitian politics in the eyes of the international community. In many locales, but especially in Haiti, disasters are not only physical events but agents of cultural formation. Cultures of disaster happen in places where "frequently occurring natural hazards are integrated into the schema of daily life" (M. Anderson 2011: 8; Bankoff 2002: 3–4). Haiti exists in something of a state of "permanent catastrophe" (Laënnec Hurbon, quoted in Munro 2015: 515); there is not a "non-catastrophic normality" in Haiti. Hence, in Haiti, "crises are not abnormal or periodic interruptions" (Beckett 2013: 40). However, if Haiti has been struck by many "disasters" in its history, the earthquake of January 12, 2010, stands apart in a long list of catastrophes that have impacted the country; it "changed everything, thrusting the country into a new time, one of an ongoing aftermath" (Mika 2019: 1). The degree of infrastructural destruction and human life lost warranted that specific status: estimates oscillate between 200,000 and 300,000 persons injured and 65,000 to 316,000 deaths, and most of the state apparatus was destroyed along with the destruction of close to 260,000 structures in the earthquake zone. While estimates provide only a "rough indication of the situation," some 3 million people (out of a total population of 10 million) are believed to have been affected in some way by the earthquake, with an economic toll of the devastation estimated to be around US$14 billion. The loss amounts to an average of up to 12 percent of Haiti's gross domestic product over the period of 2010–15 (Best and Burke 2017).

The aftermath of the earthquake prompted discussions about returning to normalcy, with various international NGOs aiming to re-create a semblance of normalcy for Haitians. The same conversations erupt from time to time after every single catastrophe, whether it is a tropical storm or a contested election process. However, post-Duvalier Haiti—which really started in 1986, after a popular revolt against President Jean-Claude "Baby Doc" Duvalier (1971–86), the son of President François "Papa Doc" Duvalier (1957–71)—has never been considered a "normal state." To the contrary, if one wants to categorize states, post-Duvalier Haiti clearly falls into the abnormal category, being dubbed either as "a nightmare, predator, collapsed, failed, failing, parasitic, kleptocratic, phantom, virtual, or pariah" or even a "perennial failed state" or "a basket-case" (see Lemay-Hébert 2014: 210n7). In the same vein, disaster-related terms continued to proliferate in relation to Haiti (Munro 2015: 509), considered either an "ecological disaster," a "humanitarian disaster," or a prime example of "disaster capitalism" at its worst. The word *disaster* has become a "kind of metonymy for the Haitian state and its history" (Jenson 2010: 103), closing the loop with the earlier tradition regarding the advent of a black state—the only successful slave revolt in the modern world and the first decolonized republic to have banned slavery—as "the disasters of Saint-Domingue" (Jenson 2010: 103) or as a "monstrous anomaly" (Nesbitt 2013).

While there have always been "dreams of normalcy" in Haiti (Wargny 2008), the normal state of politics in the country is closer to what the International Committee of the Red Cross has dubbed a state of "bad normalcy" (Taillefer 2004). Under Duvalierism, Haiti managed to crystallize many features of the predatory state. Michel-Rolph Trouillot (1990: 161) calls that crystallization the "formalization of the crisis," the "capacity of Duvalierism to transform the aberrant into the normal," including the centralization of the state around the figure of the president, the corruption of the ruling class, and the violence displayed in governing relations between the state and nation. President Jean-Bertrand Aristide (1994–96, 2001–4) continued in the tradition of the personalization of power (Dupuy 2007; Nicholls 1996), which had been "the normal practice in Haiti since independence" (Nicholls 1996: xxxii).

After the 2010 earthquake, the essential questions were, "What to leave under the rubble? What to pick up?" (Dorlus 2010: 14; our translation). In that context, there has been a vibrant discussion in Haiti—mostly led by Haitian intellectuals—over the necessity for the "refoundation of the state," going beyond the mere reconstruction process. The roots of this discussion lie in the fall of the Duvaliers in 1986 and in the sociopolitical debates that arose about the nature of the new state emerging after years of autocracy (Hector 2012: 252). In the Haiti government's national plan for reconstruction, "rebuilding Haiti does not mean returning to the situation that prevailed before the earthquake. It means addressing all these areas of vulnerability, so that the vagaries of nature or natural disasters never again inflict such suffering or cause so much damage and loss" (Government of the Republic of Haiti 2010: 5). The concept of the "refoundation of the state" conveys the intention of going beyond the status quo ante to reach a state of new normalcy, presumably more inclusive and participatory. As Haitian president René Préval quipped, the earthquake is "a rendezvous with history that Haiti cannot miss" (Government of the Republic of Haiti 2010: 3). For Oxfam (2010), the disaster provided "a once-in-a-century chance for change." Bill Clinton observed, "This country has the best chance to escape its past that it's ever had. . . . As horrible as this is, it gives them a chance to start again" (quoted in Fletcher and Guyler Delva 2010). In line with the previously discussed rhetoric of "windows of opportunity" spoken in the sociology of disasters, many analysts coming from very different backgrounds and with different agendas in mind jumped on the fact that the disaster constitutes an opportunity to build a different Haiti (Bourguignon 2010; Castor 2011: 107; Ulysse 2015: 8).

Compassionate onlookers have proliferated new normality visions for Haiti, including plans to relocate the capital entirely or redistribute its citizens in the country (Lindsay 2010; for similar plans for New Orleans, see Foster and Giegengack 2006: 55–58). The semantics of "building back better" were also pervasive in the years following the earthquake. The appointment of Bill Clinton as special envoy to Haiti (2009–11) was certainly one of the reasons for the migration of that framework from post-tsunami recovery (as discussed earlier) to Haiti. In the thinking of former prime minister Michèle Pierre-Louis, which is in line with Foucault's response to the incorrigible figure, building back better must start within Haiti (United States Institute of Peace 2010); the technology of rectification needs to be internalized and appropriated by Haitians. After the earthquake, the Haitian Ministry of Tourism launched an international housing competition, Building Back Better Communities, funded primarily by the Clinton Foundation and the Inter-American Development Bank and seeking to construct four hundred new homes in one hundred days, using designs and structural engineering provided almost solely by foreign firms (UIC Barcelona 2011). Many participants and even some organizers characterized the exposition as a "farce," a "disaster," and a "waste of money" (Regan 2012). The project was supposed to lead to the establishment of an "exemplar community" in the Zoranje region (a floodplain), this time funded by Deutsche Bank. A team from Harvard University and the Massachusetts Institute of Technology "spent exactly one afternoon meeting with existing residents in Zoranje" (Bell 2012) and produced a plan for a "model community" that was never funded or constructed.

Debates about housing and urban planning serve as "a revealing case study wherein foreigners with little understanding of Haitian needs are designing the kinds of communities Haitians should live in" (Bell 2012). Under the pretense of reducing risks, New Urbanist–inspired plans effectively make large segments of the capital's population disappear, presumably reshuffled elsewhere in Haiti. One month after launching Building Back Better Communities, Haitian president Michel Martelly unveiled a bold plan, sponsored by the Prince's Foundation for the Built Environment, to completely redesign Port-au-Prince's downtown. The plan was penned by the "founding father" of New Urbanism, Duany. His idea for a "Port-au-Prince 2.0" involved self-sufficient "urban villages," each with its own separate condominiums and neighborhood watches, for "middle class people" (Lindsay 2011). In 2011, Port-au-Prince mayor Muscadin Jean-Yves Jason suspended all relations with the Prince's Foundation, noting that he was "tired of foreign domination of the reconstruction process" (Haiti Grassroots Watch 2011). But the "foreign domination" in Haiti works hand in hand with a specific local elite. The reconstruction guidelines drafted after the earthquake by a group of urban planners from the Haitian government (again in conjunction with New Urbanist architects, from Miami) treated the recent disaster as an opportunity (Ourousoff 2010), with plans to shift the population across the country. Finally, Duany designed a "Haitian Cabin," a variation of the Katrina Cottage and the Mississippi Cottage. His goal was to tailor the cabin to the Haitian "way of life." As stated on the New Urbanist website, with "attention to how haitians [*sic*] live In [*sic*] Haiti, the shelter designed by Duany Plater-Zyberk & Co. (DPZ) is more rudimentary than anything on the Gulf Coast" (Langdon 2010). Known as "Le Cabanon" (which could potentially be a nod to Le Corbusier 1951 Cabanon de vacances), Duany's cabin was designed in partnership with InnoVida Holdings, and the initial reconnaissance mission for the project included such "celebrities" as retired general Wesley Clark and retired Miami Heat basketball player Alonso "Zo" Mourning. The project entailed a gift of one thousand units and a plan to build ten thousand houses a year, but apart from a small cluster of units built as a reference, it remains only potential. The draft design document for the Haitian Cabin clearly indicates, "First, one must confront that there is a category for whom housing provision is wasted. There are persons that would sell the housing or the donated material and remain homeless. This is listed as a Class I situation. These people find rudimentary and temporary shelter in unhealthy and unsafe locations. They would do much better in the countryside" (Duany Plater-Zyberk and Company 2010: 3). Duany candidly recognized that in Haiti, "the problem is the sociology," and "the reason that it is so hard to design these dwellings is that there . . . these people live in ways that are unlike ours" (Infinity Filmworks 2010: 3m45s). Like many other idealistic notions of societal transformation in Haiti, the various plans for housing and urban development were quickly tabled, and no reconstruction plans for downtown Port-au-Prince have materialized. Meanwhile, the Clinton Bush Haiti Fund invested US$2 million to finish the construction of a luxury hotel in Pétionville, the most affluent part of Port-au-Prince, toward which most of the local elite and expatriates gravitate. Paul Altidor, vice president of the fund, boasted that the 130-room Oasis Hotel "symbolizes Haiti 'building back better' and sends a message to the world that Haiti is open for business" (Reitman 2011). The hotel might be a better indication of what "building back better" really means in Haiti.

Other urban planning nightmares include the development of Morne-à-

Cabris (Village Lumane Casimir), now a ghost town on the road from Port-au-Prince to Mirebalais. Inaugurated by President Martelly, it was supposed to lead to a community of three thousand houses (less than half of which have been constructed), all equipped with modern amenities. Doors have been stolen, plumbing has been dismantled, and many squatters occupy the houses. The project cost US$49 million, taken from the PetroCaribe Fund, now linked to corruption charges in Haiti (Payton 2019). Most of the grand plans for refoundation of the nation—locally or internationally led—and many of the campaigns to radically transform the country (reminiscent of the Marshall Plan) ended up being expensive and wasteful pipe dreams. The "new" normalcy, which is not unlike New Orleans after Hurricane Katrina, resembles the old normalcy and disappointed Haitians, who desperately wanted to see something "new" emerge from one of the worst cataclysms of the twentieth century. In that context, dreaming of a new, radical normalcy for Haitians becomes more important and relevant.

CONCLUSION

In this chapter, we have abundantly referred to New Urbanism and its failure to create communities through design, especially in the context of the post-disaster urban planning of New Orleans and Port-au-Prince. If architectural modernism (exemplified by Le Corbusier, for instance) was grounded in the mildly authoritarian idea of producing a universal subject—a "new man"—then New Urbanism falls into the same modernist fallacy, replacing the "new man" figure with an ideal happy consumer committed to traditional family values. For the architecture critic Michael Sorkin (2013: 230), both movements fall on the same sword: their inability to understand architecture in its messy, delightful diversity. The New Urbanist vision of normality is simply disconnected with the "incontrollable diversity" that makes every city its own social laboratory. Nowhere is that trend more clear than when New Urbanists put forward plans to build a new normalcy for disaster-stricken cities, such as New Orleans and Port-au-Prince. The proactive strand of restoring normalcy does not sit far from practices of imposing normalcy, especially in its aspirational transformativity. However, using the vocabulary of restoring normalcy and coming to terms with a permanent state of crisis and instability made of contingency, adaptability, and vulnerability is the trademark of the framework of restored normalcy.

The technology of restoring normalcy entails a general withdrawal of responsibility for previous failures to impose normalcy—as discussed in chapter 3—as well as a new tactical interventionism, which seeks to impose normalcy through building resiliency and self-sufficiency. In other words, international efforts to restore normalcy represent a renewed rationale to govern risks and vulnerabilities at their source and to suspend any modernist fallacy about progress or stability. In that context, restoring normalcy is generally considered successful if it entails a return to dismal pre-conflict levels or if it manages to stabilize a country enough to enable an exit strategy. Even in more transformative and intrusive practices of building "new normalcy," we generally see the same old normalcy template creeping back. Restoring normalcy fits neatly with the growing emergence of "cut-and-run" stabilization missions, with international actors exhibiting declining confidence in their ability to influence events on the ground, as well as increasing reluctance to accept responsibility for perceived failures of transformative international stabilization efforts. Modest ambitions and a lower degree of normativity make stability a popular concept for international actors, mirroring the concept of resilience (Bachmann 2014: 122–23). As such, stability becomes a matter of balance between politically desirable objectives and empirical realities (Hills 2011: 2), which makes it fit neatly within the framework of restored normalcy.

The concept of containment is inherently connected with normalcy-restoring practices and encapsulates policy recommendations in the context of a permanent state of crisis and instability. From the first time that modern principles of relief were applied—arguably during the Indian famine of 1837–38—"humanitarian action by the state was essentially an issue of *containment*" (Walker 2007: 2; see also Betts 2009: 56). It was seen as an opportunity to encourage discipline and obedience to authority within the confines of controlled relief camps (see also Agier 2011; Dubernet 2017). Some even argue that host countries in the Middle East form a regional "Super-Camp" that is, in effect, an immense zone of containment (Chr. Michelsen Institute 2018). In turn, containment is an integral part of the theories of "new barbarism" or "ancient hatred," discussed in the introduction to this chapter; within such a framework, "the best policy response is containment, i.e. protecting the borders of the West from this malady" (Kaldor 2013). The growing importance of containment strategies is recognized by policymakers. For example, former UN Secretary-General Kofi Annan (2000) noted to member states that "you have become part of a 'containment strategy,' by which this world's more fortunate and powerful countries seek to keep the problems of the poorer at arm's length." The "containment of the dispossessed" is deplored by Nicholas Stockton, emergencies director for Oxfam UK and Ireland (1996: 147). Seen through the prism of new containment strategies to deal with the incorrigible turbulent states and populations in the periphery, normalcy-restoring practices aim to create or return to a societal equilibrium that, while not ideal, enables international actors to keep those "problems" at "arm's length."

5 ✦ Accepting Normalcy

This chapter explores the discourses and practices contributing to the acceptance of certain states as normal subjects in world politics though they share many anomalies with states and societies subject to normalizing interventions. We focus on the acceptance of states that are implicated in breaching the international human rights norms, as an example of uneven politics of normalcy in international relations. Regardless of normative or geopolitical agendas, human rights have become one of the main indicators for measuring the normalcy of states and for justifying international interventions. There are, however, states that manage to retain their international acceptance and seek to forge a sense of normalcy regardless of their human rights record. This chapter demonstrates that the politics of forging a particular meaning of normalcy—thus making it acceptable to others— takes place through a complex set of discourses and political-legal mechanisms. The discourses at play here mainly surround confessional narratives, and the political-legal mechanisms consist of commissions of inquiry and other ad hoc measures to make a particular normalcy acceptable to others. At the heart of discourses of accepted normalcy is a specific production of knowledge that justifies state behavior and political practices deemed as legal, legitimate, and in accordance with the rule of law and international norms. The key technique for states to retain their international acceptance and normalcy is constant surveillance, by themselves and others, through various forms of self-transformation. In that regard, the scope for disciplinary intervention is narrowed to mechanisms and bodies that seek to correct only a particular set of practices deemed abnormal.

The first part of this chapter examines the politics of acceptability in international affairs, to set the context for exploring situations that might be deemed abnormal but are accepted as normal. Michel Foucault's third figure of the abnormal (the onanist) provides relevant resemblances to the subject matter of this chapter. Foucault (2003) stipulates that onanist practices came to be prohibited by society and were subject to prohibitory norms. Unlike forms of abnormalcy that were controlled via external interventionary measures, such as judicial-medical institutions and community, onanist practices were problems to be resolved and controlled by family, parents, and pastoral figures. They required not total control or transformation of the body but individualized and targeted behavioral change. At the heart of the change process has been self-control and confession, truth-telling, and other lite modes of intervention. The focus of such normalization is more individualized and atomized into specific segments of the social practices deemed unacceptable. It is about accepting subjects as equal members while still requiring measures to control and overcome specific practices deemed abnormal.

Translating those features into contemporary world politics, we find striking parallels for understanding a set of discourses and practices that underpin the normalization of states. Human rights abuses are widely practiced among states and, over time, have come to be seen as an unacceptable and abnormal practice, subject to international and national condemnation. Yet some of the many states implicated in human rights abuses retain the status of sovereign, independent, and recognized states, enjoying most of the benefits in the international system and remaining accepted members of the club of states. A normative conflict between sovereign equality of states and the primacy of human rights is at the heart of the struggle for normalization in world politics. On the one hand, principles such as recognition of state sovereignty and noninterference in internal affairs of other states serve as a basis for a pluralist international order with different conceptions and degrees of normalcy. On the other hand, human rights protection has emerged as a major concern underpinning state relations. That normative dualism provides the basis for simultaneous contestation and acceptance of state normalcy. The main carriers of the normative dualism are the politics of friendship and strategic alliances between states. Accepting the behavior of certain countries as normal while labeling others as abnormal springs partially from the relationship between states at hand. Dominant states within alliances and families of states tend to take pastoral roles in normalizing states implicated in human rights abuses. Ultimately, the figuration of international order that selectively accepts certain states as normal and labels others as abnormal reproduces power relations between states.

The second part of this chapter examines the politics of truth-telling and state confession, to uncover some of the core discourses and practices that underpin the acceptance of states as normal entities. In Foucault's work, truth-telling and confession represent central features for understanding the efforts for normalization and self-transformation of individuals. Judging states' behavior and normalcy inevitably requires a normative framework or a set of norms to situate the position of states. Norms such as human rights, political liberties and democracy, and social justice have become some of the key global benchmarks for measuring quality and normalcy of statehood in world politics. Truth-telling and confession is seen as vital for states to retain their status as normal and acceptable members of the international community. In world politics, the confessionary practice of making state reports to different human rights bodies tends to be a major source of seeking to retain international legitimacy and acceptance as a normal state. Yet the very practice of seeking to report to international bodies on human rights compliance enables states to forge their own narrative of normalcy while simultaneously undertaking recommendations for self-regulation and transformation. It is a practice of restoring state subjectivity by being subject to a lite and collective mode of submission. By default, the practice of state reporting and confession for human rights has led to the emergence of human rights diplomacy and has become a major field of foreign policy, where normalization of state compliance with human rights norms is at the heart of international relations. Attempts to forge normalcy usually take place through the production of counterfactuals as well as narratives that reduce the harmful effects of competing narratives. To make sense of those dynamics, this chapter examines states' discourses, rituals, and performances as part of the UN universal periodic review on human rights compliance. Although not the focus of our analysis here, there are also other instances when states are encouraged to establish national truth-seeking commissions or specialized war crimes courts, through which those states retain international acceptance in exchange for internal self-transformation and hybrid forms of normalization (see Visoka 2017a).

Often, state confession and truth-telling is dubiously filled with alternative truths and strategic counternarratives, resulting in accelerating the mode of international normalizing interventions from state confession to a temporal fact-finding inquiry by a separate mechanism. The third part of this chapter examines lite interventionism through commissions of inquiry and fact-finding mechanisms, as an optimal technique for retaining the state's international acceptance while forging small corrective and regulatory impositions from outside. The discussion shows that one function of commissions of inquiry is examination, which is a practice of knowing states according to observation by power holders and is based on certain criteria of normality. Commissions of inquiry can be instruments of political coercion but also suitable mechanisms that enable restoring a state's international status and justifying its normalcy. International normalizing society uses formal inquiries and fact-finding missions as a disciplinary power that describes and analyzes the norm and identifies and examines its breaches. Yet, compared to other types of normalization practices examined earlier in this book, states that are subject to such inquiry are given the opportunity to shape the process of examination through the process of confessional practices. Commissions of inquiry represent a platform for practicing truthtelling by states. The normalcy-maintaining technology at the heart of commissions of inquiry consists of addressing individual cases and redistributing power in those deemed as harming domestic and international norms. In other words, it concerns taking action against individuals and not against an entire society. Situations of accepting normalcy are sustained by appearing to take into account various external judicial-political opinions, findings, and decisions, while holding onto the sovereign right to implement them. That approach enables creating the impression of intervention to correct an abnormalcy without tackling broader political, structural, cultural, and societal features that permit such anomalies.

ONANIST STATES AND THE CONSTITUTION OF ACCEPTABILITY IN WORLD POLITICS

In world politics, it has become a norm that a state wanting to be considered normal and acceptable must promote and protect the human rights of its citizens. Human rights have come to be understood as "internationally agreed values, standards or rules regulating the conduct of states towards their own citizens and noncitizens" (Baehr and Castermans-Holleman 2004: 3). Contemporary state practices show that a large number of states are implicated in human rights abuses—albeit in different degrees—yet often try to pretend to be defenders of human rights, while also covering up or justifying such abuses on exceptional grounds. Thus, the issue of human rights reflects a broader struggle of states for retaining the image and status of a normal state while continuing certain practices deemed abnormal. This section of this chapter draws parallels between states with human rights abuses (a type of global abnormalcy) and Foucault's third figure of the abnormal, associated with onanist practices and also referred to as the figure of the "masturbator."

In essence, the figure of the masturbator represents a common practice widely judged as abnormal but also silently accepted and practiced by many. As Stuart Elden (2001: 103) maintains, that figure of abnormalcy "is looked at as a very frequent occurrence, almost a universal individual." Foucault (2003) shows that the major condition enabling the acceptance of onanist practices is the fact that they are considered private and individual affairs within a particular family and community, to be resolved through individualized interventions. It is a parent-child affair resolved through restorative, corrective, and noncorporal measures. As Robbie Duschinsky and Leon A. Rocha (2012: 7) show, "Foucault places the family as an absolutely integral institution to judgements in modern societies regarding the normal and the abnormal, the acceptable and the unacceptable." Thus, the scale of intervention is localized, and the family becomes the primary location for regulating social conduct among a particular regime of normalcy. We here use the figure of the onanist as a departure for exploring a distinct set of discourses and practices associated with selective acceptance of normalcy among certain states and societies. The discursive practices in the case of accepting normalcy are different from the two sets of practices examined so far. In the case of imposing normalcy, the frame of reference was the abnormalcy of the entire society and the state. The frame in the case of restoring normalcy was the goal to correct certain social structures, norms, and practices. In the case of accepting normalcy, the focus is on a much narrower set of interventions, to change individual and segmental practices while still accepting the actor as normal.

In understanding practices of accepting normalcy, we find clues on how interstate relations are structured: namely, how different normative and discursive practices join with the politics of friendship and alliances to constitute acceptability in world politics. In essence, norms set dispositions of what is expected to be acceptable and normal conduct. International acceptance is the basis of international relations, where mutual recognition and commitment to respect of territorial integrity and sovereignty are the core norms of the existing state system (see Visoka, Doyle, and Newman 2020). Bridget Coggins (2014: 26–27) maintains, "International society's acceptance is a fundamental component of any actor's realizing full statehood. . . . Without external recognition, even the most internally sovereign actor cannot function as a state outside of its borders." After the end of the Second World War, the international order was designed around three principles: developing friendly relations among nations, based on respect for the principle of equal rights and self-determination of peoples; achieving international cooperation in peacefully solving international problems of economic, social, cultural, or humanitarian character; and promoting and encouraging respect for human rights and fundamental freedoms for all. These norms often end up contradicting one another or creating conflictual relations between states. They encourage nonintervention and acceptance of pluralism and diversity among states as long as the states adhere to certain universal values and norms of human rights and freedoms. As R. J. Vincent (1986: 117) maintains, nonintervention is meant to promote pluralism and accept "variety within states." Pluralism acknowledges that "states have different political, economic, and cultural systems but holds that even diverse States can form an international society with moral and legal rules" (Fidler 2001: 145). John Rawls (1999: 59) points out that those who tolerate non-liberal societies not only "refrain from exercising political sanctions— military, economic, or diplomatic—to make a people change its ways"; they also "recognize these nonliberal societies as equal participating members in good standing of the Society of Peoples."

At the heart of international order is a struggle to balance unity and diversity of political units (Rosenboim 2017: 4). Formally, diversity regime is at the heart of the UN-based post-1945 world order of sovereign equality of states, but in practice, such a regime is deeply hierarchical, power-ridden, and culturally infused. By exploring states' uneven and selective invocation of different norms, we can observe that the current international order comprises a multilayered register of norms, which provides rationales for justifying intervention or nonintervention in other states' affairs. In specific instances, when dominant states want to impose a sense of normalcy in a particular society, they tend to suspend the importance of principles of sovereignty, nonintervention, and sovereign equality. In instances of restoring normalcy, such principles are hallowed and selectively invoked. Accepting certain states as normal while labeling others as abnormal is central to what Christian Reus-Smit (2018: 13, 215) calls a "diversity regime," which involves "the construction and ranking of legitimate (and illegitimate) difference by 'order builders.'" Reus-Smit points out that "while diversity regimes recognize and empower certain forms and expressions of difference, they also create social and political hierarchies, and generate patterns of inclusion and exclusion" (225). He further maintains, "International societies are member-ship associations: they recognize some polities as legitimate and others as illegitimate, and these decisions are always based on substantive political, social, or cultural criteria—pluralism is always pluralism of the elect" (115). The pragmatic nature of state acceptability is also prevalent in the argu-ment made by John Rawls (1999: 59) in his liberal theory: "If all societies were required to be liberal, then the idea of political liberalism would fail to express due toleration for other acceptable ways . . . of ordering soci-ety." From that perspective, selectively accepting diversity and pluralism and having the power to make exceptions on toleration enables liberal states to hold the upper hand and retain privileged states in world politics. Moreover, tolerance and partial recognition of difference and pluralism are tactics for avoiding the accusation of imposing liberal principles on non-Western soci-eties. As Annette Förster (2014: 47) argues, "denying them toleration (and respect) would violate the principle of reasonable pluralism," and "imposing liberal principles on them would constitute a form of liberal imperialism."

In world politics, the metaphors of international membership and fam-ily roughly resemble political, military, economic, and cultural alliances. Notably, members of an international alliance have different perceptions of normalcy, and what enables their acceptance as normal by other states is the broad support from other members of the alliance. They are different but still part of a common family. The reciprocal recognition and accep-tance of their status of normalcy becomes a crucial mechanism at play in the acceptance category of normalization in world politics. Alliances are groups of states that may have common goals and values in terms of the international system and that may share a common political system or be part of common regional and international institutions. Yet alliances and friendship between states tend to be pragmatic and tactical in nature (see Ghez 2011: 6). A central feature of alliances is instrumental friendship based on mutual interests and utility, not necessarily historical, cultural, and political bonds. For dominant states to remain in charge, they have to find a solution to diversity and must institute boundaries of "different degrees of permeability" (Barkey 2008: 13).

Under the discursive register of diversity, dominant states tend to accept and treat certain friendly states as normal while labeling or treating adversary states as abnormal. In the logic of normalcy, extremes are considered abnor-mal and thus undesirable, but in the current conditions, diversity discourse in world politics enables toleration of difference and pluralism. In practice, international acceptability entails acceptance of a state by other states as a normal member of the international community, based not only on the state's track record and performance on the implementation of norms, rules, and values guiding the society of states but also on strategic friendship and affinity. The politics of friendship and alliances are crucial for explaining state selectivism with regard to judging or attempting to normalize other states, as states tend to have different political reactions toward allies as opposed to adversaries. For example, Nancy Qian and David Yanagizawa (2009: 456) have presented evidence indicating that "the U.S. shows significant favouritism towards countries that it values strategically." Allies are less likely to be exposed to sanctions and various other interventionary practices than are nonmembers of an alliance. Through different registers of truth-making, such as annual human rights reports, the United States tends to normalize state behavior with regard to human rights in allied countries more positively, as opposed to a more negative framing and abnormalizing tendency for unfriendly states (see Qian and Yanagizawa 2009: 446–47).

Thus, what prevails within communities and families of states is not only sameness and like-mindedness but the strategic acceptance of difference. In the cases of imposing and restoring normalcy, difference is a risk and threat to the Western way of life and its foreign policy interests, but in the instance of accepting normalcy, the mechanisms of interventionism are different. The ability to produce discourses and mechanisms of truth-making and to have the backing of strong allies determines the extent to which a state under scrutiny is able to retain international acceptance and the status of a normal state. In Foucault's research, parents and priests are the enforcers of normalcy by disciplining the governance of the body of individuals as members of a family or the church. In world politics, superficial disciplining measures undertaken by friendly states and through special ad hoc mechanisms are seen as sufficient for retaining international acceptance. The proceeding section examines how the existing international human rights order, especially the instrument of state confession and inquiries, facilitates the acceptance of states through lite intervention, self-regulation, and self-normalization.

TRUTH-TELLING AND STATE CONFESSION

The protection of human rights is considered one of the core international responsibilities for all UN member states. Part of the international system is a multilayer architecture for state reporting on human rights situations in their respective countries. Almost all global and regional organizations have set up mechanisms for states to tell their truth and confess about compliance with human rights norms and regimes. A report of the UN General Assembly (2006: 2) stated, "The promotion and protection of human rights should be based on the principles of cooperation and genuine dialogue and aimed at strengthening the capacity of Member States to comply with their human rights obligations for the benefit of all human beings." Countries often engage in rhetorical inquiries to examine how they and other states comply with human rights violations. In particular, Western states tend to use human rights as a foreign policy instrument, to judge, examine, and justify intervention in foreign nations. In the context of accepting normalcy, human rights tend to be used for two different and simultaneous purposes: as a disciplinary rhetoric to justify interference within other states' internal affairs and as a mechanism to portray their own internal situation as normal and demonstrating compliance with international norms. The politics of truth are central to understanding the politics of normalization in international politics. As Torben B. Dyberg (2014: 51) maintains, "truth-seeking knowledge" goes "hand in hand with disciplinary apparatuses of surveillance and normalization." Acceptance of states as normal depends on being seen as trustworthy and telling the truth. Parrhesia, or truth-telling, features prominently in some of the later works of Foucault, as an attempt to capture the interaction between power, knowledge, and ethics.

Foucault's take on truth-telling seeks to examine the performative conditions for democratic life and the vitality of critique for resisting normalization tendencies. In global politics, however, truth-telling has become a mechanism for states to forge their narrative and sense of normalcy. Accepting certain states as normal takes place through a broad range of discourses and strategic narratives. Brent Steele (2008: 10) shows that "all states justify their actions, even when such actions compromise existing international principles." State justifications and truth-telling are often rhetorical endeavors entailing the appearance of telling the truth, and the game of truth-telling enables the state to enjoy external legitimacy and acceptance. Similar to cases of human rights activists, certain states involved in "witnessing and testifying have an opportunity for creating counter-discourses," which help question "dominant discourses and offer alternative worldviews" (Lyon and Olson 2011: 209). Strategic narratives construct "a sequence of events and identities, a communicative tool through which political elites attempt to give determined meaning to past, present, and future in order to achieve political objectives" (Miskimmon, O'Loughlin, and Roselle 2015: 59). Often, the political objective is to promote a particular narrative that is acceptable by other states and that delivers acceptability for the concerned state.

Strategic narratives tend to be used mostly to deter the international community from placing a state on its agenda of troublesome regions and thus subjecting the state to international intervention. One of the main ways of understanding practices of forging international acceptance of domestic normalcy is to look at the confessionary politics manifested through state reporting to international human rights bodies. For Foucault (2003: 169), practices of identifying and labeling misconduct and prohibited acts shifted from silencing "abnormalities" to "obligatory confession as a procedure of power." In that context, the effectiveness of confession lies in the ability to acknowledge a condition without resorting to punitive measures. The function of confession is to restore inner peace and retain social acceptance. Foucault (2003: 176) argues, "Confession occupies the central place in the mechanism of the remission of sins." To a certain point, as Foucault (2003: 173) claims, "confession is already a kind of penalty and the beginning of expiation." It relates to the acceptance of guilt and shame but short of any putative measures. While confession is meant to have a self-transformative effect, it can be turned, as Sigmund Freud warned, into an obsessive practice where one continues to do what one has always done, without substantive change in conduct (see Neu 1991). As a form of acceptance, confession thus creates the false belief of normalcy and permits indulgent actions.

Applying that understanding of confession in the context of our study, we can observe that a state's continued international acceptance and its retention of the status of a normal state requires confessing to international bodies on state performance and the implementation of international norms and rules. Reporting to international bodies as a form of confession has emerged as a regular mechanism regardless of the human rights situation on the ground. State confession of "sins" has become a method to ensure international acceptance. It enables states to retain normalcy at the international level without needing to change their practices. The ritual of confessing in compliance with international norms suffices to retain acceptance and renew normalcy. More often than not, as discussed by Foucault (2003: 186), practices of confession result in forgetting "everything that has been said." Similarly, states often forge rhetorical confessions, commitments, and promises that serve their acceptance at the international level, and "confession may offer little more than an opportunity for perpetrators to cling to the legality of their actions" (Doxtader 2011: 276).

States are forced to engage in confessional practices to forge their narrative of normalcy. Stephanie Lawson and Seiko Tannaka (2010: 422) argue that "'normality' is not something that every state is simply free to define for itself, thus highlighting the fact that the social construction of meaning in the international sphere is formulated via much broader intersubjective dynamics." Confession contributes to the acceptance and normalization of subjects under investigation. As Lena Sjöberg (2014: 63–64) maintains, "the practice of the confession functions as a technology where the person confessing, in a very concrete and active manner, participates in processes of both creating and displaying the self." Confession is a mode of self-intervention and self-regulation mediated by external forces. It prevents radical external intervention and contributes to the retention of self-perceived normalcy. "Through the confession," Sjöberg (2014: 64) goes on to explain, "the individual creates a narrative about him or herself that s/he is then implicitly or explicitly expected by the receivers of the confessions and by the subject itself to inhabit and make a part of his or her own 'truth.'" For states to retain their status of relatively sovereign entities and enjoy external acceptance and legitimacy, they must engage in confessional practices. One of the main purposes of confession is learning through truth-telling. It is identifying vulnerabilities and turning them into targets for self-transformation (Besley 2005). At its core, then, practices of state confession intend state self-transformation. For a state to be accepted as normal, it has to perform various technologies on itself—on its institutions, structures, individuals, and conduct—that demonstrate its willingness to transform, modify, and perfect itself in accordance with externally tailored requirements and perceptions of how a normal state should behave in the international system.

Confessional practices consist of two interacting forces: those who confess and those to whom one confesses (Edwards 2008: 31). In international affairs, the role of confessor is often taken by commissions of inquiry reporting to an international or regional organization. Confessions give those international bodies grounds for their existence and a purpose to govern (Landry 2009). As Foucault (1998: 62) stipulates, confessors' are prescribed the role to "judge, punish, forgive, console and reconcile." Simultaneously, those international mechanisms represent a suitable platform for states to use for demonstrating their agency and retaining international acceptance. On the one hand, confessional practices in world politics are intended to satisfy the concerns of external audiences on a specific issue that is deemed abnormal and to satisfy the will of those audiences to govern and intervene in the internal affairs of other countries. Such practices perform the function of stating the norm and defining the abnormal. On the other hand, they enable states to forge their strategic narratives and official versions of truth, thereby reconstituting their own subjectivity as well as enjoying their status as a recognized state, accepted by the international community. In that regard, confessions play a role in the constitutions of states in world politics, enabling states to confess a certain truth and accept individual responsibility (see Lorenzini and Tazzioli 2018: 74). Confession by states seeks their purification, which can be interpreted as their normalization and acceptance by the wider international community. For instance, as part of a UN universal periodic review, Myanmar confessed that it "is making every effort to become a democratic society and, therefore, the international community is expected to continue their constructive engagement with and assistance to Myanmar" (UN Human Rights Council 2015a: 22).

Because confession is about modification rather than radical change, it enables a sense of normalcy to be retained. As Richard Edwards (2008: 30) points out, "confession actively codes a subject as productive and autonomous" but "already governed through participating in confessional practices." The very act of confession is seen as sufficient to retain international acceptance, regardless of the outcomes of that "truth-telling" process, because the process of confession and inquiry entails a degree of mutual recognition between parties concerned. Consequently, confession is "a practice of subjectification by which the subject authenticates in himself, and for himself, the truths of his own discourse" (Avelino 2015: 21). Thus, the very act of being subject to an investigation and given the opportunity to confess is a form or acceptance of subjectivity. Confession enables the proclamation of commitment for self-discipline without being required to undergo serious changes imposed by external interventions. States' commitment to self-regulation, self-improvement, and self-development plays a central role in deterring external intervention. As the international normalizing society encourages the self-mastery of states, it contributes to the production and reproduction of states' sovereignty and legitimizes governance over their subjects. In that regard, confession is meant to lead to the establishment of self-controlling states, which is key to the global civilizing process.

Universal periodic reviews on human rights compliance to the stipulations of the UN Human Rights Council represent one of the main institutionalized forms of state confession on the protection and promotion of human rights and reveal numerous discourses and practices invoked to retain international acceptance. The universal periodic review provides an opportunity for all UN member states "to declare what actions they have taken to improve the human rights situations in their countries and to over-come challenges to the enjoyment of human rights" (UN Human Rights Council 2020). It is envisaged to be "a cooperative mechanism, based on an interactive dialogue, with the full involvement of the country concerned and with consideration given to its capacity-building needs" (UN General Assembly 2006: 3). However, as James Crawford (2000: 8) points out, the system of human rights reporting to the UN "encourages states to view com-pliance only in the context of a rather sporadic reporting procedure, with a lack of follow-up mechanisms for both periodic reports and communica-tions." In the past, as admitted by UN Secretary-General Kofi Annan (2005: para. 182), mechanisms such as the UN Commission on Human Rights were used by states "not to strengthen human rights but to protect them-selves against criticism or to criticize others." Deliberations and discussions by working groups as part of the universal periodic review serve as a space for praising states for their efforts to promote and protect human rights. They often channel light criticism or whitewash failures. Those interactions often result in recommending the concerned state to continue and take actions for protecting human rights. Most often, universal periodic reviews result in the UN Human Rights Council adopting review documents, which is marked by states as an important renewal of their international standing and human rights record. State confessions commit to undertaking small actions (such as institutional reforms, training on human rights, and consultation with civil society) that constitute sufficient measures for a state to be seen as complying with international human rights obligations.

In principle, states do not want to be subject to selective processes of international examination or intervention. They prefer universal and equal measures delivered to all the nations. In particular, they prefer universal peri-odic reviews, seen as a normal process because of their universal character, to any country-specific mandates or inquiries, which risk flagging elements of state abnormalcy. In an attempt to retain their international status, states often try to remove themselves from specific agendas, investigations, or inquiries. For that reason, many states have no problem being part of univer-sal scrutiny on human rights or receiving ambiguous and universal criticism directed to all the states. Putting states into a spotlight undermines both the domestic and the international legitimacy of the incumbent government and ruling elite and could have a destabilizing effect for the targeted state, as is clearly the case with Myanmar, which considers the "Universal Periodic Review the most dependable mechanism for every country to discuss human rights issues on an equal footing in a constructive manner," while stating that "it is high time to end the tabling of resolutions against Myanmar, based on the principles of universality, impartiality and non-selectivity in addressing human rights issues together with undeniable progress Myanmar has achieved" (UN Human Rights Council 2015a: 13).

These reservations notwithstanding, state confession enables states to promote their strategic narratives. By default, international confessionary mechanisms such as the UN Human Rights Council enable states to promote their official narrative and confess their version of normalcy. For example, Myanmar has used the UN universal periodic review to promote the narrative of itself as a responsible state, arguing that "as a member of the United Nations promoting and protecting human rights, Myanmar has been working to become a state party to the remaining core international human rights treaties" (UN Human Rights Council 2015a: 5). Similarly, Israel's confession held that the country maintains "close relations with a variety of international and domestic human rights bodies, compiles detailed state reports and conducts dialogues with high-ranking foreign delegations as an expression of its appreciation for transparency" (UN Human Rights Council 2017: 3). Moreover, states such as Myanmar, Bahrain, Israel, or even North Korea, which are implicated in serious human rights abuses against their subjects, tend to commit or report proudly on their compliance with certain human rights norms (such as those concerning children's and women's rights or people with disabilities), in an effort to satisfy external expectations while continuing to suppress the vital rights of suppressed ethnic groups and minorities within their jurisdiction as sovereign or occupying authority. Focusing on nonpolitical rights provides a platform for like-minded states to commend the concerned state for protecting those rights, while ignoring serious human rights abuses against ethnic minorities or suppressed groups.

State-based mechanisms for monitoring human rights compliance not only perform the function of promoting alternative truths but play a vital role in the constitution and reproduction of other states' statuses as normal regardless of the facts on the ground. Western and northern states, in particular, have demonstrated their ability to use confessionary technologies to target and push for intervention against opponents' human rights abuses while simultaneously remaining silent against and discharging allies and friends. For example, in the UN Human Rights Council's review of Israel's human rights compliance, the vast majority of states aligned with Israel internationally almost entirely ignore Israel's violations of international and human rights law in the Occupied Palestinian Territory, including the construction of illegal settlements and apartheid-like policies (see

UN Human Rights Council 2018), while Palestine's international allies explicitly deplore Israel's refusal to recognize and protect the rights of Palestinians. In reports for universal periodic reviews, countries such as Myanmar and Israel completely misrecognize the status of Rohingya and Palestinians (see UN Human Rights Council 2015), using those confessionary mechanisms as platforms for portraying those minorities as security threats and for victimizing majority communities, at home and abroad, as the subject of discriminatory policies. In its annual report, Amnesty International (2018: 14) noted that "narratives of national security and counter-terrorism have continued to provide justification to governments seeking to reconfigure the balance between state powers and individual freedoms." Another illustrative example is North Korea, which maintains a reputation as one of the world's worst human rights violators. As Jonathan T. Chow (2017: 159) argues, "North Korea seems to participate in the UPR [Universal Periodic Review] because it can gain the benefits of cooperation with international human rights mechanisms without having to drastically reform its human rights policies, all while working to undermine more rigorous human rights mechanisms." Chow (2017: 157) shows that North Korea willingly participates in the review as an opportunity to "positively frame its human rights record" and to utilize the state-based reporting system "as a platform for advancing North Korea's sovereign-centric view of human rights." The UN's state-based periodic review "is not an incentive for North Korea to improve its human rights record but instead a step toward undermining stronger human rights mechanisms" (Chow 2017: 158).

The universal periodic review resolves the dilemma of reconciling human rights protection while respecting the national sovereignty of states (see Cowan 2014: 54). The principle of universality and equality is at the heart of that review process. That principle and the requirement for constructive criticism offered to all states tend to place all the states on a level playing field, a crucial feature for accepting normalcy. As Jane Cowan (2014: 60) argues, the universal periodic review "reinforces through repetition not only the normality of being a sovereign state, but also the idea that it is the state, and its policies, which are responsible for both violations and realisations of human rights." The reiterative review process enables the normalization of states, regardless of their implementation of human rights norms. The review has also been weaponized as a foreign policy instrument of states, to forge the normalcy of their allies while demonizing their adversaries. The peer review process at the heart of the universal periodic examination of human rights compliance helps like-minded states and regional neighbors to normalize themselves by praising their forged narratives of human rights protection and expressing solidarity. For example, "African states have acted to defend each other's images in the face of critical comments from non-African states rather than using the system to exchange substantive and honest criticism" (Bulto 2014: 253). In another example, some states with weak human rights records praised North Korea for "its education, health care, or accession to international human rights instruments while omitting questions of civil and political rights" (Chow 2017: 151). States also regularly criticize other states for failures on human rights for which the criticizers themselves do not provide adequate protection. The peer review process that is part of the UN's universal periodic examination of human rights enabled North Korea to criticize the human rights records of other countries, most notably the United States and South Korea, two of its major adversaries. As Chow (2017: 154) shows, peer review allowed "North Korea to undercut its international pariah status and undermine its rivals' human rights records."

International reporting on human rights may merely be a ritual for forging, accepting, or rejecting the normalcy of states. Hilary Charlesworth and Emma Larking (2014: 10) show that in the context of the universal periodic review, "ritualism may mean participation in the process of reports and meetings, but an indifference to or even reluctance about increasing the protection of human rights." Turned into a ritual, the review often shows how, for instance, states "shield their friends under review by taking up the available time for questions, comments and recommendations"; claim that "they are already recognising rights when this is clearly not the case"; "entrench an understanding of states as the primary duty bearers in relation to human rights, and ignore systemic and structural contributors to rights failures," or even criticize "other states for rights failures when they themselves do not provide adequate protection for the rights in question" (Charlesworth and Larking 2014: 14–15). The totality of those mechanisms, practices, and rituals form an international confessing society (see also Fejes and Dahlstedt 2013). In particular, "repeated participation in the ritual of the UPR serves to make habitual, customary and normal a specific discourse regarding the nature of sovereignty in relation to human rights" (Cowan 2014: 52). In a nutshell, confessing on human rights compliance, regardless of how truthful such claims may be, helps states gain "the positive reputational benefits" (Charlesworth and Larking 2014: 18).

By being self-critical as well as self-congratulatory, states tend to be seen as responsible and self-regulating and thus as normal members of the international community. As Cowan (2014: 57) shows, "in the UPR the state itself is asked to marshal and coordinate people, objects and resources into multiple tasks of scrutiny, assessment and action plans for self-improvement." Short of any enforcement mechanisms, "the reviewed state bears the primary responsibility for implementing the recommendations it has accepted, and of reporting during subsequent periodic reviews on the progress of implementation, as well as more broadly on its human rights situation" (Charlesworth and Larking 2014: 6). That a state under review is responsible for self-transformation results in lack of implementation of recommendations and makes it difficult "to gain an accurate picture of the status of human rights in the state in question" (Chauville 2014: 96). As Charlesworth and Larking (2014: 18) show, while "rituals may similarly be a step on a journey toward substantive transformation," universal periodic review "can also deflect or postpone human rights observance." Morten Kjærum (2009: 20) adds that "most State Parties submit reports which are satisfactory in relation to information regarding the legal regime governing the specific area under consideration, but less so when it comes to actual implementation on the ground." Chow (2017: 149) summarily explains, "The UPR's promise lies in disseminating best practices for implementing human rights norms rather than enforcing them or adjudicating competing factual claims about violations. When states fundamentally disagree on human rights principles or matters of fact, the UPR can degenerate into a series of mutually contradictory rhetorical claims."

LITE INTERVENTIONISM THROUGH COMMISSIONS OF INQUIRY

Accepting normalcy is also facilitated through a process that gives the impression of satisfying external expectations that states under scrutiny behave in accordance with the rule of law and other legal standards. Struggles for normalization or to forge acceptance of a situation as normal go through judicious processes, whether those of ordinary legal institutions or ad hoc mechanisms. The body of knowledge that enables accepting normalcy consists of reports, protocols, and other micropolitical and judicial decisions seeking to address individualized misconduct without affecting structural features that enable such practices in the first place. Commissions of inquiry seem to emerge as a mechanism in service of accepting normalcy of a state undergoing protracted or temporal internal conflict and troubles. Established by either international or domestic actors, commissions seek to establish the facts and circumstances of alleged human rights violations by military and security forces, with the view of ensuring full accountability of perpetrators and justice for victims. In some instances, a commission of inquiry plays the function of restoring international credibility of the affected state, thus resulting in accepting local normalcy. In other instances, such mechanisms may serve to delegitimize and abnormalize particular societies.

Existing research on international fact-finding commissions of inquiry tends to focus on the role and impact of those mechanisms for promoting human rights and setting the stage for "prosecutions for war crimes and other international crimes" (Frulli 2012: 1323). A fact-finding mechanism is seen as "a process distinct from other forms of dispute settlement in the sense that it is aimed primarily at clarifying the disputed facts through impartial investigation, which would then facilitate the parties' objective of identifying the final solution to the dispute" (Frulli 2012: 1324). However, the function of a fact-finding commission in restoring a state's credibility or retaining the acceptance of its status of normalcy is largely overlooked. Christine Schwöbel-Patel (2017: 146) argues that commissions of inquiry are not only "complicit in a narrowing understanding of accountability" but also "complicit in a global power struggle in favour of the great political and economic powers." Other scholars note that "the decision to launch an investigation, the choice of investigators, the actual focus of the inquiry, the resources devoted to it, and so on, all contribute to constructing the 'reality' that will emerge from any given fact-finding exercise" (Alston and Knuckey 2016: 8). Commissions of inquiry and fact-finding mechanisms continue to perform their function of pacifying and defusing a conflict and conciliating the differences among states (see van den Herik 2014: 536). The task of commissions of inquiry to identify anomalies in the system and propose ways for domestic reforms enables targeted states to retain international acceptance without requiring major structural changes, particularly because "most recommendations are addressed to the State concerned, and their implementation is dependent on the political will of the authorities" (OHCHR 2015: 101).

A number of illustrative examples show that the performative function of commissions of inquiry are to simultaneously retain international acceptance and forge a sense of self-transformation. The Arab Spring's wave of instability in the Middle East temporarily spread to Bahrain, where the Shia population and their political and social leaders took to the streets protesting to end structural inequalities, corruption, oppression, and a lack of government representation in that Arab monarchy. To contain the popular contention, the government mobilized its police and special forces to arrest protestors and other senior political and clerical leaders of the opposition. In response to growing international pressure, the Bahrain Independent Commission of Inquiry (BICI) was established in 2011 by Bahraini king Hamad bin Isa bin Salman Al Khalifa, in an effort to investigate the allegations of human rights abuses and to ensure international acceptance. The BICI consisted of a team of internationally respected jurists and legal scholars who conducted "more than 9,000 interviews to investigate the events of 2011" (BICI 2011: 3). The BICI's final report held both government and opposition groups partially responsible for the violent events. It found that government forces used deliberate and extensive use of force to torture people in custody. However, the report "stopped short of the most sensitive issues. It did not incriminate those at the very top of the decision-making process, the senior members of the ruling family such as the king and the prime minister" (Matthiesen 2013: 69).

An important feature of normalization practices in world politics is the question of individual and collective responsibility for wrongdoings and the interventionary measures thereafter. As Priscella B. Hayner (2001: 192) shows, reports by commissions of inquiry "have recommended specific reforms in the judiciary, armed forces, and political sector; the prosecution of perpetrators or their removal from the military, police, or political posts; reparations; measures to instil a human rights culture, including through human rights education; the ratification of international human rights treaties; and apologies from officials." To facilitate interventions in troublesome places, the international community often attributes responsibility for delinquent acts to collective social and political structures. That attribution primarily serves the purpose of facilitating a much broader form of intervention to reform the state and reengineer social relations via peacebuilding and statebuilding techniques. In contrast, when the international community is committed not to intervene in troubled societies comprised of allies and friends, a greater focus is placed on addressing individual responsibility for wrongdoings. That focus tends to reduce the problems to a handful of individuals whose prosecution or removal from office would cure the wider social and political problems and restore normalcy in the country as well as continue unchallenged international acceptance. As Thomas Weatherall (2015: 275) shows, "individual responsibility for international crimes carries the expectation of accountability, thereby deterring delinquent behaviour by combating impunity." Carsten Stahn (2018: 123–24) similarly argues, "Individualization of wrongdoing makes it possible to render retributive justice and to introduce incentives for deterrence. It seeks to prevent formal assignment of blame or guilt to collectivities, such as entire nations, societies or whole ethnic and religious groups." Yet Stahn (2018: 124) also notes that "an exclusively individualist approach fails to take into account the group dynamics of crime, including the relations among individual members."

In world politics, retaining states' acceptance and accepting their normalcy undergoes a complex process of attribution of responsibility for breaching international norms. In most cases—even when a state is held responsible, as a joint enterprise, for violations of international norms—there is a tendency to shift toward seeking individual responsibility or holding a small number of individuals accountable for their wrongdoings. At the heart of the UN commissions of inquiry, fact-finding missions, and human rights investigations lies the priority of identifying the people responsible for violations and crimes. The logic of chasing individuals is to address their wrongdoings and deter similar practices from reoccurring in the future. The pursuers seek to transform the body politic via individualized attributions of responsibility without significantly undermining a state's international standing or requiring major external intervention. The Office of the United Nations High Commissioner for Human Rights (OHCHR 2018: 21) maintains, "Efforts to assign individual responsibility for serious international crimes and violations do have a deterrent effect, in particular on those not yet implicated in violations. Some refer to the power of stigma which may result from the individual having been named, or having being personally affected by travel bans, economic sanctions or even criminal prosecution, should the information be shared with the bodies responsible for such mechanisms." There are examples where the international community has employed the rubric of transitional justice to undertake all-encompassing measures to deal with the past. But that approach is more exemplary to countries subject to international interventions aimed at imposing an externally designed normalcy. The UN human rights bodies admit that "information on individuals allegedly responsible for serious crimes, which has been gathered in an investigation, might feed into such processes, importantly reinforcing the notion of individual, as opposed to group, responsibility" (OHCHR 2018: 18). In that context, naming individuals for breaching international norms is as much about laying the grounds for justice and accountability as it is about exempting an entire state or society from collective guilt for past wrongdoings. Attributing individual responsibility is about avoiding collective sanctions against the state and society concerned. It also enables vetting of alleged perpetrators and potentially removes malign elements from institutions, resulting in partial state reforms while retaining general normalcy.

Fact-finding assessments that examine exceptional incidents also form the basis of forging a particular meaning of normalcy. As long as states are able to identify criminal wrongdoings and human rights abuses and to undertake individualized forms of sanctions, they are accepted as normal states. That approach plays a major role in retaining the status of a normal state, while the situation on the ground or state behavior might be far from what a normal society should be. In his capacity as UN special rapporteur on extrajudicial, summary, or arbitrary executions, Philip Alston concluded, "Commissions can be used very effectively by Governments for the wrong purposes: to defuse a crisis, to purport to be upholding notions of accountability and to promote impunity. . . . An ineffective commission can be more than just a waste of time and resources; it can contribute to impunity by deterring other initiatives, monopolizing available resources and making subsequent endeavours to prosecute difficult or impossible" (UN Human Rights Council 2008: 18).

To retain wide international acceptance following the violent events of 2011, Bahrain undertook symbolic and gradual measures to reform parts of its institutional structure and thereby created the impression that the country promotes and protects human rights, has a culture of accountability and rule of law, and has legal avenues for handling and disciplining misconduct (Bahrain Embassy in Washington 2015). A Bahraini official stated, "Our country accepted its errors and implemented far-reaching reforms to ensure they don't occur again. . . . The entire nation—or substantial portions of it—acted with great dedication to implement the bulk of the BICI recommendations" (UK Parliament 2012). Yet, more often than not, commissions of inquiry offer general and sweeping recommendations that have never been implemented in practice (see Hayner 2001: 193). Although domestic and international human rights groups have demonstrated that the Bahraini government "has failed to fully address many of the recommendations of the commission" (ADHRB, BIRD, and BCHR 2015: 3), the government has managed to persuade external audiences that the country has addressed the anomalies of the 2011 violence. For instance, the Bahraini government passed anti-terror laws in July 2013 to "criminalize public demonstrations and free speech" (Nuruzzaman 2015: 544), and "instead of starting a process of transitional justice, the BICI has become a symbol of the political stalemate in Bahrain" (Matthiesen 2013: 70). One of the major functions of the BICI was to satisfy the international community and help retain its close ties with the United States and the United Kingdom, among other international allies. By offering a complete narrative of the events and conclusions about the allegations, the BICI managed to develop a strategic narrative that served to silence local resistance and retain international acceptance. As a fact-finding mechanism, the BICI helped show that Bahrain was willing to engage with its violent response to the riots and to undertake measures to ensure some degree of individual accountability for human rights abuses, without needing to structurally change the setup of the state or address the power imbalance and structural discrimination in the society.

The United States and the United Kingdom consider Bahrain a strategic partner due to its strategic location and alignment in the Gulf region. Both those Western countries have military bases in Bahrain. As stated by US assistant secretary of state Michael H. Posner, his country's "longstanding alliance with Bahrain is based on shared political, economic, and security interests. And it is in part because of this important strategic relationship that we have devoted so much attention to Bahrain" (US Department of State 2013: 18). He also stated, "Many people wish to compare Bahrain to other countries in the region such as Tunisia or Egypt. While some comparisons may be valid, it also is very important to recognize the unique history and political and economic development in each of these countries, and to shape our policies accordingly" (US House of Representatives 2012: 21). Posner went on to add, "As a partner and friend, the United States stands ready to support the government and the people of Bahrain as they seek pathways toward meaningful dialogue about the future of the country" (US House of Representatives 2012: 21). For instance, US congressman Dan Burton stated that "Bahrain is trying to fix this problem and make sure that the situation is improved dramatically" (US House of Representatives 2012: 6). In Bahrain, the United States found itself in "the undesirable position of maintaining close ties with a repressive regime that has skilfully avoided meaningful reforms while engaging in a concerted public relations campaign to burnish its image" (Wehrey 2013: 109). Similarly, the United Kingdom considers its relationship with Bahrain "one of its oldest and closest in the Gulf," admitting that "Bahrain plays a key role in regional security, largely by merit of its location in the Arabian Gulf and its openness to international partners and coalition operations" (UK Parliament 2013: 71, 84). The UK Foreign and Commonwealth Office (FCO 2012) argued,

> While we have many common interests, there are differences between us. The essence of any state to state relationship is respect for each other's cultures and an ability to deal with difference honestly and frankly. We do not aim to use our relationships with other

states to demand that they mirror us. But we do engage in frank discussion, defending and promoting our own values at all times, and encouraging other governments towards policies we believe to have merit and relevance to them. When we disagree with our partners in the Gulf on human rights-related issues, we make our concerns clear to each other.

The BICI report enabled Bahraini authorities to mostly please its international allies by admitting that mistakes were made in the past and by promising modest reforms. The government claimed that the BICI was not forced from outside but was a domestic initiative and an unprecedented step in the region. Matthiesen (2013: 81) observes, "When asked about Bahrain, Western officials are quick to point to the National Dialogue and the Bahrain Independent Commission of Inquiry (BICI) as proof of progress; both are in fact cornerstones of the Bahraini regime's public relations strategy." In 2013, the US Department of State released a report stating, "In general terms, the Government of Bahrain has taken some important steps towards implementing BICI recommendations, but much work remains." It concluded that "King Hamad deserves credit . . . for accepting the recommendations put forward in the report, and for committing to implement the reforms" (US Department of State 2013: 12). Assistant Secretary Posner held that "the Government of Bahrain has taken many important steps toward the long-term institutional reforms identified in the report, such as removing arrest authority from the national security agency, drafting legislation concerning the investigation and prosecution of torture, and drafting a code of conduct for police based on international best practices" (US House of Representatives 2012: 20). Similarly, in the United Kingdom, the FCO (2012) hailed the BICI report as "the first time that any government in the region had set up an international investigation into allegations of state abuse."

Following the 2011 violence in Bahrain, EU member states, the United States, and other states issued critical statements but were opposed to undertaking more serious measures, in contrast to "the actions taken against the, admittedly more repressive, regimes in Libya and Syria" (Matthiesen 2013: 78). For example, the EU's high representative for foreign and security policy, Catherine Ashton, "refused to blame the government for the violence and the failure of dialogue" (Matthiesen 2013: 80). In 2014, the EU awarded the Chaillot Prize to Bahrain's National Institution for Human Rights and Ombudsman Office, acknowledging and further encouraging the efforts and work of those new institutions, which were created as a result of the

BICI's recommendations. Soon after, the European Parliament issued a resolution raising concerns that those bodies have repeatedly justified the human rights violations undertaken by the Bahraini government (European Parliament 2018). In response to growing criticism of the EU's soft stance, the EU responded that it "will continue to encourage the Government of Bahrain to meet all of its human rights obligations, as well as to implement the recommendations of the National Institute for Human Rights" (European Parliament 2017). Similarly, in a joint statement, thirty-three states of the UN Human Rights Commission recognized and welcomed "the positive steps taken by the Government of Bahrain in order to improve the human rights situation," while stating that "the human rights situation in Bahrain remains an issue of serious concern to us" (Swiss Confederation 2015).

A central feature among all countries that are accepted as normal—which share many features with other states that are subject to imposing or restoring normalcy through interventionary practice—is the effort of retaining such a status of normalcy by using individualized and limited legal and bureaucratic measures to correct a practice deemed abnormal. The UN's Independent Commission of Inquiry on the 2014 Gaza conflict revealed the scale of abnormalcy in the Israel/Palestine situation and the human rights violations, killings, indiscriminate attacks, and destruction of the livelihood of Palestinian civilians in Gaza (UN Human Rights Council 2015b). To counter the commission's findings and to avoid responsibility for the Gaza conflict, the Israeli Ministry of Foreign Affairs (MFA) engaged in an extensive campaign of forging a counternarrative that justified its indiscriminate use of force against civilians. It stated that "in order to protect its civilians and restore an acceptable level of protection and normalcy to the civilian population, the Government of Israel ordered an expanded aerial campaign to degrade the military capacity of Hamas and other terrorist organisations in the Gaza Strip to conduct such attacks" (MFA of Israel 2015: 37). The Israeli government and other groups, such as the nongovernmental organization Monitor, have constantly criticized international human rights groups about their reporting on Israel and often have accused them of advocating for the Boycott, Divestment, Sanctions movement against companies that operate in the settlements. That government response is widely seen as an example of state policy to silence criticism that is seen as a serious threat to the state's international reputation and status. Israel's counterstrategy of assertively reacting to the criticism of other states and international organizations has resulted in neutralizing and often silencing international organizations' reporting on the human rights situation in the country. For instance, the

EU tends to use rather vague and neutral language when reporting on Israeli settlements. The EU considers Gaza's blockade and total control by Israeli forces as "enclosure" and "barriers" (European Heads of Mission 2017: 15, 17). Following the 2014 Gaza conflict, the United States publicly supported what they called "Israel's right to defend itself against attacks by rockets overhead or through tunnels below," stating that "no country in the world would tolerate a relentless barrage of attacks on its citizens" (UN Security Council 2014a: 12).

Yet Israel's discursive reaction was not sufficient to satisfy the international community. To retain the status of a normal state that undertakes actions in compliance with the law and strict institutionalized procedures, Israel claimed that it regularly conducts lesson-learning exercises to review its operational directives (MFA of Israel 2015: xvi). That learning process indicates self-enforced and internal transformation and change in order to ensure Israel's status as a normal state. Over the years, Israel has established internal accountability mechanisms—such as the Military Advocate General's Corps, the Military Police Criminal Investigation Division, and military courts—to deal with cases of legal issues arising from the use of force. In the case of the 2014 Gaza conflict, Israel admitted and was "aware of allegations that certain IDF [Israeli Defense Force] actions during the 2014 Gaza Conflict violated international law." Yet, to retain the status of a normal state, Israel stipulated that it "reviews complaints and other information it receives suggesting IDF misconduct, regardless of the source, and is committed to investigating fully any credible accusation or reasonable suspicion of a serious violation of the Law of Armed Conflict" (MFA of Israel 2015: xix).

Israel's holding to account a small number of individuals was praised by its international allies as a sign of a legible and democratic response. In August 2018, the IDF Military Advocate General reported that out of five hundred filed complaints, it referred only seven "incidents" for criminal investigation. The majority of cases were closed due to the lack of what the IDF referred to as "reasonable grounds for suspicion of criminal behaviour" (IDF 2018: 2). The US Department of State (2018b: 1) recognized that reason by arguing, "Israel is a multiparty parliamentary democracy. . . . The government took steps to prosecute and punish officials who committed abuses within Israel regardless of rank or seniority." Most important, in an attempt to retain external acceptance of its actions in Gaza and, more broadly, its state prosecution, the IDF held that it maintains "a robust process for implementing lessons learned from contending with the events. When relevant lessons are identified, they are implemented immediately and disseminated among all relevant forces" (Government of Israel 2018: 19). In an attempt to justify Israeli actions undertaken as part of Operation Protective Edge, Israel's ambassador to the UN claimed that his government "established a fact-finding mechanism in accordance with international law to investigate exceptional incidents. Those incidents include, among others, cases which resulted in harm to civilians or damage to civil or United Nations facilities." He wrote, "As a democracy, Israel upholds and abides by the rule of law. We would hope that the international community would support us in this effort. Premature and unfounded accusations serve no purpose other than to inflame tensions in the region." The ambassador went on to call international commissions of inquiry on Gaza "just one more example of the anti-Israel bias" (UN Security Council 2014b: 9).

Another relevant and illustrative example of lite interventionism and acceptance of normalcy through commissions of inquiry involves Myanmar. Since 2015, that country has experienced one of the most brutal state-led atrocities against the Rohingya, following attacks on police and military posts by local insurgent groups. The government of Myanmar is accused of committing ethnic cleansing and genocidal acts against Rohingya civilians, resulting in large-scale killings, a refugee crisis, destruction of property, and extensive discriminatory practices. Despite large-scale human rights abuses, the international community has remained divided about how to respond to the unfolding atrocities in Myanmar. While the United States, the United Kingdom, and the majority of European powers condemned Myanmar's actions, China and Russia justified the acts. At the end of 2019, Gambia filed a lawsuit against Myanmar before the International Court of Justice, for genocide against Rohingya people. As with other contemporary conflicts examined in this chapter, contestation of the scale and the responsibility for the conflict in Myanmar were shaped by commissions of inquiry and fact-finding missions.

Since 2012, Myanmar has created several special government-led inquiries to investigate violence in Rakhine State. Yet the Advisory Commission on Rakhine State, established by Myanmar in 2016 and chaired by the late Kofi Annan, stands out as an important mechanism. That commission was mandated to "examine the complex challenges facing Rakhine State and to propose responses to those challenges" (Advisory Commission on Rakhine State 2017: 6). It produced a report that tended to put the responsibility for ethnic cleansing in Rakhine State on the attacks on security personnel and that offered interim recommendations to help Myanmar restore its international credibility. The commission's report sought to identify the broad and structural factors that led to intercommunal tensions and the intervention of the Myanmar Army in Rakhine State. By trying to demonstrate the complex and deeply contested relations between communities in Rakhine State and the mutual exclusivity of its historical narratives, the report unintentionally legitimized some of the actions of the Myanmar government against the civilian population. Utilizing the personal credibility of Annan as a former UN Secretary-General and global peacemaker, the commission offered rather vague measures for building lasting peace in Rakhine State. It sought to save the credibility of, among others, Aung San Suu Kyi, who, as state counsellor, has been widely criticized for her silence and complicity in atrocities against the Rohingya.

The commission tried to balance its assessment of the situation by recognizing Myanmar's "right to defend its own territory" with the "militarised response," commending the government's "public endorsement of the report" and "willingness to implement 'the large majority' of the recommendations" (Advisory Commission on Rakhine State 2017: 10). The report tends to blame the Rohingya people and the Muslim community for threatening peace and security in Rakhine State. The report admitted that under the instruction of Su Kyi, the Myanmar government would refer to the local Rohingya population not as Rohingya but as Muslims, whereas non-Muslim communities were referenced in relation to the land, as the Rakhine community. To retain its international legitimacy and acceptance, the commission called the international community "to fully understand the sensitivities that prevail in Rakhine State and work with the Government to achieve a positive vision for the future," while also advising Myanmar to "be open to advice and support from the international community, recognising that what it does or does not do has ramifications far beyond the borders of the country" (Advisory Commission on Rakhine State 2017: 11). The commission proposed small changes that seemed to serve the regime well by whitewashing impunity for ethnic cleansing, war crimes, and serious human rights abuses. It proposed that Myanmar provide "training on human rights awareness to Myanmar security personnel," "improve the monitoring of the performance of security forces," "establish a national complaint mechanism," and "provide adequate training to members of Rakhine's judiciary" (Advisory Commission on Rakhine State 2017: 54–56). Such measures are evident across all cases where domestic or international actors seek external audiences to accept their normalcy.

The Advisory Commission on Rakhine State and all other government-led investigations into widespread abuses by security services against the

Rohingya failed to attribute responsibility for serious crimes and were deeply flawed. Still, China and Russia, strategic rivals of the United States and major European powers, proactively defended Myanmar's interests and its international standing at the UN Security Council. They openly opposed the independent international fact-finding mission on Myanmar established by the UN Human Rights Council. Russia considered "the work of the fact-finding mission on Myanmar . . . harmful and counterproductive" (UN Security Council 2018: 2). Trying to tame the international community's response to the crisis, China commented, "When it comes to the issue of Rakhine state, the Security Council should play a constructive role, and any action it takes should help to resolve the issue" (UN Security Council 2018: 2). Praising the commission, Russia maintained that "the Myanmar leadership is working systematically to implement the recommendations of the Advisory Commission on Rakhine State with a view to achieving a comprehensive settlement of the crisis, and 81 of the 88 recommendations have been implemented so far" (UN Security Council 2018: 20–21). Claims such as those made by Russia on the implementation of recommendations of commissions of inquiry have become a major discursive feature for accepting normalcy of certain states. Along the same lines, China claimed, "The recommendations made by the Advisory Commission on Rakhine State in its report are being implemented. Myanmar's independent commission of inquiry on Rakhine state recently began work and held a meeting" (UN Security Council 2018: 21).

In March 2017, the UN Human Rights Council established a fact-finding mission to establish the facts and circumstances of the abuses and the alleged human rights violations by the military and security forces in Myanmar. The UN independent international fact-finding mission on Myanmar found that "war crimes and crimes against humanity have been committed in Kachin, Shan and Rakhine states" (UN Security Council 2018: 5). Its report suggested that the "mission also found sufficient information to warrant the investigation and prosecution of senior officials in the Tatmadaw on charges of genocide. That means that we consider that genocidal intent—meaning the intent to destroy the Rohingya in whole or in part—can be reasonably inferred" (UN Security Council 2018: 5). The report in which the UN Human Rights Council (2018) detailed findings of the independent international fact-finding mission on Myanmar confirms that the government of Myanmar has failed to implement most of the recommendations set out by the Advisory Commission on Rakhine State. Myanmar has categorically objected to independent international fact-finding missions. They have called the UN mission a "totally biased and one-sided . . . investigation" that "targeted only Myanmar security forces and excluded the violations committed by the Arakan Rohingya Salvation Army (ARSA)" (UN Security Council 2019: 19). To counterbalance the UN Human Rights Council's Independent Investigative Mechanism for Myanmar, the government of Myanmar established its own Independent Commission of Enquiry (ICOE), tasked to "investigate the allegations of human rights violations and related issues following terrorist attacks by ARSA with a view to assigning accountability for any human rights violations and related issues that may have occurred" (Republic of the Union of Myanmar 2018). As stipulated by a spokesperson for the Office of the President of Myanmar, the ICOE was "to respond to false allegations made by the UN Agencies and other international communities" (ICOE 2018). The significance of commissions of inquiry in retaining international acceptance is clearly illustrated by a statement delivered by Myanmar's representative at a UN Security Council meeting.

> The Myanmar Government is committed to bringing to justice the perpetrators of human rights violations on a basis of solid evidence. It has established an independent commission of inquiry on Rakhine state, which has extensive international participation and has promised to submit a report within a year. The international community should respect Myanmar's sovereignty and encourage the commission to work independently, establish the truth and hold the perpetrators of human rights violations accountable. (UN Security Council 2018: 22)

As the Myanmar example indicates, the outcome of state confessions may result, more often than not, in a state accepting responsibility for past wrongdoings and apologizing and expressing remorse while also defying or resisting other narratives, thereby pushing for normalizing its status and conduct (Daase, Engert, and Renner 2016).

CONCLUSION

This chapter has examined dominant discourses and practices underpinning, on the one hand, the struggle of some states to forge their narrative of normalcy and, on the other, the restraint and lite interventionism employed by other states. We have shown that to justify acceptance of friendly and ally states complicit in human rights abuses (and thus deemed suppressive), dominant states use lite forms of interventionism, such as commissions of inquiry or special confessionary and investigative mechanisms. That approach is a form of both governing their friendly states and protecting them by deterring harsher forms of interventionism by international organizations or other adversaries. In the age of human rights, state normalcy is associated with the promotion and protection of human rights. Although the promotion of human rights is grounded on principles of universality and equality, it embeds an ideological desire for transforming states into liberal democracies where civil society and liberalism are the core pillars of society (Mutua 2002). By default, non-Western states tend to see any criticism from Western states on human rights as a foreign policy instrument for regime control and change, although that perception is overcompensated by the politics of pluralism and tolerance of difference in the international system. Some see Western states' tolerance of the existence of different regimes of normalcy as emblematic of a post-liberal order (see Coker 2019), while others regard it as an optimal technology of state dominance in world politics (see Reus-Smit 2018). Accepting alterity and a pluriversal of normalcy springs from a backlash that the liberal international order has faced in the last two decades, especially the agenda to globalize human rights. Accepting other states as normal is a strategic withdrawal of Western powers from the grand project of liberal internationalism and is certainly a post-interventionist strategy of damage control. A transition to a post-American and post-Western order whereby the rules imposed by the existing hegemons may no longer be respected, it is a realization that "this liberal international order is in crisis," that "liberal democracy itself appears to be in retreat" as "populist, nationalist and xenophobic strands of backlash politics have proliferated" (Ikenberry 2018: 7).

Also shown in this chapter is how the meaning of normalcy is discursively, institutionally, and politically constructed. In particular, accepting the normality of states complicit in serious human rights abuses is a strategic move that fulfills a number of functions. It plays out as a regime of accepting cultural difference and political autonomy of states with uneven human rights records. That regime helps disguise imperialist agendas. It tends to decouple the Western states from colonial-like practices, interventionism, and utilization of human rights as an ideological and foreign policy instrument, and it feeds well into the narrative of decolonization and pluralization of international norms and rules. By loosely and unevenly advocating for human rights protections, the regime of discourses and practices underpinning the acceptance of normalcy of deviant states lures non-Western states to be part of human rights regimes and to be subjected to various hierarchies of norms, institutions, and power bases. Moreover, acceptance of states with dubious records on human rights renews the power of dominant states, as it forces affected states to take a subordinate position toward powerful states and to comply with the latter's political, economic, and security agendas. Ultimately, accepting other states as normal is also a precondition for engaging in strategic relationships, which is crucial for the survival and preservation of the status of dominant power. Yet, by invoking the notion of non-intervention but demanding self-transformation, dominant states perform a form of disguised intervention on themselves.

For states under scrutiny for abuses, offering their narrative on human rights protection is key to international acceptance. By forging and demonstrating human rights protections, states guard their domestic affairs from interference by other states. While "the purpose of human rights is to protect all people everywhere from severe political, legal, and social abuse" (Lefebvre 2018: 3), the discourse and practices of suppressive regimes, articulated within UN institutional bodies, reveal human rights as a mechanism to protect the state from external interference (deemed abuse). The analytics of accepting normalcy require states to assess, criticize, transform, and hold themselves to account. States are accepted as normal as long as they undertake a commitment to self-improvement and change along a set of norms and standards. For states offering and states fielding them, state confessions produce discourses and regimes of truth that shape perceptions of what is normal and what is abnormal state behavior. Institutional platforms, such as UN universal periodic reviews or national commissions of inquiry, facilitate the self-mastery of states' denial of human rights abuses. State confessions enable distribution of power (at least discursive and relational power) along structures, hierarchies, and alliances, thereby producing new forms of dependency toward other states while also constituting new forms of agency. In particular, the confession of failures and the promise to become a better state is sufficient proof for retaining the status of a normal state. At the heart of the technology of accepting normalcy is not the occurrence of abnormal state practices but the capacity and determinism to respond to such abnormalcies. A state's self-application of that technology is an attempt to achieve self-mastery through truth-telling, confession, and a voluntary commitment to change. As the technology of forging normalcy is participatory and inclusive, it is seen as a less intrusive and interventionist method of normalization. Yet, whenever there are excusive bodies, such as commissions of inquiry, the technology of self-transformation changes dynamics, demonstrating a greater degree of external interference and stronger degree of resistance and contestation.

6 ✦ Toward a Society of Docile States

In this book we have explored different discourses and practices of normalization in world politics. In contrast to approaches emphasizing the novelty of specific interventionary forms, the alternative perspective offered here focused on how narratives and practices of normalization include elements of both continuity and change—encompassing both the continuation of "traditional" interventionary dynamics and the emergence of new, post-interventionary dynamics. In casting the technologies of normalization in turbulent societies, this book focused on a number of distinctive sets of discourses and practices: interventions that seek to reform and transform "abnormal" societies through the imposition of external blueprints of normalcy, interventions that seek to restore normalcy to pre-disaster states, and newly emerging features of accepting normalcy. Focusing on Michel Foucault's method of problematization enabled us to unravel the dominant discourses and to explore how knowledge production is co-constitutive of real-world events and actions. We embarked on a type of critique seeking simultaneously to deconstruct discourses and practices of normalization and to reconstruct them in an order that reveals how normalization interventions operate in world politics. In this chapter, we reprise our key arguments and findings and reflect on the prospects and limits of trying to develop a society of docile states.

THE WILL TO (AB)NORMALIZE

The terms *normal* and *normalcy* are some of the most commonly used in social and political life. Yet they remain highly contested. As discussed in chapter 2, normalization discourses encompass a number of paradoxes. While the term *normal* is a description of the opposite of what is perceived as abnormal or unacceptable, normalization discourses also inherently contribute to the prescription of the normal and the abnormal. The concepts of normal, normalcy, and normalization reveal the problematic and intermingled dynamics of sameness versus difference, homogeneity versus heterogeneity, order versus disorder, universalism versus pluralism, and values versus interests. In this book, we have focused on the international dynamics of states' normalization. Mapping the scope and variety of normalization interventions in world politics, we have explored some of the key features of what may be referenced as an international normalizing society, consisting of an assemblage of political actors governed by a set of evolving socio-legal, political-diplomatic, and military norms, standards, and practices. In principle, normalization interventions are meant to contribute to the formation of a society of states expected to share common values and interests and governed by a common set of rules and institutions. They pull all the states in the direction of a universal world order embedded in the unity and sameness of values, norms, and institutions considered good, progressive, and in service of peace, justice, and order. Yet, as examined in this book, the continuum of normalizing interventions—ranging from those seeking to impose a new order of normalcy over fragile states to those seeking to restore or develop a more resilient normalcy in disaster-affected states or to accept an existing order of normalcy in suppressive states—is embedded in multiple teleologies, which optimize the norms and ethics of normal subjects around the world (see also da Mota 2018).

The analysis in this book focused on problematizing and disentangling normalization discourses and practices as technologies of social control and manifestations of disciplinary power. Our framework for analyzing normalization in world politics revolved around the work of Foucault, which offers valuable conceptual and epistemological tools for studying normalization discourses and practices. For Foucault, normalization represents one of the most complex and advanced techniques for governing of all aspects of life without using coercive power and punishment. In a nutshell, normalization consists of discursively setting an optimal model and measure of what ought to be normal and using that model to encourage subjects to conform to the norm. Thus, dynamics of normalization are determined by iterative processes of posing particular norms as standard and universal and of labeling subjects who fall outside such norms as abnormal. To ascertain a norm as a code of conduct and to determine which subjects should fall outside its remit requires the deployment of three disciplinary techniques. The first is obtaining hierarchical observations of targeted subjects through surveillance, tracking mechanisms, and data collection, to survey broad trends and dynamics. The second is using normalizing judgment to ensure that subjects engage in educational and transformative activities and to deploy corrective, punitive, and rewarding mechanisms to move the subjects, metaphorically speaking, within the remit of the normal. The third is examining subjects exposed to a set of interventionary practices that seek to place subjects into specific trajectories of normalization, combining elements from the two previous techniques of normalization.

In mapping normalization discourses and practices in world politics, we assembled knowledge frameworks of different labels of state abnormalcy linked to different techniques of normalization. All normalization interventions are informed by a discourse of intelligibility seeking to enable a set of actions that make imposing, restoring, or accepting normalcy conceivable and justifiable. State labeling and grading are techniques of hierarchical observation and examination that serve as international disciplinary mechanisms of normalization. Existing scholarship on international norms, order, and statehood tends to take the perspective of liberal states as the starting position from which to examine how the rest of the world fares vis-à-vis liberal norms, values, and principles. The figure of the normal state in world politics is predominantly the Western state, constituting the yardstick by which to measure all other forms of abnormality in world politics. Once states fall outside the perceived realm of normalcy, they are considered abnormal and are subjected to intervention and exclusion. Abnormal states are not seen as legitimate states and are not treated as equals in world politics. They are subject to different disciplinary interventions to contain and, when possible, transform the conditions of normalcy, with the ultimate goal of building a decent society sufficient to coexist with other (liberal) societies. In this book, we challenge that methodological positionality and reveal how taking liberal states' perception of others as a starting point contributes to the otherization process. We used Foucauldian analytics on normalization to dissect and problematize efforts of liberal societies to impose their normalcy over conflict-affected and failed states, restore normalcy in disaster-affected states, and accept normalcy among suppressive states deemed as decent allies.

Predominantly, global gradeability regimes regard Western states as models to be emulated, whereas non-Western states feature at the bottom of most indexes. Such benchmarks and grading metrics foreground a symbolic judgment that serves as a mode of discipline, forcing states to alter their conduct in order to retain their international status. Gradeability has significant implications, as it tends to produce and reproduce hierarchical orders of normalcy that render certain actors, practices, regions, and cultures as abnormal. States that fall outside the perceived model of statehood are often stigmatized and labeled as norm violators, pariahs, and uncivilized states. In that regard, the normalization process becomes the governance of social relations by creating otherness and then putting pressure on different subjects to follow a particular order, standard, and logic of normalcy. Indexes such as the Failed States Index, the Global Peace Index, Freedom in the World, the Corruption Perception Index, and many other metrics contribute to the stratification of states along different categories, whereby those ranked above the average are praised as normal states while those below the average are seen as abnormal. Grading states along lines of normalness and peacefulness is a form of distant, indirect, and transnational governmentality. It simultaneously shapes what state wellness should look like and constructs narratives and labels of undesirables in world politics.

The disciplinary process central to international interventions entails hierarchical observation by external actors on the political and social structures of societies targeted for normalization. That observation can be carried out by powerful states but can also operate through the intervening structures of international or regional organizations. It relies on codified international norms and practices, as well as particularly assembled knowledge as a justificatory base for intervention. International structures and conventions provide the socio-material foundation for surveillance, judgment, and alteration of targeted societies. In the international normalizing society, UN agencies, regional organizations, and nongovernmental organizations and think tanks contribute to the identification, classification, and intervention of societies that are deemed either normal or abnormal. By those actions, they contribute to setting the criteria of normalcy in world politics.

In this book, we have focused on three categories of states—failed, disaster-prone, and suppressive—that are subject to different techniques of normalization. They further correspond to Foucault's three figures of the abnormal. States labeled failed or fragile are often associated with monstrous creatures that are abnormal, unnatural, and criminal, contravening and breaching the laws, rules, and norms governing the international community. Failed states are often ranked and placed at the bottom of the hierarchical labeling of states in world politics. Prevalent in the colonial era, the discourse of monstrosity and uncivilized nations served as a justification for European imperialism and geopolitical and economic expansion and exploitation. In the postcolonial era, such discourse was replaced by more technocratic language pathologizing states that had limited capacity to govern their own affairs or that turned into zones of violent conflicts. Following anticolonialism and antiracism discourse on the global stage, it is no longer deemed acceptable to label states as savages and barbarians, and the discourse has shifted toward concepts such as "failed," "collapsed," or "rogue." The discourse of failed states, which corresponds to Foucault's figure of the monster, represents the most extreme form of abnormalcy, which is dealt with through judicial-political methods, entailing law enforcement, courts, and other corrective instruments. Thus, state failure emerged as a condition diagnosed through techno-political and epistemic methods of hierarchical observation and examination, opening up the possibility for intervention to "cure" that abnormalcy through statebuilding and peacebuilding activities.

States associated with disasters and emergencies are also subject to normalization discourse. In our analysis, we have associated such states with Foucault's figure of the incorrigible, dealt with through interventions that seek to reorganize and manage anomalies through various functional changes. Disaster-affected states are associated with catastrophic events, for which external assistance is required to provide humanitarian relief and build resilience among affected populations. The normalization discourse regarding such states envisages crisis management and structural, institutional, and political adjustments within the state and society, to enhance resilience, transformation, and social change. In other words, it calls for the establishment of complex governance and self-reliance systems for societies to correct themselves without needing constant external assistance and support. The discourse shifts between "bouncing back" to a pre-crisis normalcy and "bouncing forward" to a new normalcy with enhanced resilience to adapt to future episodes of crisis.

Finally, the third category of states covered in this book are mostly accepted as being normal but are known to be suppressive of their populations and rely on authoritarian governance. Due to strategic alliances and politics of friendship, those states are predominantly exempt from significant external intervention. That category of states is associated with Foucault's figure of the onanist, handled through noncoercive, self-helping, and transformative measures and by redistributing power at the level of the individual, without affecting the entire society. That governmentality is expressed through lighter forms of intervention, manifested, in the current international context, through individual responsibility for misconduct or ad hoc disciplinary measures against misbehaving subjects. The will of those states for self-transformation and modification, expressed through confessionary practices and verified through commissions of inquiry, is seen as sufficient to allow the states to be accepted back, at the international level, as "normal" and "healthy" subjects.

In this book, we have argued that one key feature of world politics has been the process of setting boundaries around normalcy, defining who and what is normal, and developing international mechanisms for governing normalcy. That process entails imposing a certain regime of normalcy on particular societies, seeking to restore normalcy in another set of circumstances, or even accepting normalcy in specific contexts. The will to normalize results in empowering certain states and societies while marginalizing others and has far-reaching implications for rights, entitlements, resources, opportunities, and the status of states and societies in world politics. Practices of normalization have long-lasting impact on the identity and recognition of targeted states and populations. At a more grounded level, normalizing efforts lead to structural forms of disqualification, discrimination, suppression, and alienation that harm the collective identity, dignity, and standing of certain social groups. Regardless of changes over time, conflict-affected or disaster-prone states continue to be discursively and politically separated and even discriminated against in the international system. Once present, the stigma attached to the status of abnormalcy can last for decades after specific interventions. The normalization of state status in world politics is prolonged by the protracted nature of normalization interventions. As we have shown in our work, intervention tends to have a dual nature: it may start as a reaction to a perceived state of abnormalcy, but the focus of the intervention can change when new conditions of abnormalcy are revealed or to preempt any future issues. That the object of normalization constantly shifts and that the actual normalization remains potential and aspirational opens endless opportunities for normalization interventions.

Normalization has the potential to become an umbrella notion for multifaceted interventions, from peacemaking, peacekeeping, stabilization missions, and peacebuilding, to resilience building and monitoring fact-finding missions. The discourse of normalization is gradually replacing references to peace, order, and stability, which could represent a reduction of expectations vis-à-vis affected societies as well as a realization of the limits of interventionism and could serve as a tactical withdrawal from special responsibilities. Therefore, there is the possibility to shift the different rationales of normalcy in a particular society at different stages of intervention. What was once seen as abnormal suddenly becomes normal and acceptable, and vice versa. Victims of conflict become either resilient subjects or referents of insecurity. Peace spoilers become either peace enablers or imminent security threats. In the context of all-encompassing attempts to govern risks, discourses of resilience, acceptance of difference, and permanence of crisis become enabling frameworks that legitimize optimal normalization expressed in more radical and fluid forms of intervention.

The politics of normalization reveal how international authority is constructed through exercising power by abnormalizing certain societies, countries, and situations while avoiding any accountability of the potential harm caused in the process. That discourses of normalization in world politics produce epistemic violence goes without saying. The very practice of labeling states as failed, disaster-prone, and suppressive can create opportunities for regimes in need of resources or international backing (see, for example, Fisher 2014), but local populations are the first casualties of that labeling, restricting everyday practices. Such labeling results in "othering" the local communities while ultimately opening the possibility for intervention, imposition, and discrimination. The subjects of international interventions are then exposed to multilayered forms of discrimination and suspension of freedoms, not only from their own national governments, but from external actors who come to impose, restore, or accept a particular order of normalcy.

TECHNOLOGIES OF NORMALIZATION IN WORLD POLITICS

Mapping normalization practices around the world—spanning conflict-afflicted, disaster-affected, and suppressive states—reveals how the quest for normalcy tends to be optimized by actors based on situational conditions. In societies labeled fragile and failed, the focus and scope of intervention tends to be deep, seeking to spread and impose an external regime of normalcy. We found that fragile and failed states labeled as monstrous subjects are exposed to a set of extensive measures for imposing normalcy from outside, guided by liberal interventionism (statebuilding and peacebuilding) as a knowledge and practice regime. For societies labeled broken or disaster-prone, the focus of intervention is on consolidating and improving their resilience and capacity to bounce back and forward. We found that disaster-affected states are associated with incorrigibility and thus exposed to different regimes for restoring normalcy, through resilience building and emergency management. In societies that are accepted as normal despite their irregularities, the focus of intervention is on deepening normalcy through confessionary and self-regulatory processes. We found that states associated with suppressive policies and authoritarian regimes while remaining allies with dominant states in the international system tend to be accepted as normal states through a regime of confessionary practices and international pastoral politics. Accordingly, this book has shown that the fluidity and optimization of discourses and practices of normalcy articulated through an assemblage of interventionary measures represent a will to govern that is not necessarily or exclusively attached to liberal normative frameworks and that constantly changes the referent objects of intervention. Those discourses and practices point to an understanding of world politics as constituted through uneven and optimized politics, rather than consistently following a unique normative register often associated with the liberal rule-based international order.

One defining feature of normalization interventions as explored in this book is the mechanism(s) through which such interventions take place. In chapter 3, we explored the most intrusive techniques of normalization interventions that take place in states categorized as failed or collapsing and incapable of acting as normal states. Through that lens, peacebuilding and statebuilding become all-encompassing rationales for justifying liberal interventions, from global to local levels. Through peacebuilding and statebuilding activities, the international community seeks to create institutionalized and legal conditions for governing, disciplining, and normalizing the local population. The imposition of a new normalcy in conflict-affected societies is facilitated through a wide array of interventions that share elements of interim rule (through transitional administration), delegated rule (through controlling national elites and the peace-supporting behavior), and proxy rule (through civil society organizations and self-disciplining local groups). Rationales for imposing normalcy spring from a standpoint of liberal exceptionalism: namely, the perception that the intervener's values and political system should act as a yardstick for evaluating the progress of societies in world politics. That exceptionalism is also linked to the idea that powerful Western states have "special responsibilities" to police international order—in a sense, a new version of the "White Man's Burden."

Despite efforts to impose normalcy, the current record shows that societies labeled as fragile do not necessarily internalize international norms or become liberal states. They end up in an ambivalent state of liminality and instability. We often see a process of transformation of and hybridization between local and international norms. Whenever international missions fail to impose norms on conflict-affected societies, the mission leaders tend to blame the hostile local context or the inability of local actors to improve. Failure is normalized and treated as something to be expected in fragile states. Discourses of normalization permit normative fluidity and flexibility, which can result in turning failed interventions into opportunities for new forms of intervention. The very mechanisms that ought to promote normalization, such as hierarchical observation, normalizing judgment, and examinations, become sources for further abnormalization of fragile societies and thus justify reconfigured forms of intervention. Peacebuilding and statebuilding have emerged as technologies of power to control and discipline fragile states through external direct and indirect methods of imposition, governance, regulation, and supervision. Once states are set on a course of statebuilding and peacebuilding and are subject to extensive social reconstruction and institutional reforms, they become subject to never-ending examination from outside. They are distrusted subjects in world politics and are expected to accept external interventions for their own benefit and for the benefit of the international community.

In chapter 4, we analyzed the techniques of normalization that operate through discourses and practices of restoring normalcy, aimed at facilitating a return to a status quo ante or at establishing a new, more resilient normal order. Starting from the premise that international actors have limited capacity to transform "turbulent societies" into fully accepted, normal actors in the international arena, that bundle of practice in regard to normalization represents a different qualitative engagement from social transformation objectives inherent in imposing normalcy practices. In that framework of international engagement, there is an understanding of restoring normalcy as a way to deal with the normalization of instability in the world. Discussion based on that understanding echoes the portrayal of "difficult" or "turbulent" states as normal in their abnormality, harboring violence as a constitutive trait, and normalizing instability to the extent that what constitutes an "emergency" becomes the new normal. In the face of growing normalization of emergencies, there is undoubtedly a certain capitulation by powerful actors, as one can see through discussions of "donor fatigue" and the tendency to disengage with difficult regions of the world. Policymakers' capitulation in the face of that complexity echoes Foucault's discussion around the figure of the incorrigible, who requires correction because all the usual techniques, procedures, and attempts at training within the family have failed as correction attempts. Such "correction," or "technology of rectification," operates through a logic that difficult subjects of world politics need to "be restrained" while failing to be completely transformed. International interventions that operate in such an environment work through logics of resilience building, aimed at restoring a semblance of normalcy to protect intervening actors from any negative implications of instability. Restoring normalcy practices also work through a recognition that we are operating in a complex environment, where linear models of intervention—buttressing imposing normalcy practices, for instance—are repudiated in a bid to recognize our limited ability to manage the sheer complexity of social systems. But operating in a complex environment does not mean the end of intervention; the complexity framework enables new forms of intervention, moving away from international liberalism and toward alternative practices of intervention.

Despite the efforts of many societies to construct alternative normalities, the quest for governmentality of different ways of life has found ways of intervening with ever-shifting rationales and justifications. As discussed in this book, technologies of normalization in world politics do not seek the abandonment of all other competing norms and cultures. Because many states experiencing failure-like symptoms are part of a particular geopolitical and security alliance and have particular geographical, military, and economic strength, they may be deemed as normal regardless of their human rights record or suppressive policies. The analysis in chapter 5 focused on the techniques for accepting the normalcy of suppressive states through pastoral international mechanisms, with a particular focus on truth-telling and state confession and on lite forms of interventionism through commissions of inquiry. State confession rituals within multilateral forums feed into the technology of normalization, whereby international bureaucracies perform hierarchical observation over member states to ensure compliance with international norms, standards, and regimes. Processes such as universal periodic reviews, together with more targeted reviewing and reporting protocols, serve as state examination instruments determining states' normalcy and acceptability. Moreover, commissions of inquiry and fact-finding missions jointly enable normalizing judgment, allowing for strategic narratives that whitewash human rights abuses and for pastoral politics that deliver subjective assessment of normalcy for alliance members. The combination of those instruments satisfies external actors' desire for intervention and local actors' plea for recognition and acceptance without undergoing major social transformation.

Although the politics of alliances, friendship, and self-interest expose the hypocrisy of powerful states for selectively accepting certain states as normal despite the presence of human rights abuses, they enable dominant states to defuse power by encoding it into different normalization technologies. Accepting other states as normal and coexisting with others in the international system is not symptomatic of the tolerant character of dominant powers; on the contrary, it is a reflection of their weakness and inability to govern and impose their regime of truths, practices, and institutions in all circumstances. States that dominate the existing international order seek to retain their global status through their own suspension and exceptionalism toward certain suppressive states. They exploit diversity as a mechanism for preserving hierarchical supremacy through pastoral politics that inflict minimal intervention and forge self-normalization of suppressive states. Asking other states to transform themselves without meaningful external intervention is not a sign of self-restraint but a symptom of trying to govern the ungovernable. It is also a symptom of a transitional international order, which seeks self-legitimization through accepting others' normalcy. In other words, accepting other states as normal might be perceived as a strategic withdrawal of Western powers from the already fading project of liberal internationalism and is certainly a post-interventionist strategy for damage control. It marks a transition to a post-American and post-Western order whereby the rules imposed by the existing hegemons may no longer be respected. One strategy for prolonging the liberal order is to optimize interventions abroad and lure alliances and partnerships through a mixture of diplomatic, economic, and security incentives. It is an attempt to rebrand liberal internationalism by "reconciling the dilemmas of sovereignty and interdependence, seeking protections and preserving rights within and between states" (Ikenberry 2018: 8).

Looking at this broad range of contemporary dynamics of normalization, our analysis points out that the will to normalize highlights hegemonic tendencies for disciplining the conduct of states through the optimization of technologies. Efforts for normalization of states point to the desire for the creation of a world community through a combination of different technologies of power, in order to mitigate perceived anomalies within and among states without perceiving such interventions as impositions from outside. Normalization practices in world politics have both homogenizing and heterogenizing functions. Interventions for imposing normalcy seek to heterogenize states into distinct categories, whereas interventions for restoring and accepting normalcy tend to focus on homogenizing aspects. The former interventions invoke differentiating discourses to justify suspension of norms governing state sovereignty, whereas the latter interventions tend to focus on mutual recognition and validation among nations. The heterogenizing effects of normalization seek to preserve the hierarchical position of dominant states who are often among the interveners. Those effects retain the ontological status of dominant states as benchmark countries, status made possible through abnormalizing and excluding other states from the same status on the world stage. Homogenizing effects are evident when, for instance, dominant states seek to retain and expand their pastoral influence over other states simply by protecting and treating their allies as normal states regardless of their suppressive and delinquent conduct.

Normalization practices constitute power relations between, on the one hand, states that take on the roles of observing, judging, and examining other states and thus of producing discursive knowledge on normalcy and, on the other hand, states that are targets of normalization and that are expected to transform themselves into docile subjects through various technologies of power. Ultimately, the discourses of abnormalcy enable the former to (re)constitute a Schmittian sovereign power by deciding on the normal and the exception, while subjugating the latter into a process of social transformation and self-alienation. Those who judge, examine, and diagnose which states are normal and abnormal perform temporal sovereign exceptions. In the name of promoting the normal, societies subjected to normalization interventions become exceptions on which impositions can be made without being perceived as imperial and coercive in nature. In the context of international interventions, the politics of exceptionality are well engrained within the political and moral theology of liberal interventionism, disaster management, and human rights promotion, where crises, catastrophes, threats, and risks constitute solid bases for emergency powers (see Agamben 1998).

TOWARD A SOCIETY OF DOCILE STATES:
PROSPECTS AND LIMITS

Ultimately, normalization in world politics is closely linked to normative goods, such as peace, order, and stability. While that outcome might appear to be reasonable and uncontroversial, matters open to debate and appropriate for scrutiny are how the society of normal states is formed, which interventionary techniques shape it, and who has or claims the authority to implement such changes and at what cost. As we have shown in this book, technologies of normalization often enshrine various forms of exceptional, arbitrary, and violent politics. Our analysis shows that normative stances on world politics can easily be co-opted by certain states to frame their geopolitical interventions within a more acceptable discourse. On the surface, normalization interventions aspire to promote the condition of sameness in world politics. That condition takes the shape of higher ethical and normative aspirations expressed in the form of rights, values, and codes of conduct. However, since those aspirations conditioned on sameness are applied to different societies and contexts with distinct historical, political, cultural, and socioeconomic dynamics, they expose the impossibility, in practice, of ascertaining homogeneity. Therefore, looking at international interventions from the prism of normalization has exposed the will to create docile states that, in many cases, are not necessarily liberal or do not mirror the intervener's identity and values. The exceptional politics of international interventions do not necessarily mirror the dynamics of normalization in liberal countries but, rather, develop distinct, arbitrary, hybrid technologies of normalization. The states of exception underpinning international interventions range from suspending democratic decision-making processes to imposing various norms, rules, and institutional regimes on local vulnerable societies in the name of their stabilization, pacification, and self-transformation. Discourses and practices of normalization and disciplinary techniques at the disposal of the international community represent an attempt to limit the sovereign power of states and turn them into docile subjects with relative autonomy.

Thus, practices of normalization seek to create states that conduct their affairs as "docile bodies." As Foucault (1991: 136) points out, a docile body is "the body that is manipulated, shaped, trained, which obeys, responds, becomes skillful and increases its forces." A docile body, able to be analyzed and manipulated, can be "subjected, used, transformed and improved" (Foucault 1991: 136; see also Foucault 1988b; Olivier 2010; Stewart 2017). The will to create docile states through normalization interventions is a will to establish an international society that is constantly subject to external examination and imposition. Such a state of docility is enforced through external coercion as well as internal transformation from critical constituencies. Docile states are those viewed as decent, rational, or responsible and as capable of self-transformation through learning, self-regulation, or self-discipline. In mapping different varieties of normalization practices, we have observed a link between discourses and technologies of intervention: namely, how the invocation of certain state labels reconstitutes the significance of certain ascribed norms that, in turn, justify a specific regime of intervention, reshuffle social hierarchies of states, and determine new realities of what is accepted as normal or abnormal. Most important, our analysis demonstrates how the politics of the abnormalization of states results in producing new vulnerabilities and dependencies among states.

Docility in world politics—as the end goal of normalization interventions—enables dominant states to exercise power at the lowest cost and with as little resistance as possible. Hence, self-governance of the subject is the natural end point of normalization. Institutions and practices of social control aim at reflective, penitent, and self-regulating subjects, who do not contest and question power dynamics and relations behind the construction and maintenance of the normal and abnormal in society. As Janie Leatherman (2008: 4) argues, "one of the ubiquitous effects of much of the disciplining in global politics is the rendering of docile bodies and the internalization of regimes of supervision so that at the individual level they become self-regulating." Docile states are capable of determining what measures to implement and from which norms and values to depart. They are self-corrective actors seeking to adopt regulatory norms depicted globally as normal. They are adaptable states, open to external regulation, examination, and control. Such obedience is seen as an ultimate form of satisfying both local and international requirements for peace, order, and development. In practice, as shown in this book, docility is cultivated through different techniques, such as therapeutic governance, the normalization of emergencies or the cycles of repetition of disciplinary techniques from periodic and annual reports on state performance, and regular intergovernmental and multilateral events and meetings where states have to present and compare themselves with other states and thus expose themselves to peer pressure and embarrassment.

The ultimate condition of docility is to design states and societies able to follow rules, norms, and institutional regimes that mostly originate from the outside but are also implicated within, through self-disciplinary and renormalization mechanisms. State docility is well engrained within the principles of Hedley Bull's (1977) conception of the international society of states, where observance of peace and limitation of interstate violence constituted some of the main goals of normalcy and order in world politics. States are encouraged and gently coerced to become peaceful, turn their power away from war and conflict, and focus on economic utility. Hence, interventions are articulated through a disciplinary will to render populations docile or "literally peaceful" (Howell 2011: 145). Peace-loving nations are considered to be not only those that perform self-restraint and resolve interstate conflicts through peaceful methods but those that do not engage in conflicts in the wider sense of incompatible or contradictory goals. They are seen as acting in compliance with international norms, rules, and laws governing relations between states. Failed or weak states are de facto subjects of liberal interventions molding them into new normal actors in world politics. States exposed to natural catastrophes and disasters are encouraged to become resilient and to turn a negative event into a positive outcome, bouncing forward to a more sustainable normalcy. Suppressive states are encouraged to address human rights abuses and engage in mimicries of self-transformation so that they can be taken away from the international abnormalization agenda. Accordingly, the ultimate goal of normalization interventions is to create docile states capable of self-normalizing and self-disciplining and tame enough to accept constant external supervision.

Docile states are meant to be passive yet productive. To retain a sense of independence and sovereignty, docile states have to constantly engage in political adjustment and self-transformation as the result of new forms of knowledge and measurements of normalcy imposed on them. Yet having agency is necessary for docile states to fulfill their norm-taking function. They are expected to act as norm takers and to display a submissive attitude toward norm-making states. In that context, norm taking entails acceptance and adaptation of foreign norms through a mixture of imposed and voluntary strategies. As Annika Björkdahl et al. (2015: 2) argue, "norm export and import takes place in a relationship between norm-maker and norm-taker that is defined by interdependence, asymmetry and power." Thus, norm makers act as teachers and supervisors, whereas norm takers are seen as learners and recipients of norms.

Not sovereign states in the classical sense, docile states traditionally undergo different degrees of normalization interventions, eventually become peripheral members of alliances, and are expected to be norm takers and to follow leading members of an alliance. Often losing control over their foreign policy conduct, docile states are subject to supranational regimes that monitor and supervise the internalization of norms in the name of, for instance, international cooperation, democratic accountability, or good governance. Furthermore, normalization practices are iterative and tend to result in prolonged interventions, entrapping subjects into essentialized positions of privilege (for those deemed normal) and disadvantage (for those deemed abnormal). The will to create docile states goes back to the conception of normality as repeatability—the predictable reoccurrence of events and situations or even the projection and anticipation of social behaviors and attitudes. The repeatability segment of normality concerns the expectation of how a state and society should act and perform their duties. It is about decontextualizing and transferring context-specific conceptions of the normal and the stereotypical to other places and societies in an effort to expand and maintain the self-centric need for the repeatability of the state of affairs.

Despite the normative and cosmopolitan resonance of normalizing interventions intended to promote peace, justice, development, and order, the international normalizing order is deeply contested. In principle, normalizing interventions are framed as a function of creating a society of states sharing common values and interests and governed by a common set of rules and institutions. That society might seem to be a reasonable outcome, but highly problematic are how it is formed, what interventionary techniques shape it, and who has the authority to implement such changes and at what cost. Normalcy that Western states view as desirable in one part of the world may not be valued the same in another part of the world. The differentiated view of what constitutes normalcy is the defining feature of contemporary interventions in world politics. The very process of normalization of turbulent societies reinforces and creates hierarchical relationships and uneven power dynamics between states and societies. Moreover, practices of normalization in world politics point to complex disciplinary systems that constrain state autonomy and regulate the conduct of both domestic and foreign affairs, thus revealing tendencies of global carcerality (see Foucault 1988b) and the development of what Hans Gerth and C. W. Mills called "internal whips" (cited in Corbett 2012: 316).

In sum, the politics of normalization embodies aspects of symbolic violence, as those politics enshrine a tendency for subordination through imposing the gradual internationalization and acceptance of certain discourses, ideas, and structures that have constraining and controlling outcomes. Judith Butler (1990) has warned that a norm becomes violent and legitimizes violence when it is naturalized or when it imposes a pattern of normality that is portrayed as natural, objective, ahistorical, and universal instead of cultural, constructed, and contingent (see also Ingala 2019: 193). Resistance to such an imposition is to be expected and is concomitant to the traditional view of power in the well-known understanding of Foucauldian theory. Hence, Jens Bartelson (2009: 2) argues that "every effort to impose a given set of values on the existing plurality of communities in the name of a common humanity is likely to be met with resistance on the grounds of its own very particularity." He concludes that "a real and genuinely inclusive world community is a dream incapable of realization, since every attempt to transcend the existing plurality in the name of some set of universal values is likely to create conflict rather than harmony." Since the project of creating a community of states that operates through a universal system of values, norms, and institutions is not feasible in the foreseeable future, we see the discourse and practices of normalization operating as optimized technologies of power between governing the self and others. In a world of relative sovereignty and autonomy, states are allowed to perform self-mastery and care for themselves only insofar as they are seen as normal and docile subjects. To retain relative autonomy, states are pushed to develop forms of self-knowledge and self-examination and, thus, to exercise self-normalization.

References

Abdul-Ahad, G. 2009. "Somalia: One Week in Hell—Inside the City the World Forgot." *The Guardian*, May 29.

ADHRB, BIRD, and BCHR (Americans for Democracy and Human Rights in Bahrain; Bahrain Institute for Rights and Democracy; and Bahrain Center for Human Rights). 2015. *Shattering the Façade: A Report on Bahrain's Implementation of the Bahrain Independent Commission of Inquiry (BICI) Recommendations Four Years On*. Washington, DC: Americans for Democracy and Human Rights in Bahrain. http://birdbh.org/wp-content/uploads/2015/11/Shattering_the_Facade_Web.pdf

Adler, E. 2019. *World Ordering: A Social Theory of Cognitive Evolution*. Cambridge: Cambridge University Press.

Adler-Nissen, R. 2017. "Are We 'Lazy Greeks' or 'Nazi Germans'? Negotiating International Hierarchies in the Euro Crisis." In *Hierarchies in World Politics*, edited by A. Zarakol, 198–218. Cambridge: Cambridge University Press.

Advisory Commission on Rakhine State. 2017. *Towards a Peaceful, Fair and Prosperous Future for the People of Rakhine: Final Report of the Advisory Commission on Rakhine State*. August. https://docs.wixstatic.com/ugd/0aa62d_044cf438d35d4becb030519c72b8db9d.pdf

Agamben, G. 1998. Homo Sacer: *Sovereign Power and Bare Life*. Translated by D. Heller-Roazen. Stanford: Stanford University Press.

Agier, M. 2011. *Managing the Undesirables*. London: Polity.

Albert, M. 2016. *A Theory of World Politics*. Cambridge: Cambridge University Press.

Albert, M., B. Buzan, and M. Zürn. 2013. "Introduction: Differentiation Theory and International Relations." In *Bringing Sociology to International Relations: World Politics and Differentiation Theory*, edited by M. Albert, B. Buzan, and M. Zürn, 1–26. Cambridge: Cambridge University Press.

Alesch, D. J., J. N. Holly, E. Mittler, and R. Nagy. 2001. *Organizations at Risk: What Happens When Small Businesses and Not-for-Profits Encounter Natural Disasters*. Fairfax, VA: Public Entity Risk Institute.

Alexander, P. 1973. "Normality." *Philosophy* 48 (184): 137–51.

Alston, P., and S. Knuckey. 2016. "The Transformation of Human Rights Fact-Finding." In *The Transformation of Human Rights Fact-Finding*, edited by P. Alston and S. Knuckey, 3–23. Oxford: Oxford University Press.

Alter, L. 2015. "So What Ever Happened to Katrina Cottages?" *Treehugger*, August 14. https://www.treehugger.com/tiny-houses/so-what-ever-happened-katrina-cottages.html

Alvesson, M., and J. Sandberg. 2013. *Constructing Research Questions*. 3rd ed. London: SAGE.

Amnesty International. 2018. *The State of the World's Human Rights (2017/2018)*. London: Amnesty International. https://www.amnesty.ie/wp-content/uploads/2018/02/AIR201718_English_2018_EMBARGOED-22-FEB.pdf

Anderson, B. 2015. "What Kind of Thing Is Resilience?" *Politics* 35 (1): 60–66.

Anderson, M. 2011. *Disaster Writing: The Cultural Politics of Catastrophe in Latin America*. Charlottesville: University of Virginia Press.

Annan, K. 2000. "Secretary-General Addresses Executive Committee of UNHCR." UNIS/SG/2678, October 3.

Annan, K. 2005. "In Larger Freedom: Towards Development, Security and Human Rights for All." A/59/2005, March 21.

Anton, M. 2019. "The Trump Doctrine." *Foreign Policy*, April 20. https://foreignpolicy.com/2019/04/20/the-trump-doctrine-big-think-america-first-nationalism/

APEC (Asia-Pacific Economic Cooperation). 2018. *Casebook of Infrastructure Build Back Better from Natural Disasters: Enhancing Rural Disaster Resilience through Effective Infrastructure Investment*. Singapore: APEC Secretariat.

Apter, D. E. 2008. "Duchamp's Urinal: Who Says What's Rational When Things Get Tough?" In *The Oxford Handbook of Contextual Political Analysis*, edited by R. E. Goodin and C. Tilly, 767–96. Oxford: Oxford University Press.

Aradau, C., J. Huysmans, A. Neal, and N. Voelkner, eds. 2014. *Critical Security Methods: New Frameworks for Analysis*. London: Routledge.

Arato, A. 2009. *Constitution Making under Occupation: The Politics of Imposed Revolution in Iraq*. New York: Columbia University Press.

Arribas-Ayllon, M., and V. Walerdine. 2008. "Foucauldian Discourse Analysis." In *The SAGE Handbook of Qualitative Research in Psychology*, edited by C. Willig and W. Stainton-Rogers, 91–108. London: SAGE.

Ashcroft, B., G. Griffiths, and H. Tiffin. 2000. *Post-Colonial Studies: The Key Concepts*. 2nd ed. Abingdon: Routledge.

Asma, S. T. 2009. *On Monsters: An Unnatural History of Our Worst Fears*. New York: Oxford University Press.

Australian Volunteers for International Development. 2015. *Build Back Better Operations Manual*. http://yolanda.neda.gov.ph/wp-content/uploads/2016/02/BBB-Operations-Manual-Rev1.0-July-2015-small-file-size.pdf

Avelino, N. 2015. "Confession and Political Normativity: Control of Subjectivity and Production of the Subject." *Soft Power: Revista euro-americana de teoria e historia de la politica* (Grupo Planeta) 2 (1): 14–38.

Bachmann, J. 2014. "Policing Africa: The US Military and Visions of Crafting 'Good Order.'" *Security Dialogue* 45 (2): 119–36.

Baehr, P. R., and M. Castermans-Holleman. 2004. *The Role of Human Rights in Foreign Policy*. 3rd ed. Basingstoke: Palgrave Macmillan.

Bahrain Embassy in Washington. 2015. "Highlights of Bahrain's Reform Progress 2015." *Medium*, September 17. https://medium.com/@bahrainembdc/highlights -of-bahrain-s-reform-progress-2015-d1863093b945

Bain, W. 2003. *Between Anarchy and Society: Trusteeship and the Obligations of Power*. Oxford: Oxford University Press.

Bankoff, G. 2002. *Cultures of Disaster: Society and Natural Hazard in the Philippines*. London: Routledge.

Barkey, K. 2008. *Empire of Difference: The Ottomans in Comparative Perspective*. Cambridge: Cambridge University Press.

Barnett, M. 2010. *The International Humanitarian Order*. London: Routledge.

Barnett, M., and R. Duvall. 2005. "Power in International Politics." *International Organization* 59 (1): 39–75.

Barnett, T. 2004. *The Pentagon's New Map: War and Peace in the Twentieth Century*. New York: Berkley Books.

Barrios, R. 2016. "Expert Knowledge and the Ethnography of Disaster Reconstruction." In *Contextualizing Disaster*, edited by G. Button and M. Schuller, 134–52. New York: Berghahn Books.

Barston, R. P. 2013. *Modern Diplomacy*. London: Routledge.

Bartelson, J. 2009. *Visions of World Community*. Cambridge: Cambridge University Press.

Baumgartner, F., B. Jones, and P. Mortensen. 2017. "Punctuated Equilibrium Theory: Explaining Stability and Change in Public Policymaking." In *Theories of the Policy Process*, edited by C. Weible and P. Sabatier, 55–101. New York: Westview.

Beal, T. 2001. "Our Monsters, Ourselves." *Chronicle of Higher Education*, November 9.

Bear, A., and J. Knobe. 2016. "Normality: Part Descriptive, Part Prescriptive." *Cognition* 167 (October): 25–37. https://doi.org/10.1016/j.cognition.2016.10.024

Beck, U. 2006. "Living in the World Risk Society." *Economy and Society* 35 (3): 329–45.

Beck, U. 2015. "Emancipatory Catastrophism: What Does It Mean to Climate Change and Risk Society?" *Current Sociology* 63 (1): 75–88.

Becker, H. S. 1963. *Outsiders: Studies in the Sociology of Deviance*. New York: Free Press.

Beckett, G. 2013. "Rethinking the Haitian Crisis." In *The Idea of Haiti: Rethinking Crisis and Development*, edited by M. Polyné, 27–49. Minneapolis: University of Minnesota Press.

Behler, G. 1987. "The Nuclear Accident at Three Mile Island: Its Effects on a Local Community." Ph.D. diss., University of Delaware.

Behrent, M. C. 2013. "Foucault and Technology." *History and Technology: An International Journal* 29 (1): 54–104.

Bell, B. 2012. "'Best Practices' and 'Exemplar Communities': Ivory Tower Housing Solutions for Haiti." *World Pulse*, February 2. https://www.worldpulse.com/com munity/users/beverly-bell/posts/19444

Bendix, A. 2019. "Brad Pitt's Post-Katrina Housing Project Faces Even More Backlash after Residents Discover Their Homes Are Rotting and Caving In." *Business Insider*, February 2.

Berke, P. R., and T. J. Campanella. 2006. "Planning for Postdisaster Resiliency." *Annals of the American Academy of Political and Social Science* 604:192–207.

Besley, A. C. 2005. "Self-Denial or Self-Mastery? Foucault's Genealogy of the Confessional Self." *British Journal of Guidance and Counselling* 33 (3): 365–82.

Best, R., and P. J. Burke. 2017. "Macroeconomic Impacts of the 2010 Earthquake in Haiti." Working Papers in Trade and Development 2017/15, Australian National University, December. https://acde.crawford.anu.edu.au/sites/default/files/publi cation/acde_crawford_anu_edu_au/2018-01/2017-15_best_burke_wps.pdf

Betts, A. 2009. "Institutional Proliferation and the Global Refugee Regime." *Perspectives on Politics* 7 (1): 53–58.

BICI (Bahrain Independent Commission of Inquiry). 2011. *Report of the Bahrain Independent Commission of Inquiry*. December 10. http://www.bici.org.bh/BIC IreportEN.pdf

Bigo, D. 2008. "Security: A Field Left Fallow." In *Foucault on Politics, Security and War*, edited by M. Dillon and A. W. Neal, 93–114. Basingstoke: Palgrave Macmillan.

Björkdahl, A., N. Chaban, J. Leslie, and A. Masselot. 2015. "Introduction: To Take or Not to Take EU Norms? Adoption, Adaptation, Resistance and Rejection." In *Importing EU Norms: Conceptual Framework and Empirical Findings*, edited by A. Björkdahl, N. Chaban, J. Leslie, and A. Masselot, 1–12. Cham: Springer International.

Blair, T. 1999. "The Blair Doctrine." Global Policy Forum, April 22. https://archive .globalpolicy.org/empire/humanint/1999/0422blair.htm

Blum, A. 2008. "Saint Brad." *Metropolis*, March 1. https://www.metropolismag.com /uncategorized/saint-brad/

Bolopion, P. 2019. "Atrocities as the New Normal: Time to Re-energize the 'Never Again' Movement." Human Rights Watch. https://www.hrw.org/world-report /2019/essay/atrocities-as-the-new-normal

Borsekova, K., and N. Nijkamp. 2019. "Blessing in Disguise: Long-Run Benefits of Urban Disasters." In *Resilience and Urban Disasters: Surviving Cities*, edited by K. Borsekova and N. Nijkamp, 2–29. Cheltenham: Edward Elgar.

Bourguignon, F. 2010. "Haïti: Faire d'un désastre une opportunité." *Les Echos*, January 27.

Bradbury, M. 1998. "Normalising the Crisis in Africa." *Disasters* 22 (4): 328–38.

Branch, A. 2011. *Displacing Human Rights: War and Intervention in Northern Uganda*. Oxford: Oxford University Press.

Brewer, J. D., B. C. Hayes, F. Teeney, K. Dudgeon, N. Mueller-Hirth, and S. L. Wijesinghe. 2018. *The Sociology of Everyday Life Peacebuilding*. Basingstoke: Palgrave Macmillan.

Broome, A., and J. Quirk. 2015. "Governing the World at a Distance: The Practice of Global Benchmarking." *Review of International Studies* 41 (5): 819–41.

Brown, B. 2015. "Remember That Katrina Cottages Thing? Whatever Happened to That?" *Place Makers*, August 10. http://www.placemakers.com/2015/08/10/rem ember-that-katrina-cottages-thing-whatever-happened-to-that/

Brozus, L. 2011. "Applying the Governance Concept to Areas of Limited Statehood:

Implications for International Foreign and Security Policy." In *Governance without a State? Policies and Politics in Areas of Limited Statehood*, edited by T. Risse, 262–80. New York: Columbia University Press.

Bukovansky, M., I. Clark, R. Eckersley, R. Price, C. Reus-Smit, and N. J. Wheeler. 2012. *Special Responsibilities: Global Problems and American Power*. Cambridge: Cambridge University Press.

Bull, C. 2008. *No Entry without Strategy: Building the Rule of Law under UN Transitional Administration*. Tokyo: United Nations University Press.

Bull, H. 1977. *The Anarchical Society: A Study of Order in World Politics*. London: Macmillan.

Bulto, T. S. 2014. "Africa's Engagement with the Universal Periodic Review: Commitment or Capitulation?" In *Human Rights and the Universal Periodic Review: Rituals and Ritualism*, edited by H. Charlesworth and E. Larking, 235–54. Cambridge: Cambridge University Press.

Bush, G. W. 2002. "First (Official) Presidential State of the Union Address." January 29. https://www.americanrhetoric.com/speeches/stateoftheunion2002.htm

Buzan, B., O. Wæver, and J. de Wilde. 1998. *Security: A New Framework for Analysis*. Boulder: Lynne Rienner.

Butler, J. 1990. *Gender Trouble: Feminism and the Subversion of Identity*. New York: Routledge.

Byrne, D., and G. Callaghan. 2014. *Complexity Theory and the Social Sciences: The State of the Art*. London: Routledge.

Calhoun, C. 2008. "The Imperative to Reduce Suffering: Charity, Progress, and Emergencies in the Field of Humanitarian Action." In *Humanitarianism in Question: Politics, Power, Ethics*, edited by M. Bennett and T. G. Weiss, 73–97. Ithaca: Cornell University Press.

Canguilhem, G. 1978. *The Normal and the Pathological*. New York: Zone Books.

Capasso, N. 2001. "Monsters Everywhere and Forever." In *Terrors and Wonders: Monsters in Contemporary Art*, organized by N. Capasso and J. Uhrhane, 7–11. Lincoln, MA: Decordova Museum and Sculpture Park.

Caplan, R. 2005. *International Governance of War-Torn Territories*. Oxford: Oxford University Press.

Carey, H. F. 2012. *Privatizing the Democratic Peace: Policy Dilemmas of NGO Peacebuilding*. Basingstoke: Palgrave Macmillan.

Castor, S. 2011. "Refonder la nation Haïtienne." In *Haïti aujourd'hui, Haïti demain: Regards croisés*, edited by A. Martinez, P. Beaudet, and S. Baranyi, 105–13. Ottawa: Presses de l'Université d'Ottawa.

Chambers, S. A., and T. Carver. 2008. *William E. Connolly: Democracy, Pluralism and Political Theory*. Abingdon: Routledge.

Chandler, D. 2014. *Resilience: The Governance of Complexity*. London: Routledge.

Chandler, D., and J. Reid. 2016. *The Neoliberal Subject: Resilience, Adaptation and Vulnerability*. London: Rowman and Littlefield.

Chandler, D., and O. P. Richmond. 2015. "Contesting Postliberalism: Governmentality or Emancipation?" *Journal of Development and International Relations* 18 (1): 1–24.

Charlesworth, H., and E. Larking. 2014. "Introduction: The Regulatory Power of the UPR." In *Human Rights and the Universal Periodic Review: Rituals and Ritu-*

alism, edited by H. Charlesworth and E. Larking, 1–21. Cambridge: Cambridge University Press.

Chauville, R. 2014. "The Universal Periodic Review's First Cycle: Successes and Failures." In *Human Rights and the Universal Periodic Review: Rituals and Ritualism*, edited by H. Charlesworth and E. Larking, 87–108. Cambridge: Cambridge University Press.

Chow, J. T. 2017. "North Korea's Participation in the Universal Periodic Review of Human Rights." *Australian Journal of International Affairs* 71 (2): 146–63.

Chr. Michelsen Institute. 2018. "SuperCamp: The Middle East as a Regional Zone of Containment." December 6. https://www.cmi.no/news/2094-supercamp-the -middle-east-as-a-regional-zone-of

Cilliers, P. 1998. *Complexity and Postmodernism: Understanding Complex Systems*. London: Routledge.

Cisin, I., and W. Clark. 1962. "The Methodological Challenge of Disaster Research." In *Man and Society in Disaster*, edited by G. Baker and D. Chapman, 23–54. New York: Basic Books.

City of New Orleans. 2015. *Resilient New Orleans: Strategic Actions to Shape Our Future City*. http://resilientnola.org/wp-content/uploads/2015/08/Resilient _New_Orleans_Strategy.pdf

Clark, I. 1989. *The Hierarchy of States: Reform and Resistance in the International Order*. Cambridge: Cambridge University Press.

Clinton, W. J. 2006. *Key Propositions for Building Back Better: Lessons Learned from Tsunami Recovery*. New York: Office of the UN Secretary-General's Special Envoy for Tsunami Recovery.

Clunan, A. 2010. "Ungoverned Spaces? The Need for Reevaluation." In *Ungoverned Spaces: Alternatives to State Authority in an Era of Softened Sovereignty*, edited by A. Clunan and H. A. Trinkunas, 3–13. Stanford: Stanford University Press.

Coalition Provisional Authority. 2003. Coalition Provisional Authority Order Number 39 (Foreign Investment). September 19. https://govinfo.library.unt.edu/cpa -iraq/regulations/20031220_CPAORD_39_Foreign_Investment_.pdf

Coggins, B. 2014. *Power Politics and State Formation in the Twentieth Century: The Dynamics of Recognition*. Cambridge: Cambridge University Press.

Cohen, J. 1996. "Monster Culture (Seven Theses)." In *Monster Theory: Reading Culture*, edited by J. Cohen, 3–25. Minneapolis: University of Minnesota Press.

Coker, C. 2019. *The Rise of the Civilizational State*. Cambridge: Polity.

Connolly, W. E. 1991. *Identity/Difference: Democratic Negotiations of Political Paradox*. Minneapolis: University of Minnesota Press.

Connolly, W. E. 1995. *The Ethos of Pluralization*. Minneapolis: University of Minnesota Press.

Conrad, S., and M. Strange. 2011. "Governance and Colonial Rule." In *Governance without a State? Policies and Politics in Areas of Limited Statehood*, edited by T. Risse, 39–64. New York: Columbia University Press.

Cooper, R. 2004. *The Breaking of Nations: Order and Chaos in the Twenty-First Century*. London: Atlantic Books.

Corbett, M. 2012. "Docile Bodies." In *Encyclopedia of Case Study Research*, edited by A. J. Mills, G. Durepos, and E. Wiebe, 316–18. London: SAGE.

Côté, J. 2015. *George Herbert Mead's Concept of Society: A Critical Reconstruction.* Boulder: Paradigm.

Council of the European Union. 2005. "Council Joint Action 2005/824/CFSP of 24 November 2005 on the European Union Police Mission (EUPM) in Bosnia and Herzegovina (BiH)." *Official Journal of the European Union*, L 307/55.

Council of the European Union. 2008. "Council Joint Action 2008/736/CFSP of 15 September 2008 on the European Union Monitoring Mission in Georgia, EUMM Georgia." *Official Journal of the European Union*, L 248/26.

Cowan, J. K. 2014. "The Universal Periodic Review as a Public Audit Ritual." In *Human Rights and the Universal Periodic Review: Rituals and Ritualism*, edited by H. Charlesworth and E. Larking, 42–62. Cambridge: Cambridge University Press.

Crawford, J. 2000. "The UN Human Rights Treaty System: A System in Crisis?" In *The Future of UN Human Rights Treaty Monitoring*, edited by P. Alison and J. Crawford, 1–12. Cambridge: Cambridge University Press.

CRED and UNISDR (Center for Research on the Epidemiology of Disasters and United Nations Office for Disaster Risk Reduction). 2016. *Poverty & Death: Disaster Mortality 1996–2015.* Brussels and Geneva: CRED and UNISDR.

Cryle, P., and E. Stephens. 2017. *Normality: A Critical Genealogy.* Chicago: University of Chicago Press.

Curtis, W. 2009. "Houses of the Future." *Atlantic*, November. https://www.theatlantic.com/magazine/archive/2009/11/houses-of-the-future/307708/

da Mota, S. 2018. *NATO, Civilisation and Individuals: The Unconscious Dimension of International Security.* Basingstoke: Palgrave Macmillan.

Daase, C., S. Engert, and J. Renner. 2016. "Introduction: Guilt, Apology and Reconciliation in International Relations." In *Apology and Reconciliation in International Relations*, edited by C. Daase, S. Engert, M.-A. Horelt, J. Renner, and R. Strassner, 1–28. Abingdon: Routledge.

Davidson, J. W. 2011. *America's Allies and War: Kosovo, Afghanistan, and Iraq.* Basingstoke: Palgrave Macmillan.

Davis, L. J. 1995. *Enforcing Normalcy: Disability, Deafness, and the Body.* London: Verso.

Davis, L. J. 2014. *The End of Normal: Identity in a Biocultural Era.* Ann Arbor: University of Michigan Press.

Davoudi, S. 2012. "Resilience: A Bridging Concept or a Dead End?" *Planning Theory and Practice* 13 (2): 299–333.

Day, G. 2000. "The Training Dimension of the UN Mission in Bosnia and Herzegovina (UNMIBH)." *International Peacekeeping* 7 (2): 155–68.

de Guevara, B. B. 2014. "Studying the International Crisis Group." *Third World Quarterly* 35 (4): 545–62.

Del Castillo, G. 2008. *Rebuilding War-Torn States: The Challenge of Post-Conflict Economic Reconstruction.* Oxford: Oxford University Press.

Delgado, R., and J. Stefancic. 2013. *Critical Race Theory: The Cutting Edge.* 3rd ed. Philadelphia: Temple University Press.

Dellinger, M. 2006. "The Terrible Opportunity: How a Crisis for the Gulf Coast Became a Defining Moment for New Urbanism." *Oxford American* 53 (Spring): 108–17.

Devetak, R. 2005. "The Gothic Scene of International Relations: Ghosts, Monsters, Terror and the Sublime after September 11." *Review of International Studies* 31 (4): 621–43.

Dillon, M., and A. Neal, eds. 2008. *Foucault on Politics, Security and War*. Basingstoke: Palgrave Macmillan.

Dobbins, J., J. G. McGinn, K. Crane, S. G. Jones, R. Lal, A. Rathmell, R. M. Swanger, and A. R. Timilsina. 2003. *America's Role in Nation-Building: From Germany to Iraq*. Santa Monica, CA: RAND.

Dorlus, W. 2010. Introduction to *Entre refondation et reconstruction: Les problématiques de l'avenir post-sismique d'Haïti*, edited by W. Dorlus, 11–19. Port-au-Prince: Editions de l'Université d'Etat d'Haïti.

Doxtader, E. 2011. "A Question of Confession's Discovery." *Rhetoric Society Quarterly* 41 (3): 267–81.

Doyle, M. W. 1983. "Kant, Liberal Legacies, and Foreign Affairs." Part 2. *Philosophy and Public Affairs* 12 (4): 323–53.

Doyle, M. W. 2012. *Liberal Peace: Selected Essays*. London: Routledge.

Doyle, M. W. 2015. *The Question of Intervention: John Stuart Mill and the Responsibility to Protect*. New Haven, CT: Yale University Press.

Duany, A. 2009. "Restoring the Real New Orleans." *New Geography*, March 17. https://www.newgeography.com/content/00673-restoring-real-new-orleans

Duany Plater-Zyberk and Company. 2010. *Haitian Cabins / Les cabanons d'Haiti*. https://massengale.typepad.com/files/haitian_cabins.pdf

Dubernet, C. 2017. *The International Containment of Displaced Persons: Humanitarian Spaces without Exit*. London: Routledge.

Duffield, M. 1996. "The Symphony of the Damned: Racial Discourse, Complex Political Emergencies and Humanitarian Aid." *Disasters* 20 (3): 173–93.

Duffield, M. 1999. "The Crisis of International Aid." In *Responding to Emergencies and Fostering Development: The Dilemmas of Humanitarian Aid*, edited by C. Pirotte, B. Husson, and F. Grunewald, 19–21. London: Zed Books.

Duffield, M. 2001. *Global Governance and the New Wars: The Merging of Development and Security*. London: Zed Books.

Duijsens, R., and M. Faling. 2014. "Humanitarian Challenges of Urbanization in Manila: The Position of the Philippine Red Cross in a Changing Disaster and Aid Landscape." *Resilience* 2 (3): 168–82.

Dunne, T., and M. MacDonald. 2013. "The Politics of Liberal Internationalism." *International Politics* 50 (1): 1–17.

Dupuy, A. 2007. *The Prophet and Power: Jean-Bertrand Aristide, the International Community, and Haiti*. London: Rowman and Littlefield.

Durkheim, É. 1982. *The Rules of Sociological Method and Selected Texts on Sociology and Its Method*. New York: Macmillan.

Duschinsky, R., and L. Rocha. 2012. "Introduction: The Family in Foucault's Work." In *Foucault, the Family and Politics*, edited by R. Duschinsky and L. Rocha, 1–18. Basingstoke: Palgrave Macmillan.

Dyberg, T. B. 2014. *Foucault on the Politics of Parrhesia*. Basingstoke: Palgrave Macmillan.

Edmunds, T., and A. E. Juncos. 2020. "Constructing the Capable State: Contested Discourses and Practices in EU Capacity Building." *Cooperation and Conflict* 55 (1): 3–21.

Edwards, R. 2008. "Actively Seeking Subjects?" In *Foucault and Lifelong Learning: Governing the Subject*, edited by A. Fejes and K. Nicoll, 21–33. Abingdon: Routledge.

Elden, S. 2001. "The Constitution of the Normal: Monsters and Masturbation at the Collège de France." *Boundary 2* 28 (1): 91–105.

Elliott, L. 2003. "The United Nations and Social Reconstruction in Disrupted States." In *From Civil Strife to Civil Society: Civil and Military Responsibilities in Disrupted States*, edited by W. Maley, C. Samford, and R. Thakur, 257–78. Tokyo: United Nations University Press.

Ellis, S. 2005. "How to Rebuild Africa." *Foreign Affairs* 84 (5): 135–48.

Enarson, E. 2006. "Women and Girls Last? Averting the Second Post-Katrina Disaster." *Items: Insights from the Social Sciences*, June 11. https://items.ssrc.org/underst anding-katrina/women-and-girls-last-averting-the-second-post-katrina-disaster/

Escobar, A. 1984. "Discourse and Power in Development: Michel Foucault and the Relevance of His Work to the Third World." *Alternatives* 10 (3): 377–400.

ESSC (Environmental Science for Social Change). 2016. "Implementing the 'Building Back Better' Agenda: Moving from Policy to Practice." November 20. https://essc.org.ph/content/archives/8969/

European Heads of Mission. 2017. *European Joint Strategy in Support of Palestine 2017–2020*. https://eeas.europa.eu/sites/eeas/files/final_-_european_joint_strate gy_english.pdf

European Parliament. 2017. "Answer Given by High Representative / Vice-President Mogherini." Doc. E-006917/2016, January 12. https://www.europarl.europa.eu /doceo/document/E-8-2016-006917-ASW_EN.html

European Parliament. 2018. "Resolution on the Human Rights Situation in Bahrain, Notably the Case of Nabeel Rajab." Doc. 2018/2755(RSP). https://oeil.secure.eu roparl.europa.eu/oeil/popups/ficheprocedure.do?lang=en&reference=2018/275 5(RSP)

Evans, B., and J. Reid. 2014. *Resilient Life: The Art of Living Dangerously*. Cambridge: Polity.

Evans-Cowley, J., and M. Zimmerman Gough. 2009. "Evaluating New Urbanist Plans in Post-Katrina Mississippi." *Journal of Urban Design* 14 (4): 439–61.

Ewald, F. 1990. "Norms, Discipline, and the Law." *Representations* 30 (Spring): 138–61.

Fair, B. 2009. "After Katrina: Laying Bare the Anatomy of American Caste." In *Hurricane Katrina: America's Unnatural Disaster*, edited by J. Levitt and M. Whitaker, 35–49. Lincoln: University of Nebraska Press.

FAO, IFAD, UNICEF, WFP, and WHO (Food and Agriculture Organization of the United Nations, International Fund for Agricultural Development, United Nations Children's Fund, World Food Programme, and World Health Organization). 2017. *The State of Food Security and Nutrition in the World 2017: Building Resilience for Peace and Food Security*. Rome: FAO.

FCO (Foreign and Commonwealth Office). 2012. "Written Evidence from the Foreign and Commonwealth Office." November 19. https://publications.parliame nt.uk/pa/cm201314/cmselect/cmfaff/88/88we14.htm

Fejes, A., and M. Dahlstedt. 2013. *The Confessing Society: Foucault, Confession and Practices of Lifelong Learning*. Abingdon: Routledge.

Fidler, D. P. 2001. "The Return of the Standard of Civilization." *Chicago Journal of International Law* 2 (1): 137–57.

Finnemore, M. 2003. *The Purpose of Intervention: Changing Beliefs about the Use of Force*. Ithaca: Cornell University Press.

Firchow, P. 2018. *Reclaiming Everyday Peace: Local Voices in Measurement and Evaluation after War*. Cambridge: Cambridge University Press.

Fisher, J. 2014. "When It Pays to Be a 'Fragile State': Uganda's Use and Abuse of a Dubious Concept." *Third World Quarterly* 35 (2): 316–32.

Fletcher, P., and J. Guyler Delva. 2010. "Haiti, Donors Face Huge Task to 'Build Back Better.'" *Reuters*, March 29.

Folke, C., S. R. Carpenter, B. Walker, M. Scheffer, T. Chapin, and J. Rockström. 2010. "Resilience Thinking: Integrating Resilience, Adaptability and Transformability." *Ecology and Society* 15 (4): 20. https://www.ecologyandsociety.org/vol15/iss4/art20/

Form, W., C. Loomis, R. Clifford, H. Moore, S. Nosow, G. Stone, and C. Westie. 1956. "The Persistence and Emergence of Social and Cultural Systems in Disasters." *American Sociological Review* 21 (2): 180–85.

Förster, A. 2014. *Peace, Justice and International Order: Decent Peace in John Rawls' "The Law of Peoples."* Basingstoke: Palgrave Macmillan.

Foster, K., and R. Giegengack. 2006. "Planning for a City on the Brink." In *On Risk and Disaster: Lessons from Hurricane Katrina*, edited by R. J. Daniels, D. F. Kettl, and H. Kunreuther, 41–58. Philadelphia: University of Pennsylvania Press.

Foucault, M. 1972. *The Archaeology of Knowledge*. New York: Pantheon Books.

Foucault, M. 1985. *The Use of Pleasure*. Vol. 2 of *The History of Sexuality*. New York: Vintage Books.

Foucault, M. 1988a. *The Care of the Self*. Vol. 3 of *The History of Sexuality*. Translated by R. Hurley. New York: Vintage Books.

Foucault, M. 1988b. "Technologies of the Self." In *Technologies of the Self: A Seminar with Michel Foucault*, edited by L. Martin, H. Gutman, and P. H. Hutton, 16–49. Amherst: University of Massachusetts Press.

Foucault, M. 1991. *Discipline and Punish: The Birth of the Prison*. London: Penguin.

Foucault, M. 1998. *The Will to Knowledge*. Vol. 1 of *The History of Sexuality*. London: Penguin.

Foucault, M. 2002. *The Order of Things: An Archaeology of the Human Sciences*. Abingdon: Routledge.

Foucault, M. 2003. *Abnormal: Lectures at the Collège de France, 1974–1975*. Translated by G. Burchell. New York: Picador.

Foucault, M. 2007. *Security, Territory, Population: Lectures at the Collège de France, 1977–78*. London: Palgrave Macmillan.

Foucault, M. 2008. *The Birth of Biopolitics: Lectures at the Collège de France, 1978–1979*. New York: Picador.

Fox, G. H. 2008. *Humanitarian Occupation*. Cambridge: Cambridge University Press.

Friedman, M. 2005. "The Promise of Vouchers." *Wall Street Journal*, December 5.

Frulli, M. 2012. "Fact-Finding or Paving the Road to Criminal Justice? Some Reflections on United Nations Commissions of Inquiry." *Journal of International Criminal Justice* 10 (5): 1323–38.

Fukuyama, F. 1992. *The End of History and the Last Man*. New York: Free Press.

Fukuyama, F. 2004. *State-Building: Governance and World Order in the 21st Century*. Ithaca: Cornell University Press.

Fukuyama, F. 2015. *Political Order and Political Decay*. New York: Farrar, Straus and Giroux.

Garfinkel, H. 1964. "Studies in the Routine Grounds of Everyday Activities." *Social Problems* 11 (3): 225–50.

Gheciu, A. 2005. "International Norms, Power and the Politics of International Administration: The Kosovo Case." *Geopolitics* 10 (1): 121–46.

Gheciu, A., and J. Welsh. 2009. "The Imperative to Rebuild: Assessing the Normative Case for Postconflict Reconstruction." *Ethics and International Affairs* 23 (2): 121–46.

Ghez, J. 2011. *Alliances in the 21st Century: Implications for the US-European Partnership*. Santa Monica, CA: RAND.

Goffman, E. 1959. *The Presentation of Self in Everyday Life*. Garden City, NJ: Doubleday.

Goffman, E. 1983. "The Interaction Order: American Sociological Association, 1982 Presidential Address." *American Sociological Review* 48 (1): 1–17.

Goldberg, D. T. 2001. *The Racial State*. Malden, MA: Blackwell.

Golder, B. 2015. *Foucault and the Politics of Rights*. Stanford, CA: Stanford University Press.

Government of Israel. 2018. "The Violent Riots and Attacks in the Border Area between Israel and the Gaza Strip: Summary of the Government of Israel's Submissions to the Israeli Supreme Court (HCJ 3003/18)." https://www.idf.il/media/48315/petition-gaza-border-events-summary-of-state-position.pdf

Government of the Republic of Haiti. 2010. *Action Plan for National Recovery and Development of Haiti: Immediate Key Initiatives for the Future*. March.

Grigat, S. 2014. "Educating into Liberal Peace: The International Crisis Group's Contribution to an Emerging Global Governmentality." *Third World Quarterly* 35 (4): 563–80.

Groß, L. 2015. "The Journey from Global to Local: Norm Promotion, Contestation and Localisation in Post-War Kosovo." *Journal of International Relations and Development* 18 (3): 311–36.

Group for Political and Legal Studies. 2020. *Rule of Law Performance Index in Kosovo*. 5th ed. Pristina: Group for Political and Legal Studies. http://www.legalpoliticalstudies.org/wp-content/uploads/2020/01/RoLPIK_Edition-5-1.pdf

Gunitsky, S. 2017. *Aftershocks: Great Powers and Domestic Reforms in the Twentieth Century*. Princeton: Princeton University Press.

Gutting, G. 2005. *Foucault: A Very Short Introduction*. Oxford: Oxford University Press.

Hacking, I. 1990. *The Taming of Chance*. Cambridge: Cambridge University Press.

Haigh, R., and D. Amaratunga. 2011. Introduction to *Post-Disaster Reconstruction of the Built Environment: Rebuilding for Resilience*, edited by D. Amaratunga and R. Haigh, 1–12. London: Wiley-Blackwell.

Haiti Grassroots Watch. 2011. "Impasse? What's Blocking the Capital's Path to Reconstruction?" June 9. http://haitigrassrootswatch.squarespace.com/7pap2eng

Haraway, D. 1991. *Simians, Cyborgs, and Women: The Reinvention of Nature*. Abingdon: Routledge.

Hardt, M., and A. Negri. 2009. *Commonwealth*. Cambridge, MA: Harvard University Press.

Harper, M. 2012. "Getting Somalia Wrong." *E-International Relations*, May 9. https://www.e-ir.info/2012/05/09/getting-somalia-wrong/

Hartnell, A. 2015. "New Orleans, 2005 and Port-au-Prince, 2010: Some Reflections on Trans-American Disaster in the Twenty-First Century." In *The 'Katrina Effect' on the Nature of Catastrophe*, edited by W. M. Taylor, M. Levine, O. Rooksby, and J.-K. Sobott, 49–70. London: Bloomsbury.

Hartnell, A. 2017. *After Katrina: Race, Neoliberalism, and the End of the American Century*. Albany: State University of New York Press.

Havis, D. N. 2014. "Discipline." In *The Cambridge Foucault Lexicon*, edited by L. Lawlo and J. Nale, 110–19. Cambridge: Cambridge University Press.

Hayner, P. B. 2001. *Unspeakable Truths: Transitional Justice and the Challenge of Truth Commissions*. 2nd ed. London: Routledge.

Hector, C. 2012. "Les perspectives de la reconstruction/refondation: 'Rabattre les cartes'?" In *Haïti, réinventer l'avenir*, edited by J.-D. Rainhorn, 251–59. Paris: Editions des Sciences de l'Homme.

Hellmüller, S. 2013. "The Power of Perceptions: Localizing International Peacebuilding Approaches." *International Peacekeeping* 20 (2): 219–32.

Helman, G. B., and S. R. Ratner. 1992–93. "Saving Failed States." *Foreign Policy* 89 (Winter): 3–20.

Henry, J. 2011. "Continuity, Social Change and Katrina." *Disasters* 35 (1): 220–42.

Herbst, J. 2004. "Let Them Fail: State Failure in Theory and Practice." In *When States Fail: Causes and Consequences*, edited by R. Rotberg, 302–18. Princeton: Princeton University Press.

Hewitt, K. 1983. "The Idea of Calamity in a Technocratic Age." In *Interpretations of Calamity from the Viewpoint of Human Ecology*, edited by K. Hewitt, 1–32. Boston, MA: Allen and Unwin.

Heyes, C. J. 2007. *Self-Transformations: Foucault, Ethics, and Normalized Bodies*. Oxford: Oxford University Press.

Hills, A. 2011. "'War Don Don': Stability, Normalcy and Sierra Leone." *Conflict, Security and Development* 11 (1): 1–24.

Hoffman, S. 2002. "The Monster and the Mother: The Symbolism of Catastrophe." In *Catastrophe and Culture: The Anthropology of Disaster*, edited by S. Hoffman and A. Oliver-Smith, 113–42. Santa Fe, CA: School of American Research Press.

Holling, C. 1973. "Resilience and Stability of Ecological Systems." *Annual Review of Ecological Systems* 4:1–23.

Holmqvist, C. 2014. *Policing Wars: On Military Intervention in the Twenty-First Century*. Basingstoke: Palgrave Macmillan.

Holsti, K. J. 2004. *Taming the Sovereigns: Institutional Change in International Politics*. Cambridge: Cambridge University Press.

Horwitz, A. W. 2016. *What's Normal? Reconciling Biology and Culture*. New York: Oxford University Press.

Howell, A. 2011. *Madness in International Relations: Psychology, Security, and the Global Governance of Mental Health*. Abingdon: Routledge.

Howell, A., and M. Richter-Montpetit. 2019. "Racism in Foucauldian Security Studies: Biopolitics, Liberal War, and the Whitewashing of Colonial and Racial Violence." *International Political Sociology* 13 (1): 2–19.

Howell, A., and M. Richter-Montpetit. 2020. "Is Securitization Theory Racist? Civilizationism, Methodological Whiteness, and Antiblack Thought in the Copenhagen School." *Security Dialogue* 51 (1): 3–22.

Hughes, C., and V. Pupavac. 2005. "Framing Post-Conflict Societies: International Pathologisation of Cambodia and the Post-Yugoslav States." *Third World Quarterly* 26 (6): 873–89.

Humphreys, S. 2010. *Theatre of the Rule of Law: Transnational Legal Intervention in Theory and Practice.* Cambridge: Cambridge University Press.

ICOE (Independent Commission of Enquiry). 2018. "Press Conference, Nay Pyi Taw." August 16. https://www.facebook.com/theirrawaddyburmese/videos/218544952337657/

IDF (Israeli Defence Force). 2018. "Decisions of the IDF Military Advocate General regarding Exceptional Incidents That Allegedly Occurred during Operation 'Protective Edge.'" Update no. 6, August 15. https://www.idf.il/media/40288/examination_and_investigation_of_exceptional_incidents_from_operation_protective_edge.pdf

Ignatieff, M. 1999. *The Warrior's Honor: Ethnic War and the Modern Conscience.* London: Vintage.

Ikenberry, G. J. 2018. "The End of Liberal International Order?" *International Affairs* 94 (1): 7–23.

Infinity Filmworks. 2010. *Rebuilding Haiti.* https://vimeo.com/9339977

Ingala, E. 2019. "Judith Butler: From a Normative Violence to an Ethics of Non-Violence." In *The Meanings of Violence: From Critical Theory to Biopolitics*, edited by G. Rae and E. Ingala, 191–208. Abingdon: Routledge.

Ioannides, I., and G. Collantes-Celador. 2011. "The Internal–External Security Nexus and EU Police / Rule of Law Missions in the Western Balkans." *Conflict, Security and Development* 11 (4): 415–45.

Islamic Relief Worldwide. n.d. "Building Back Better in the Philippines." https://www.islamic-relief.org/building-back-better-in-the-philippines/

Jabri, V. 2006. "War, Security and the Liberal State." *Security Dialogue* 37 (1): 47–64.

Jacob, D. 2014. *Justice and Foreign Rule: On International Transitional Administration.* Basingstoke: Palgrave Macmillan.

Jacobs, K. 2010. "Rebuilding Haiti." *Metropolis*, April 1. https://www.metropolismag.com/uncategorized/rebuilding-haiti/

James Lee Witt Associates. 2005. *Building Back Better and Safer: Private Sector Summit on Post-Tsunami Reconstruction.* May 12. https://www.preventionweb.net/files/2070_VL108700.pdf

Jeng, A. 2012. *Peacebuilding in the African Union: Law, Philosophy and Practice.* Cambridge: Cambridge University Press.

Jenson, D. 2010. "The Writing of Disaster in Haiti: Signifying Cataclysm from Slave Revolution to Earthquake." In *Haiti Rising: Haitian History, Culture and the Earthquake of 2010*, edited by M. Munro, 102–12. Liverpool: Liverpool University Press.

Jessop, B. 2016. *The State: Past, Present, Future*. Cambridge: Polity.

Johnson, C. 2011. "Charming Accommodations: Progressive Urbanism Meets Privatization in Brad Pitt's Make It Right Foundation." In *The Neoliberal Deluge: Hurricane Katrina, Late Capitalism, and the Remaking of New Orleans*, edited by C. Johnson, 187–224. Minneapolis: University of Minnesota Press.

Johnson, J., and S. Wiechelt. 2004. "Introduction to the Special Issue on Resilience." *Substance Use and Misuse* 39 (5): 657–70.

Jørgensen, M., and L. Phillips. 2002. *Discourse Analysis as Theory and Method*. London: SAGE.

Joseph, J. 2009. "Governmentality of What? Populations, States and International Organisations." *Global Society* 23 (4): 413–27.

Joseph, J. 2012. *The Social in the Global: Social Theory, Governmentality and Global Politics*. Cambridge: Cambridge University Press.

Joseph, J. 2013. "Resilience as Embedded Neoliberalism: A Governmentality Approach." *Resilience* 1 (1): 38–52.

Kaldor, M. 1996. "A Cosmopolitan Response to New Wars." *Peace Review* 8 (4): 505–14.

Kaldor, M. 2012. *New and Old Wars*. 3rd ed. Cambridge: Polity.

Kaldor, M. 2013. "In Defence of New Wars." *Stability: International Journal of Security and Development* 2 (1). https://www.stabilityjournal.org/articles/10.5334/sta.at/

Kamin, B. 2005. "Mississippi Rocks the Boat with Bold Coastal Designs." *Chicago Tribune*, October 18.

Kaplan, F. 2016. "Obama's Way: The President in Practice." *Foreign Affairs* 95 (1): 46–63.

Kaplan, R. D. 1994. "The Coming Anarchy: How Scarcity, Crime, Overpopulation, Tribalism, and Disease are Rapidly Destroying the Social Fabric of Our Planet." *Atlantic Monthly*, February. https://www.theatlantic.com/magazine/archive/1994/02/the-coming-anarchy/304670/

Kaplan, R. D. 2014. "Why So Much Anarchy?" *Stratfor Worldview*, February 5. https://worldview.stratfor.com/article/why-so-much-anarchy#/home/error

Kappler, C. 1980. *Monstres, démons et merveilles à la fin du moyen-age*. Paris: Payot.

Kelley, J. G. 2017. *Scorecard Diplomacy: Grading States to Influence Their Reputation and Behavior*. Cambridge: Cambridge University Press.

Kennedy, J., J. Ashmore, E. Babister, and I. Kelman. 2008. "The Meaning of 'Build Back Better': Evidence from Post-Tsunami Aceh and Sri Lanka." *Journal of Contingencies and Crisis Management* 16 (1): 24–36.

Khasalamwa, S. 2009. "Is 'Build Back Better' a Response to Vulnerability? Analysis of the Post-Tsunami Humanitarian Interventions in Sri Lanka." *Norwegian Journal of Geography* 63 (1): 73–88.

Khondker, H. H. 2002. "Problems and Prospects of Disaster Research in the Developing World." In *Methods of Disaster Research*, edited by R. A. Stallings, 334–48. Bloomington, IN: Xlibris.

Kiersey, N. J., and D. Stokes, eds. 2011. *Foucault and International Relations*. Abingdon: Routledge.

Killian, L. M. 1956. *An Introduction to Methodological Problems of Field Studies in Disasters*. Washington, DC: National Research Council.

Kjærum, M. 2009. "State Reports." In *International Human Rights Monitoring Mechanisms: Essays in Honour of Jacob Th. Möller*, edited by G. Alfredsson, J. Grimheden, B. G. Ramcharan, and A. Zayas, 17–24. 2nd ed. Leiden: Martinus Nijhoff.

Klein, N. 2007. *The Shock Doctrine: The Rise of Disaster Capitalism*. New York: Picador.

Klein, R. J. T., R. J. Nicholls, and F. Thomalla. 2003. "Resilience to Natural Hazards: How Useful Is This Concept?" *Global Environmental Change Part B: Environmental Hazards* 5 (1): 35–45.

Koopman, C. 2013. *Genealogy as Critique: Foucault and the Problems of Modernity*. Bloomington: Indiana University Press.

Koro-Ljungberg, M., M. Gemignani, C. W. Brodeur, and C. Kmiec. 2007. "The Technologies of Normalization and Self: Thinking about IRBs and Extrinsic Research Ethics with Foucault." *Qualitative Inquiry* 13 (8): 1075–94.

Koslowski, T. G., and P. H. Longstaff. 2015. "Resilience Undefined: A Framework for Interdisciplinary Communication and Application to Real-World Problems." In *Disaster Management: Enabling Resilience*, edited by A. Masys, 3–20. Cham: Springer International.

Kratochwil, F. 2010. "How (Il)liberal Is the Liberal Theory of Law? Some Critical Remarks on Slaughter's Approach." In *Rule of Law and Democracy: Inquiries into Internal and External Issues*, edited by L. Morlino and G. Palombella, 185–211. Leiden: Koninklijke Brill.

Kraxberger, B. 2007. "Failed States: Temporary Obstacles to Democratic Diffusion or Fundamental Holes in the World Political Map?" *Third World Quarterly* 28 (6): 1055–71.

Kuhn, T. 1962. *The Structure of Scientific Revolutions*. Chicago: University of Chicago Press.

Laliberté, N. 2013. "In Pursuit of a Monster: Militarisation and (In)Security in Northern Uganda." *Geopolitics* 18 (4): 875–94.

Lamb, R. D. 2008. "Ungoverned Areas and Threats from Safe Havens: Final Report of the Ungoverned Areas Project." Center for International and Security Studies at Maryland, University of Maryland.

Landry, J. 2009. "Confession, Obedience, and Subjectivity: Michel Foucault's Unpublished Lectures on the Government of the Living." *Telos* 146 (1): 111–23.

Langdon, P. 2010. "After the Disaster." *Public Square: A CNU Journal*, March 1. https://www.cnu.org/publicsquare/2010/03/01/after-disaster

Larabee, A. 2000. *Decade of Disaster*. Urbana: University of Illinois Press.

Latour, B. 2011. "Love Your Monsters." *Breakthrough Journal* 2:19–26.

Lawson, S., and S. Tannaka. 2010. "War Memories and Japan's 'Normalization' as an International Actor: A Critical Analysis." *European Journal of International Relations* 17 (3): 405–28.

Leatherman, J. 2008. "Challenges to Authority in Global Politics." In *Discipline and Punishment in Global Politics*, edited by J. Leatherman, 1–25. Basingstoke: Palgrave Macmillan.

Lefebvre, A. 2018. *Human Rights and the Care of the Self*. Durham: Duke University Press.

Lemay-Hébert, N. 2011. "The Bifurcation of the Two Worlds: Assessing the Gap between Internationals and Locals in State-building Processes." *Third World Quarterly* 32 (10): 1823–41.

Lemay-Hébert, N. 2014. "Resistance in the Time of Cholera: The Limits of Stabilization through Securitization in Haiti." *International Peacekeeping* 21 (2): 198–213.

Lemay-Hébert, N. 2019. "State Fragility and International Recognition." In *Routledge Handbook of State Recognition*, edited by G. Visoka, J. Doyle, and E. Newman, 306–15. Abingdon: Routledge.

Lemay-Hébert, N., and G. Visoka. 2017. "Normal Peace: A New Strategic Narrative of Intervention." *Politics and Governance* 5 (3): 146–56.

Levine, S., and I. Mosel. 2014. *Supporting Resilience in Difficult Places: A Critical Look at Applying the 'Resilience' Concept in Countries Where Crises Are the Norm*. London: Humanitarian Policy Group, Overseas Development Institute.

Lewis, D. 2017. "The Myopic Foucauldian Gaze: Discourse, Knowledge and the Authoritarian Peace." *Journal of Intervention and Statebuilding* 11 (1): 21–41.

Lewis, J. 2006. "Battle for Biloxi." *New York Times*, May 21.

Lewis, J. D., and A. Weigert. 1985. "Social Atomism, Holism, and Trust." *Sociological Quarterly* 26 (4): 455–71.

Lindsay, G. 2010. "Is Haiti a Laboratory for New Urbanists? What the Country Really Needs Is Old Urbanism." *Fast Company*, April 6. https://www.fastcom pany.com/1607235/haiti-laboratory-new-urbanists-what-country-really-needs -old-urbanism

Lindsay, G. 2011. "Port-au-Prince 2.0: A City of Urban Villages?" *Fast Company*, January 26. https://www.fastcompany.com/1720799/port-au-prince-20-city-ur ban-villages

London Conference on Afghanistan. 2006. "The Afghanistan Compact." January 31–February 1. https://reliefweb.int/sites/reliefweb.int/files/resources/E69BFFC F9E493D17492571070006DE69-unama-afg-30jan.pdf

Lorenzini, D., and M. Tazzioli. 2018. "Confessional Subjects and Conducts of Non-Truth: Foucault, Fanon, and the Making of the Subject." *Theory, Culture and Society* 35 (1): 71–90.

Lottholz, P., and N. Lemay-Hébert. 2016. "Re-Reading Weber, Re-Conceptualizing State-Building: From Neo-Weberian to Post-Weberian Approaches to State, Legitimacy and State-Building." *Cambridge Review of International Affairs* 29 (4): 1467–85.

Lovekamp, W. 2010. "Promoting Empowerment: Social Change in Disasters." In *Social Vulnerability to Disasters*, edited by B. D. Phillips, D. S. K. Thomas, A. Fothergill, and L. Blinn-Pike, 367–81. London: CRC Press.

Luhmann, N. 1990. *Essays on Self-Reference*. New York: Columbia University Press.

Luhmann, N. 1993. *Risk: A Sociological Theory*. Translated by R. Barrett. New York: Aldine de Gruyter.

Luhmann, N. 1995. *Social Systems*. Stanford, CA: Stanford University Press.

Lupton, D. 1994. *Medicine as Culture: Illness, Disease and the Body in Western Societies*. London: SAGE.

Luttwak, E. 1999. "Give War a Chance." *Foreign Affairs* 78 (4): 36–44.

Lyon, A., and L. C. Olson. 2011. "Special Issue on Human Rights Rhetoric: Traditions of Testifying and Witnessing." *Rhetoric Society Quarterly* 41 (3): 203–12.

Lyons, M. 2009. "Building Back Better: The Large-Scale Impact of Small-Scale Approaches to Reconstruction." *World Development* 37 (2): 385–98.

Lyons, T., and A. Samatar. 1995. *Somalia: State Collapse, Multilateral Intervention, and Strategies for Political Reconstruction.* Washington, DC: Brookings Institution Press.

Mac Ginty, R. 2014. "Everyday Peace: Bottom-Up and Local Agency in Conflict-Affected Societies." *Security Dialogue* 45 (6): 548–64.

Macmillan, J. 2013. "Intervention and the Ordering of the Modern World." *Review of International Studies* 39 (5): 1039–56.

Mader, M. B. 2007. "Foucault and Social Measure." *Journal of French and Francophone Philosophy* 17 (1): 1–25.

Mandelbaum, M. 1994. "The Reluctance to Intervene." *Foreign Policy* 95 (Summer): 3–18.

Mangada, L., I. Tan, and M. dela Cruz. 2016. "The Guiuan Experience: A Story of Accountability." In *Building Back Better: A Democratic Accountability Assessment of Service Delivery after Typhoon Haiyan,* edited by E. A. Co, M. Pamintuan, and L. Diño, 17–28. Quezon City: University of the Philippines Center for Integrative and Development Studies.

Manjikian, M. 2008. "Diagnosis, Intervention, and Cure: The Illness Narrative in the Discourse of the Failed State." *Alternatives* 33 (3): 335–57.

Mannakkara, S., S. Wilkinson, and T. R. Francis. 2014. "'Build Back Better' Principles for Reconstruction." In *Encyclopedia of Earthquake Engineering,* edited by M. Beer, I. A. Kougioumtzoglou, E. Patelli, and I. Siu-Kui Au, 1–12. Berlin: Springer.

Manyena, B., G. O'Brien, P. O'Keefe, and J. Rose. 2011. "Disaster Resilience: A Bounce Back or Bounce Forward Ability?" *Local Environment* 16 (5): 417–24.

Martin, L. 2016. "Practicing Normality: An Examination of Unrecognizable Transitional Justice Mechanisms in Post-Conflict Sierra Leone." *Journal of Intervention and Statebuilding* 10 (3): 400–418.

Massoud, M. F. 2019. *Law's Fragile State: Colonial, Authoritarian, and Humanitarian Legacies in Sudan.* Cambridge: Cambridge University Press.

Matthiesen, T. 2013. *Sectarian Gulf: Bahrain, Saudi Arabia, and the Arab Spring That Wasn't.* Stanford: Stanford University Press.

McEntire, D., C. Fuller, C. W. Johnston, and R. Weber. 2002. "A Comparison of Disaster Paradigms: The Search for a Holistic Policy Guide." *Public Administration Review* 62 (3): 267–81.

McGushin, E. 2011. "Foucault's Theory and Practice of Subjectivity." In *Michel Foucault: Key Concepts,* edited by D. Taylor, 127–42. Durham: Acumen.

McHoul, A., and W. Grace. 1993. *A Foucault Primer: Discourse, Power and the Subject.* Abingdon: Routledge.

McNally, F. 2019. "The Normal Scale: From Normality to Normalcy to Normalness." *Irish Times,* November 20.

McWorter, L. 2014. "Normalization." In *Cambridge Foucault Lexicon,* edited by L. Lawlor and J. Nale, 315–21. Cambridge: Cambridge University Press.

Menkhaus, K. 2008. "Somalia: Governance vs. Statebuilding." In *Building States to Build Peace,* edited by C. T. Call and V. Wyeth, 187–215. Boulder, CO: Lynne Rienner.

Mennell, S. 2001. "The Other Side of the Coin: Decivilizing Processes." In *Norbert Elias and Human Interdependencies,* edited by T. Salumets, 32–49. Montreal: McGill-Queen's University Press.

MFA of Israel. 2015. *The 2014 Gaza Conflict: Factual and Legal Aspects*. Tel Aviv: Ministry of Foreign Affairs of Israel. https://mfa.gov.il/ProtectiveEdge/Docume nts/2014GazaConflictFullReport.pdf

Mika, K. 2019. *Disasters, Vulnerability and Narratives: Writing Haiti's Futures*. London: Routledge.

Milman, O. 2015. "Life in the Philippines: Preparing for the Next Typhoon Haiyan." *The Guardian*, March 25.

Miskimmon, A., B. O'Loughlin, and L. Roselle. 2015. "Great Power Politics and Strategic Narratives of War." In *Strategic Narratives, Public Opinion, and War Winning Domestic Support for the Afghan War*, edited by B. De Graaf, G. Dimitriu, and J. Ringsmose, 57–77. Abingdon: Routledge.

Misztal, B. 2001. "Normality and Trust in Goffman's Theory of Interaction Order." *Sociological Theory* 19 (3): 312–24.

Misztal, B. 2015. *Multiple Normalities: Making Sense of Ways of Living*. Basingstoke: Palgrave Macmillan.

Monday, J. L. 2002. "Building Back Better: Creating a Sustainable Community after Disaster." *Natural Hazards Informer* 3:1–11.

Morin, E. 2007. "Restricted Complexity, General Complexity." In *Worldviews, Science and Us: Philosophy and Complexity*, edited by C. Gershenson, D. Aerts, and B. Edmonds, 5–29. London: World Scientific Publishing.

Mouzon, S. 2015. "What Was Gained in the Katrina Cottage Loss?" *Original Green*, August 29. http://www.originalgreen.org/blog/2015/what-was-gained-in-the .html

Munro, M. 2015. "Disaster Studies and Cultures of Disaster in Haiti." *French Studies* 69 (4): 509–18.

Murray, M. 2019. *The Struggle for Recognition in International Relations*. Oxford: Oxford University Press.

Mutua, M. 2002. *Human Rights: A Political and Cultural Critique*. Philadelphia: University of Pennsylvania Press.

National Economic and Development Authority. 2013. *Reconstruction Assistance on Yolanda*. Pasig City: National Economic and Development Authority.

Neild, R. 2001. "Democratic Police Reforms in War-Torn Societies." *Conflict, Security and Development* 1 (1): 21–43.

Nesbitt, N. 2013. "Haiti: The Monstrous Anomaly." In *The Idea of Haiti: Rethinking Crisis and Development*, edited by M. Polyné, 3–26. Minneapolis: University of Minnesota Press.

Neu, J., ed. 1991. *The Cambridge Companion to Freud*. Cambridge: Cambridge University Press.

Neumann, I. B. 2008. "Discourse Analysis." In *Qualitative Methods in International Relations*, edited by A. Klotz and D. Prakash, 61–77. London: Palgrave Macmillan.

Nicholls, D. 1996. *From Dessalines to Duvalier: Race, Colour and National Independence in Haiti*. New Brunswick, NJ: Rutgers University Press.

Nigg, J. M., and K. J. Tierney. 1993. "Disasters and Social Change: Consequences for Community Construct and Affect." Preliminary Papers 195, Disaster Research Center, University of Delaware.

Nuruzzaman, M. 2015. "Rethinking Foreign Military Interventions to Promote Human Rights: Evidence from Libya, Bahrain and Syria." *Canadian Journal of Political Science* 48 (3): 531–52.

OECD (Organisation for Economic Co-operation and Development). 2011. *Future Global Shocks: Improving Risk Governance.* Paris: OECD Publishing.

OECD. 2013. "What Does 'Resilience' Mean for Donors? An OECD Factsheet." http://www.oecd.org/dac/May%2010%202013%20FINAL%20resilience%20 PDF.pdf

OECD. 2014. *Boosting Resilience through Innovative Risk Governance.* Paris: OECD Publishing.

OECD. 2016. *States of Fragility 2016: Understanding Violence.* Paris: OECD Publishing.

OHCHR (Office of the United Nations High Commissioner for Human Rights). 2015. *Commissions of Inquiry and Fact-Finding Missions on International Human Rights and Humanitarian Law: Guidance and Practice.* New York: Office of the United Nations High Commissioner for Human Rights.

OHCHR. 2018. *Who's Responsible: Attributing Individual Responsibility for Violations of International Human Rights Law and Humanitarian Law in United Nations Commissions of Inquiry, Fact-Finding Missions and other Investigations.* New York: Office of the United Nations High Commissioner for Human Rights. https://oh chr.org/Documents/Publications/AttributingIndividualResponsibility.pdf

Oksala, J. 2011. "Freedom and Bodies." In *Michel Foucault: Key Concepts*, edited by D. Taylor, 85–98. Durham: Acumen.

Olivier, B. 2010. "Foucault and Individual Autonomy." *South African Journal of Psychology* 40 (3): 292–307.

Olsson, P., L. H. Gunderson, S. R. Carpenter, P. Ryan, L. Lebel, C. Folke, and C. S. Holling. 2006. "Shooting the Rapids: Navigating Transitions to Adaptive Governance of Social-Ecological Systems." *Ecology and Society* 11 (1): 18. https://www .ecologyandsociety.org/vol11/iss1/art18/

Omand, D. 2005. "Developing National Resilience." *RUSI Journal* 150 (4): 14–18.

Onuf, N. 1989. *World of Our Making: Rules and Rule in Social Theory and International Relations.* London: Routledge.

Onuf, N. 2014. "World-Making, State-Building." In *Semantics of Statebuilding: Language, Meanings and Sovereignty*, edited N. Lemay-Hebert, N. Onuf, V. Rakić, and Petar Bojanić, 19–36. London: Routledge.

Onuf, N. 2017. "The Figure of Foucault and the Field of International Relations." In *Foucault and the Modern International: Silences and Legacies for the Study of World Politics*, edited by P. Bonditti, D. Bigo, and F. Gros, 15–31. Basingstoke: Palgrave Macmillan.

Ourousoff, N. 2010. "A Plan to Spur Growth Away from Haiti's Capital." *New York Times*, March 30.

Oxfam 2010. "Haiti: A Once-in-a-Century Chance for Change." Oxfam Briefing Paper 136, March. https://www.oxfam.org/en/research/haiti-once-century-chan ce-change

Pacholok, S. 2013. *Into the Fire: Disaster and the Remaking of Gender.* Toronto: University of Toronto Press.

Paffenholz, T. 2013. "Civil Society." In *Routledge Handbook of Peacebuilding*, edited by R. Mac Ginty, 347–59. Abingdon: Routledge.

Paris, R. 1997. "Peacebuilding and the Limits of Liberal Internationalism." *International Security* 22 (2): 54–89.

Passerini, E. 2010. "The Nature of Human Communities." In *Social Vulnerability to Disasters*, edited by B. D. Phillips, D. S. K. Thomas, A. Fothergill, and L. Blinn-Pike, 307–22. London: CRC Press.

Paternek, M. 1987. "Norms and Normalization: Michel Foucault's Overextended Panoptic Machine." *Human Studies* 10 (1): 9–121.

Patrick, S. 2011. *Weak Links: Fragile States, Global Threats, and International Security*. Oxford: Oxford University Press.

Payton, C. A. 2019. "Building Corruption in Haiti." *NACLA Report of the Americas* 51 (2): 182–87.

Pendall, R., K. A. Foster, and M. Cowell. 2010. "Resilience and Regions: Building Understanding of the Metaphor." *Cambridge Journal of Regions, Economy and Society* 3 (1): 71–84.

Peoples, C., and N. Vaughan-Williams. 2010. *Critical Security Studies: An Introduction*. Abingdon: Routledge.

Perrow, C. 1999. *Normal Accidents: Living with High-Risk Technologies*. Princeton: Princeton University Press.

Phillips, B. 2009. *Disaster Recovery*. London: CRC Press.

Phillips, B., and M. Fordham. 2010. Introduction to *Social Vulnerability to Disasters*, edited by B. D. Phillips, D. S. K. Thomas, A. Fothergill, and L. Blinn-Pike, 1–23. London: CRC Press.

Picou, J. S., B. K. Marshall, and D. A. Gill. 2004. "Disaster, Litigation, and the Corrosive Community." *Social Forces* 82 (4): 1448–82.

Piirimäe, P. 2019. "Men, Monsters and the History of Mankind in Vattel's *Law of Nations*." In *The Law of Nations and Natural Law, 1625–1800*, edited by S. Zurbuchen, 159–85. Leiden: Brill.

Pimm, S. 1984. "The Complexity and Stability of Ecosystems." *Nature* 307:321–26.

Pogrebin, R. 2006. "An Architect with Plans for a New Gulf Coast." *New York Times*, May 24.

Pouligny, B. 2014. "The Resilience Approach to Peacebuilding: A New Conceptual Framework." *Insights* (United States Institute of Peace), Summer.

President of the Philippines. 2019. "Implementing the Annex on Normalization under the Comprehensive Agreement on the Bangsamoro." Executive Order No. 79, Manila, April 24. https://www.officialgazette.gov.ph/downloads/2019/04apr/20190524-EO-79-RRD.pdf

Price, C. 2005. "Operation Rebirth." myNewOrleans.com, December 12. https://www.myneworleans.com/operation-rebirth/

Prince, S. 1920. "Catastrophe and Social Change Based upon a Sociological Study of the Halifax Disaster." Ph.D. diss., Columbia University.

Puar, J., and A. Rai. 2002. "Monster, Terrorist, Fag: The War on Terrorism and the Production of Docile Patriots." *Social Text* 20 (3): 117–48.

Pupavac, V. 2002. "Pathologizing Populations and Colonizing Minds: International Psychosocial Programs in Kosovo." *Alternatives* 27 (4): 489–511.

Qian, N., and D. Yanagizawa. 2009. "The Strategic Determinants of U.S. Human Rights Reporting: Evidence from the Cold War." *Journal of the European Economic Association* 7 (2/3): 446–57.

Quarantelli, E. L. 2006. "Catastrophes Are Different from Disasters: Some Implications for Crisis Planning and Managing Drawn from Katrina." *Items: Insights from the Social Sciences,* June 11. https://items.ssrc.org/understanding-katrina /catastrophes-are-different-from-disasters-some-implications-for-crisis-planning -and-managing-drawn-from-katrina/

Rabinow, P., ed. 1984a. *Foucault Reader.* New York: Pantheon Books.

Rabinow, P. 1984b. Introduction to *Foucault Reader,* edited by P. Rabinow, 3–29. New York: Pantheon Books.

Ramel, F. 2009. "Le barbare: Une nouvelle catégorie stratégique?" *Stratégique* 93:683–707.

Raquel Freire, M., P. Duarte Lopes, and D. Nascimento. 2015. "The EU's Role in Crisis Management: The Case of the EUMM." In *Managing Crises, Making Peace: Towards a Strategic EU Vision for Security and Defence,* edited by M. G. Galantino and M. Raquel Freire, 178–95. Basingstoke: Palgrave Macmillan.

Rawls, J. 1999. *The Law of Peoples, with "The Idea of Public Reason Revisited."* Cambridge, MA: Harvard University Press.

Regan, J. 2012. "Haiti: Housing Exposition Exposes Waste, Cynicism." *HuffPost,* December 6. https://www.huffpost.com/entry/haiti-housing-exposition_b_1911898

Reitman, J. 2011. "Beyond Relief: How the World Failed Haiti." *Rolling Stone,* August 4. https://www.rollingstone.com/politics/politics-news/beyond-relief -how-the-world-failed-haiti-242928/

Republic of the Union of Myanmar. 2018. "Government of the Republic of the Union of Myanmar Establishes the Independent Commission of Enquiry." Press Release 8/2018, July 30. http://www.president-office.gov.mm/en/?q=briefing-ro om/news/2018/07/30/id-8913

Reus-Smit, C. 2013. "The Concept of Intervention." *Review of International Studies* 39 (5): 1057–76.

Reus-Smit, C. 2018. *On Cultural Diversity: International Theory in a World of Difference.* Cambridge: Cambridge University Press.

Rich, N. 2015. "Gary Rivlin's 'Katrina: After the Flood.'" *New York Times,* August 5.

Richards, P. 1996. *Fighting for the Rain Forest: War, Youth and Resources in Sierra Leone.* Oxford: James Currey.

Richmond, O. P., ed. 2010. *Palgrave Advances in Peacebuilding: Critical Development and Approaches.* Basingstoke: Palgrave Macmillan.

Richmond, O. P. 2014. "Jekyll or Hyde: What Is Statebuilding Creating? Evidence from the 'Field.'" *Cambridge Review of International Affairs* 27 (1): 1–20.

Richmond, O. P., and G. Visoka, eds. 2021. *The Oxford Handbook of Peacebuilding, Statebuilding, and Peace Formation.* New York: Oxford University Press.

Risse, T., ed. 2011. *Governance Without a State? Policies and Politics in Areas of Limited Statehood.* New York: Columbia University Press.

Risse, T. 2015. "Limited Statehood: A Critical Perspective." In *The Oxford Handbook of Transformations of the State,* edited by S. Leibfried, E. Huber, M. Lange, J. D. Levy, and J. D. Stephens, 152–68. Oxford: Oxford University Press.

Risse, T., and E. Stollenwerk. 2018. "Limited Statehood Does Not Equal Civil War." *Daedalus* 147 (1): 104–15. https://doi.org/10.1162/daed_a_00477

Rivlin, G. 2005. "A Mogul Who Would Rebuild New Orleans." *New York Times,* September 29.

Rivlin, G. 2015. *Katrina: After the Flood.* New York: Simon and Schuster.

Rodin, Judith 2015. *The Resilience Dividend: Being Strong in a World Where Things Go Wrong.* New York: PublicAffairs.

Rodríguez, H., E. Quarantelli, and R. Dynes. 2007. Editors' introduction to *Handbook of Disaster Research*, edited by H. Rodríguez, E. Quarantelli, and R. Dynes, xiii–xx. London: Springer.

Rosenboim, O. 2017. *The Emergence of Globalism: Visions of World Order in Britain and the United States, 1939–1950.* Princeton: Princeton University Press.

Rotberg, R. 2004. "The Failure and Collapse of Nation-States: Breakdown, Prevention, and Repair." In *When States Fail: Causes and Consequences*, edited by R. Rotberg, 1–49. Princeton: Princeton University Press.

Rotfeld, A. D. 2001. "The Organizing Principles of Global Society." In *SIPRI Yearbook 2001: Armaments, Disarmament and International Security*, 1–12. Oxford: Oxford University Press.

Rubin, B. R. 2006. *Afghanistan's Uncertain Transition from Turmoil to Normalcy.* Special Reports 12. New York: Council on Foreign Relations.

Rule, J. 1992. *Theories of Civil Violence.* Berkeley: University of California Press.

Saffron, I. 2006. "Goodbye New Orleans, Hello Venice: Biennial Features WRT's Rebuilding Plan." *Skyline Online*, August 21. http://changingskyline.blogspot.com/2006/08/goodbye-new-orleans-hello-venice.html

Sahin, S. 2015. *International Intervention and State-Making: How Exception Became the Norm.* Abingdon: Routledge.

Said, E. 2003. *Orientalism.* London: Penguin.

Salter, M. 2002. *Barbarians and Civilization in International Relations.* London: Pluto.

Sandoval, C. 2000. *Methodology of the Oppressed.* Minneapolis: University of Minnesota Press.

Schmitt, C. 1985. *Political Theology: Four Chapters on the Concept of Sovereignty.* Translated by G. Schwab. Chicago: University of Chicago Press.

Schneckener, U. 2011. "State Building or New Modes of Governance?" In *Governance without a State? Policies and Politics in Areas of Limited Statehood*, edited by T. Risse, 232–61. New York: Columbia University Press.

Schwöbel-Patel, C. 2017. "Commissions of Inquiry: Courting International Criminal Courts and Tribunals." In *Commissions of Inquiry: Problems and Prospects*, edited by C. Henderson, 145–69. Oxford: Hart.

Segal, J. 2003. "Freedom and Normalization: Poststructuralism and the Liberalism of Michael Oakeshott." *American Political Science Review* 97 (3): 447–58.

Sen, A. 1999. "Democracy as a Universal Value." *Journal of Democracy* 10 (3): 3–17.

Sheridan, A. 2005. *Michel Foucault: The Will to Truth.* Abingdon: Routledge.

Simons, J. 2013. "Power, Resistance, and Freedom." In *A Companion to Foucault*, edited by C. Falzon, T. O'Leary, and J. Sawicki, 301–19. London: Wiley-Blackwell.

Simpson, G. 2004. *Great Powers and Outlaw States: Unequal Sovereigns in the International Legal Order.* Cambridge: Cambridge University Press.

Sjoberg, G. 1962. "Disasters and Social Change." In *Man and Society in Disaster*, edited by G. W. Baker and D. W. Chapman, 356–84. New York: Basic Books.

Sjöberg, L. 2014. "Confessions of an Individual Education Plan." In *Foucault and a Politics of Confession in Education*, edited by A. Fejes and K. Nicoll, 62–76. Abingdon: Routledge.

Snyder, L. 1962. Introduction to *The Imperialism Reader*, by L. Snyder, 1–15. Princeton, NJ: D. Van Nostrand.

Sorkin, M. 2013. *All Over the Map: Writing on Buildings and Cities*. London: Verso.

Sorokin, P. 1942. *Man and Society in Calamity*. New York: Greenwood Press.

Soron, D. 2007. "Cruel Weather: Natural Disasters and Structural Violence." *Transformations: Journal of Media and Culture* 14. http://www.transformationsjournal .org/wp-content/uploads/2017/01/Soron_Transformations14.pdf

Spade, D., and C. Willse. 2016. "Norms and Normalization." In *The Oxford Handbook of Feminist Theory*, edited by Lisa Disch and Mary Hawkesworth, 551–71. Oxford: Oxford University Press.

Stahn, C. 2008. *The Law and Practice of International Territorial Administration: Versailles to Iraq and Beyond*. Cambridge: Cambridge University Press.

Stahn, C. 2018. *A Critical Introduction to International Criminal Law*. Cambridge: Cambridge University Press.

Steele, B. J. 2008. *Ontological Security in International Relations: Self-Identity and the IR State*. Abingdon: Routledge.

Sterling-Folker, J., and J. F. Charrette. 2015. "Disciplining Human Nature: The Evolution of American Social Scientific Theorizing." In *Human Being in International Relations*, edited by D. Jacobi and A. Freyberg-Inan, 74–94. Cambridge: Cambridge University Press.

Stewart, D. 2017. "Producing 'Docile Bodies': Disciplining Citizen-Subjects." *International Journal of Qualitative Studies in Education* 30 (10): 1042–46.

Stirk, P. 2009. *The Politics of Military Occupation*. Edinburgh: Edinburgh University Press.

Stone, C. E., and H. H. Ward. 2000. "Democratic Policing: A Framework for Action." *Policing and Society* 10 (1): 11–45.

Suzuki, S. 2017. "'Delinquent Gangs' in the International System Hierarchy." In *Hierarchies in World Politics*, edited by A. Zarakol, 219–40. Cambridge: Cambridge University Press.

Sweetman, D. 2009. *Business, Conflict Resolution and Peacebuilding: Contributions from the Private Sector to Address Violent Conflict*. London: Routledge.

Swiss Confederation. 2015. Joint Statement on Human Rights in Bahrain. September 14. https://www.adhrb.org/wp-content/uploads/2015/09/draft-joint-statem ent-on-Bahrain_13.09_with-list-of-states.pdf

Taillefer, G. 2004. "Deux mois après la destitution d'Aristide–Haïti: Retour à une 'mauvaise normalité.'" *Le Devoir*, April 24.

Tallen, E. 2008. "New Urbanism, Social Equity, and the Challenge of Post-Katrina Rebuilding in Mississippi." *Journal of Planning Education and Research* 27:277–93.

Tamari, S. 2013. "Normalcy and Violence: The Yearning for the Ordinary in Discourse of the Palestinian-Israeli Conflict." *Journal of Palestine Studies* 42 (4): 48–60.

Tamer-Chammas, A. 2012. "Restoration of Damaged Land in Societies Recovering From Conflict: The Case of Lebanon." In *Assessing and Restoring Natural Resources in Post-Conflict Peacebuilding*, edited by D. Jensen and S. Lonergan, 203–22. London: Earthscan / Routledge.

Tanyag, M. 2018. "Resilience, Female Altruism, and Bodily Autonomy: Disaster-Induced Displacement in Post-Haiyan Philippines." *Signs: Journal of Women in Culture and Society* 43 (3): 563–85.

Taylor, D. 2009. "Normativity and Normalization." *Foucault Studies* 7 (1): 45–63.

Taylor, D., ed. 2011a. *Michel Foucault: Key Concepts.* Durham: Acumen.

Taylor, D. 2011b. "Practices of the Self." In *Michel Foucault: Key Concepts*, edited by D. Taylor, 173–86. Durham: Acumen.

Taylor, D. 2013. "Toward a Feminist 'Politics of Ourselves.'" In *A Companion to Foucault*, edited by C. Falzon, T. O'Leary, and J. Sawicki, 403–18. London: Wiley-Blackwell.

Taylor, D. 2014. "Abnormal." In *The Cambridge Foucault Lexicon*, edited by L. Lawlor and J. Nale, 3–9. Cambridge: Cambridge University Press.

Thornton, A. P. 1965. *Doctrines of Imperialism.* New York: Wiley and Sons.

Tierney, K. 2007. "From the Margins to the Mainstream? Disaster Research at the Crossroads." *Annual Review of Sociology* 33:503–25.

Timmerman, P. 1981. *Vulnerability, Resilience and the Collapse of Society.* Environmental Monographs 1. Toronto: Institute for Environmental Studies, University of Toronto.

Titchkosky, T. 2015. "Normal." In *Keywords for Disability Studies*, edited by R. Adams, B. Reiss, and D. Serlin, 130–32. New York: New York University Press.

Trouillot, M.-R. 1990. *Haiti: State against Nation.* New York: Monthly Review Press.

Tuastad, D. 2003. "Neo-Orientalism and the New Barbarism Thesis: Aspects of Symbolic Violence in the Middle East Conflict(s)." *Third World Quarterly* 24 (4): 591–99.

Tubiana J., V. Tanner, and M. A. Abdul-Jalil. 2012. *Traditional Authorities' Peacemaking Role in Darfur.* Peaceworks 83. Washington, DC: United States Institute of Peace.

Twigg, J. 2009. "Characteristics of a Disaster-Resilient Community: A Guidance Note." London: Interagency Group.

UIC Barcelona. 2011. "Haiti: Building Back Better?" July 20. http://masteremergen cyarchitecture.com/2011/07/20/haiti-building-back-better/

UK Parliament. 2012. "Written Evidence from Dr. Shaikh Khalid bin Khalifa Al-Khalifa, Chairman, Committee on Foreign Affairs, Defense and National Security, Shura Council Kingdom of Bahrain." November 17. https://publications.pa rliament.uk/pa/cm201314/cmselect/cmfaff/88/88vw17.htm

UK Parliament. 2013. *The UK's Relations with Saudi Arabia and Bahrain: Fifth Report of Session 2013–14.* London: Stationery Office. https://publications.parliament .uk/pa/cm201314/cmselect/cmfaff/88/88.pdf

Ulysse, G. A. 2015. *Why Haiti Needs New Narratives: A Post-Quake Chronicle.* Middletown, CT: Wesleyan University Press.

UNDP (United Nations Development Program). 2004. *Reducing Disaster Risk: A Challenge for Development.* New York: Bureau for Crisis Prevention and Recovery.

UNDP. 2010. *Evaluation of UNDP Contribution to Disaster Prevention and Recovery.* New York: UNDP Evaluation Office.

UNDP, UNFPA, UNOPS, UNICEF, UN-Women, and WFP (United Nations Development Program, United Nations Population Fund, United Nations Office for Project Services, United Nations Children's Fund UN-Women, and World Food Programme). 2016. "Working in Fragile Contexts, Including in Middle-Income Countries." Joint Meeting of the Executive Boards of UNDP/ UNFPA/UNOPS, UNICEF, UN-Women, and WFP, June 3. https://docs.wfp .org/api/documents/WFP-0000037716/download/

UN General Assembly. 1995. "Emergency International Assistance for Peace, Normalcy and Reconstruction of War-Stricken Afghanistan." A/50/L.60, December 13.

UN General Assembly. 1998. Resolution No. 52/211. A/RES/52/211, February 27.

UN General Assembly. 2006. Human Rights Council Resolution. UN Doc. A/RES/60/251, April 3.

UNHCR (United Nations High Commissioner for Refugees). 2001. "Afghanistan: Some Signs of Stability and Normalcy Returning." December 14. https://www.unhcr.org/news/briefing/2001/12/3c19e3124/afghanistan-signs-stability-normalcy-returning.html

UN Human Rights Council. 2008. Report of the Special Rapporteur on Extrajudicial, Summary or Arbitrary Executions. A/HRC/8/3, para 51, May 2.

UN Human Rights Council. 2015a. National Report Submitted in Accordance with Paragraph 5 of the Annex to Human Rights Council Resolution 16/21. UN Doc. A/HRC/WG.6/23/MMR/1, August 5.

UN Human Rights Council. 2015b. Report of the Detailed Findings of the Independent Commission of Inquiry Established Pursuant to Human Rights Council Resolution S-21/1." UN Doc. A/HRC/29/CRP.4, June 24.

UN Human Rights Council. 2017. National Report Submitted in Accordance with Paragraph 5 of the Annex to Human Rights Council Resolution 16/21: Israel. UN Doc. A/HRC/WG.6/29/ISR/1, November 13.

UN Human Rights Council. 2018. Report of the Detailed Findings of the Independent International Fact-Finding Mission on Myanmar. A/HRC/39/CRP.2, September 17.

UN Human Rights Council. 2019. Report of the Independent Investigative Mechanism for Myanmar. A/HRC.42/66, August 7.

UN Human Rights Council. 2020. "Basic Facts about the UPR." https://www.ohchr.org/EN/hrbodies/upr/pages/basicfacts.aspx

UNISDR (United Nations Office for Disaster Risk Reduction). 2017. *Build Back Better in Recovery, Rehabilitation and Reconstruction.* Geneva: UNISDR.

United Nations. 1999. Report of the Secretary-General on the Situation in Somalia. UN Doc. S/1999/882, 16 August.

United Nations. 2004. *Yearbook of the United Nations.* Vol. 58. New York: UN Department of Public Information.

United Nations. 2015. *Sendai Framework for Disaster Risk Reduction 2015–2030.* Geneva: UNISDR.

United Nations Office for the Coordination of Humanitarian Affairs. 2015. *An End in Sight: Multi-Year Planning to Meet and Reduce Humanitarian Needs in Protracted Crises.* OCHA Policy and Studies Series 15. New York: UN Office for the Coordination of Humanitarian Affairs. https://www.unocha.org/sites/unocha/files/An%20end%20in%20sight%20Multi%20Year%20Planning.pdf

United States Institute of Peace. 2010. "Former Haiti Prime Minister Says, 'Haiti Must Build Back Better.'" November 8. https://www.usip.org/publications/2010/11/11/former-haiti-prime-minister-says-haiti-must-build-back-better

United States Institute of Peace. n.d. "Social Reconstruction." https://www.usip.org/guiding-principles-stabilization-and-reconstruction-the-web-version/social-well-being/social-reconst

UN Secretary-General. 1992. "An Agenda for Peace: Preventive Diplomacy, Peace-making and Peace-Keeping." Report of the Secretary-General Pursuant to the Statement Adopted by the Summit Meeting of the Security Council on 31 January 1992. A/47/277–S/24111, June 17.

UN Secretary-General. 2008. "Securing Peace and Development: The Role of the United Nations in Supporting Security Sector Reform." Report of the Secretary-General. A/62/659–S/2008/39, January 23.

UN Secretary-General. 2014. "Peacebuilding in the Aftermath of Conflict." Report of the Secretary-General. A/69/399–S/2014/694, September 23.

UN Security Council. 1994. Report of the Secretary-General on the Situation in Tajikistan. S/1994/1363, November 30.

UN Security Council. 1999. Report of the Secretary-General on the United Nations Interim Administration Mission in Kosovo. S/1999/779, July 12.

UN Security Council. 2002a. Report of the Secretary-General on the United Nations Mission in Bosnia and Herzegovina. S/2002/1314, December 2.

UN Security Council. 2002b. Report of the Secretary-General on the United Nations Transitional Administration in Timor-Leste. S/2002/80, January 17.

UN Security Council. 2009a. Provisional Verbatim of the 6085th meeting. SC/9598, February 19.

UN Security Council. 2009b. Report of the Secretary-General on the United Nations Integrated Mission in Timor-Leste (for the Period from 9 July 2008 to 20 January 2009). S/2009/72, February 4.

UN Security Council. 2012. Provisional Verbatim of the 6859th meeting. S/PV/6859, November 12.

UN Security Council. 2014a. Provisional Verbatim of the 7222nd Meeting. S/PV.7222, July 22.

UN Security Council. 2014b. Provisional Verbatim of the 7281st Meeting. S/PV.7281, October 21.

UN Security Council. 2018. Provisional Verbatim of the 8381st Meeting. S/PV.8381, October 24.

UN Security Council. 2019. Provisional Verbatim of the 8477th Meeting. S/PV.8477. February 28.

USAID (United States Agency for International Development). 2015. *Organized Crime, Conflict and Fragility: Assessing Relationships through a Review of USAID Programs*. Arlington, VA: Management Systems International.

USAID. 2020. "Stabilization and Transitions." https://www.usaid.gov/stabilization-and-transitions

US Department of State. 2013. "Implementation by the Government of Bahrain of the Recommendations by the Bahrain Independent Commission of Inquiry." https://www.adhrb.org/wp-content/uploads/2015/06/State-Report-on-Implementation-of-BICI-3-2.pdf

US Department of State. 2018a. *Country Reports on Terrorism 2017*. Washington, DC: Bureau of Counterterrorism.

US Department of State. 2018b. "Israel and the Golan Heights 2018 Human Rights Report." https://www.state.gov/wp-content/uploads/2019/03/ISRAEL-AND-THE-GOLAN-HEIGHTS-2018.pdf

US House of Representatives. 2012. "Implementation of the Bahrain Independent Commission of Inquiry Report." Hearing before the Tom Lantos Human Rights Commission, August 1. https://humanrightscommission.house.gov/sites/human rightscommission.house.gov/files/documents/08_01_12_Bahrain.pdf

van den Herik, L. J. 2014. "An Inquiry into the Role of Commissions of Inquiry in International Law: Navigating the Tensions between Fact-Finding and Application of International Law." *Chinese Journal of International Law* 13 (3): 507–37.

Vejnovic, D., and V. Lalic 2005. "Community Policing in a Changing World: A Case Study of Bosnia and Herzegovina." *Police Practice and Research* 6 (4): 363–73.

Vincent, R. J. 1986. *Human Rights and International Relations*. Cambridge: Cambridge University Press.

Vintges, K. 2011. "Freedom and Spirituality." In *Michel Foucault: Key Concepts*, edited by D. Taylor, 99–110. Durham: Acumen.

Visoka, G. 2016. *Peace Figuration after International Intervention: Intentions, Events and Consequences of Liberal Peacebuilding*. Abingdon: Routledge.

Visoka, G. 2017a. *Assessing the Potential Impact of Kosovo's Specialist Court*. The Hague: PAX.

Visoka, G. 2017b. *Shaping Peace in Kosovo: The Politics of Peacebuilding and Statehood*. London: Palgrave Macmillan.

Visoka, G. 2019. "Critique and Alternativity in International Relations." *International Studies Review* 21 (4): 678–704.

Visoka, G. 2020. "Everyday Peace Capture: Nationalism and the Dynamics of Peace after Violent Conflict." *Nations and Nationalism* 26 (2): 431–46.

Visoka, G., J. Doyle, and E. Newman, eds. 2020. *Routledge Handbook of State Recognition*. London: Routledge.

Vogel, B. 2016. "Civil Society Capture: Top-Down Interventions from Below?" *Journal of Intervention and Statebuilding* 10 (4): 472–89.

Vollmer, H. 2013. *The Sociology of Disruption, Disaster and Social Change: Punctuated Cooperation*. Cambridge: Cambridge University Press.

Wæver, O., and B. Buzan. 2020. "Racism, Reading and Responsibility: Securitization Theory, Systemic Racism in Security Studies and Methodologies for Excavating Foundational Flaws in Theories." https://cric.ku.dk/publications/racismr eply/Racism_response_WebDoc_15May2020.pdf

Walker, J., and M. Cooper. 2011. "Genealogies of Resilience: From Systems Ecology to the Political Economy of Crisis Adaptation." *Security Dialogue* 42 (2): 143–60.

Walker, P. 2007. "Crisis and Normality, Two Sides of the Same Coin." Paper presented at the Brookings Institution / Ford Foundation workshop "Towards a New Poverty and Development Agenda," Washington, DC, May 30–31.

Walsh, F. 2002. "Bouncing Forward: Resilience in the Aftermath of September 11." *Family Process* 41:34–36.

Ward, J. 2002. "Back to the Future: New Urbanist Planning." *American City and Country* 117 (4): 32–43.

Wargny, C. 2008. "Rêves de normalité: Haïti, ce pays en dehors." *Le Monde Diplomatique* 653 (August): 8–9.

Weatherall, T. 2015. *Jus Cogens: International Law and Social Contract*. Cambridge: Cambridge University Press.

Webb, G. R. 2007. "The Sociology of Disaster." In *21st Century Sociology: A Reference Handbook*, edited by C. D. Bryant and D. L. Peck, 278–85. London: SAGE.

Wehrey, F. 2013. "Combating Unconventional Threats in the Gulf: Convergence and Diverence between the GCC and the West." In *The Uneasy Balance: Potential and Challenges of the West's Relations with the Gulf States*, edited by R. Alcaro and A. Dessi, 97–112. Rome: Edizioni Nuova Cultura.

Wildavsky, A. 1988. *Searching for Safety*. New Brunswick, NJ: Transaction Books.

Wilkins, B. 2007. "Principles for the Law of Peoples." *Journal of Ethics* 11 (2): 161–75.

Wille, A. 2013. *The Normalization of the European Commission: Politics and Bureaucracy in the EU Executive*. Oxford: Oxford University Press.

William, D. 2013. "Development, Intervention, and International Order." *Review of International Studies* 39 (5): 1213–31.

Wisner, B., P. Blaikie, T. Cannon, and I. Davis. 2003. *At Risk: Natural Hazards, People's Vulnerability and Disasters*. London: Routledge.

Woodward, S. 2017. *The Ideology of Failed States: Why Intervention Fails*. Cambridge: Cambridge University Press.

World Bank 2014. *Guide to Developing Disaster Recovery Frameworks: World Reconstruction Conference Version*. September. https://www.recoveryplatform.org/asse ts/publication/GFDRR/countryCS2014/DRF-Guide_FINAL_small_REVIS ED_FULL-disclaimer.pdf

Yalcin, S. 2016. "Modalities of Normality." In *Deontic Modality*, edited by N. Charlow and M. Chrisman, 230–55. Oxford: Oxford University Press.

Yates, R. 2014. "Philippines: Building Back Safer and Stronger." Plan International, November 4. https://plan-international.org/blog/2015/05/philippines-building -back-safer-and-stronger

Young, I. M. 1990. *Justice and the Politics of Difference*. Princeton: Princeton University Press.

Zanotti, L. 2006. "Taming Chaos: A Foucauldian View of UN Peacekeeping, Democracy and Normalization." *International Peacekeeping* 13 (2): 150–67.

Zanotti, L. 2011. *Governing Disorder: UN Peace Operations, International Security, and Democratization in the Post–Cold War Era*. Philadelphia: University of Pennsylvania Press.

Žižek, S. 2009. *Violence*. London: Profile Books.

Index

abnormal, 2–9, 11–12, 18, 22–24, 26, 31–33, 40–48, 67, 92–94
abnormality, 3, 5, 22, 31–33, 56, 95–96, 109
abnormalization, 3, 5–6, 13–14, 22, 43, 44, 159
acceptance, 12, 18, 40, 119–30, 138–40
accepting normalcy, 9–10, 119
adaptability, 48, 95–96, 116
Adler-Nissen, R., 5, 44
Advisory Commission on Rakhine State, 144–45
Afghanistan, 1, 11, 75, 77–78
agency, 7, 15, 21, 34, 59, 77
alliances, 120, 125
assessment, 29, 78, 84, 135
authoritarian governance, 155
average, 2, 23, 27, 34

Bahrain, 12, 18, 132, 136–40
Bahrain Independent Commission of Inquiry (BICI), 137, 141
Bangsamoro, 75
barbarian, 58
benchmarking, 43
black hole, 64
Bosnia and Herzegovina, 11, 17, 81
bottom-up interventions, 84–85
bouncing back, 89–90, 97–100
bouncing forward, 89, 97, 100–102, 106, 155
Bourdieu, P., 33
build back better, 104–6
burdened peoples, 68–69

Canguilhem, G., 31
capable state, 76–77
capacity building, 77
catastrophe, 94–95, 103, 112
categorization of states, 42
Chandler, D., xi, 7, 97
circularity, 30
civilizing process, 130
civil society, 25, 41, 46, 57, 82–85, 148, 158
classification, 25, 32, 41
colonialism, 37, 41, 55, 61
commissions of inquiry, 12, 18, 119–22, 135–39, 144, 147–48
comparison, 27–28, 45, 66
complex adaptive systems, 101
complexity, 17, 51, 90, 96–98
confession, 12, 18, 49, 120–21, 126, 128–30
confessionary practices, 40, 49, 156, 158
conformity, 21, 23, 25, 28, 30, 32
Connolly, W. E., 30–31, 36
containment, 11, 18, 48, 91, 117–18
contingency, 48, 51, 85
critical race studies, 24

Davis, L., 21, 24, 30
decolonization, 149
delinquency, 31
democracy, 5, 40, 57, 69, 72–73, 84, 87, 121
Devetak, R., 59, 61–62, 66
deviations, 11, 25, 32, 95, 97
deviance, 30, 32, 59

difference, 10, 12–13, 18, 31, 34, 36, 40, 42, 48, 57
differentiation, 30–31, 36, 39, 41, 44–45
disabilities studies, 24
disaster-affected states, 9, 40, 47, 91, 152
disaster management, 9–10, 14–15, 17, 40, 50,
    89–91, 104, 162
disasters, 2, 7, 11, 18, 43, 47–48, 90, 94–95,
    102–7
disciplinary methods, 34
disciplinary power, 7, 14, 22, 25, 27, 32, 34,
    81–82, 122
disciplinary techniques, 6, 8, 22, 26, 28, 30, 51,
    153
diversity, 124–25
docile body, 163
docile states, 13, 151, 162–67
domination, 9, 36, 115
Duany, A., 109, 111, 114–15
Duffield, M., 7, 92–93
Durkheim, É., 23

Elias, N., 26
emergency (normalization of), 1, 11, 48, 75, 90,
    92, 94–96, 105, 109–10, 118, 155, 158–59,
    162, 164
empowerment, 33, 53, 56, 62, 72
ethnic conflicts, 62, 72
EUPM, 81–82
eurocentric, 65, 86
examination, 4, 6, 8, 13–15, 22, 29, 41, 56–57,
    84, 131–32
external regulation, 42, 164

fact-finding missions, 18, 49, 121–22, 136–40,
    144–47, 156–57, 160
Finnemore, M., 38–39, 41
Foucauldian discourse analysis, 49
Foucault, M., 7–9, 17, 21–37, 40, 43, 45–52, 56,
    58–61, 68, 90–93, 96, 98, 114, 120–23, 126–
    29, 151–52, 154–55, 159, 166
fragile states, xi, 5, 9–11, 17, 40, 42–46, 53, 55–57,
    62–75, 87–88, 93–94, 152, 154, 157–59
France, 61
friendship (politics of), 120, 123, 125–26, 155,
    161

Gaza, 142–44
Georgia, 1, 79–80
Global South, 92
Goffman, E., 97, 106
governance building, 65
governance of complexity, 96–97

governmentality, 6–7, 22, 24–25, 34, 37, 52, 56–
    57, 86, 88, 154, 156, 160
gradeability, 27, 42, 154

Haiti, 91, 107, 111–16
Haiyan (Typhoon), 91, 105–6
Haraway, D., 59, 61
hell (*also:* hell on earth), 64
hierarchical observations, 8, 22, 28, 37, 41, 52,
    79, 153–55, 159–60
hierarchy, 3, 5–6, 8, 13, 22, 24, 27–30, 35–37, 39,
    41–42, 44, 51–53, 56, 66–67, 71, 77, 79, 87–
    88, 124, 149, 153–55, 159–62, 164, 166
homogeneity, 32, 35, 152, 163
Horwitz, A. W., 33, 37
human rights
    abuses, 12, 48, 62, 66, 87, 120, 160–61, 165
    general, 5, 15, 18, 40, 44, 57, 68–74, 83–84,
        119–49
    promotion or protection, 1, 4, 14, 78–80

incorrigibility, 10, 17, 91, 158
indicators (of normalcy), 26–27, 43, 85–86, 119
individualization, 34, 137
instability, 11, 31, 48, 72, 81, 90, 92, 95–96, 116–
    17, 136, 159–60
internalization, 30, 33, 67, 164–65
International administration, 46, 56, 69–72, 82
international governance, 56
international institutions, 41, 72, 125
internationalism, 39, 56, 148, 161
international normalizing order, 39–41, 48, 166
international normalizing society, 40–41, 44, 46,
    122, 152, 154
international order, 4, 12, 14, 38, 45, 55, 62, 67,
    71, 73, 78, 120, 124, 148, 158, 161
international trusteeship, 55
intervention
    administrative, 32, 77
    external, 6, 10–19, 22, 37, 43, 45–46, 56–57,
        64–65, 67, 69, 86, 120, 129–30, 138, 155,
        159, 161
    psychiatric, 32, 60
    therapeutic, 25, 32, 55, 63–64, 102, 164
intolerance, 40, 85
Iraq, 66, 75
Ireland, 118
Israel, 132–33, 142–44

Joseph, J., 7, 43, 57, 76
judgment (normalizing), 8, 14, 22, 24, 27–29, 37,
    40–41, 43, 79, 88, 153–54, 159–60

Katrina (Hurricane), 91, 94, 107–11, 115–16
knowledge
    dissemination, 30
    production, 3, 5, 7–8, 14–15, 17, 26, 41–42,
        77, 151
    systematization of, 32, 35
Kosovo, 75, 77, 82, 84

labeling
    social, 30, 60–62, 73, 120, 128, 153
    state, 4, 9, 12–13, 22, 41, 43–44, 50, 53, 55, 63,
        67, 124–25, 155, 157
Latour, B., 86
Lemay-Hébert, N., 16, 68, 77, 112
liberal interventionism, 3, 9, 15, 17, 40, 46, 50,
    56, 68–71, 74, 87–88, 157, 162
liberalization, 39, 76
liberal peace, 56, 70–71, 73–74
liberal societies, 71, 153
limited statehood, 64–66
lite interventionism, 121, 126, 135, 144
Luhmann, N., 97–98

Mac Ginty, R., 85
masturbator. *See* onanist
Mead, G. H., 33
Misztal, B., 23, 26
monster, 9, 22, 31–32, 40, 46, 55, 57–62, 64, 66,
    68, 86, 91, 155
Myanmar, 12, 18, 130–33, 144–47

narrative, 88, 121, 127–29, 132, 139–40, 147,
    149
nationalism (aggressive), 62
new barbarism, 92–93, 117
New Orleans, 91, 94, 107–9, 111, 114, 116
new urbanism, 50, 91, 108–9, 111, 114, 116
noninterference, 12, 18, 45, 56, 70–71, 120
non-Western (world), 7, 10, 12, 37, 43, 61, 72–73,
    125, 148–49, 154
North Korea, 132–34

OECD, 65, 93, 95, 99
OHCHR, 136, 138
onanist (*also:* masturbator), 9, 22, 31–32, 40,
    48–49, 120, 122–23, 155
ontological
    differentiation, 45
    indeterminancy, 44
    insecurity, 5, 53
    politics, 87
    position, 65

security, 71
    status, 162
Onuf, N., 5, 8
otherness (*also:* othering), 30, 58, 154, 157
outlaw states, 61, 66–68
OXFAM, 113, 118

Palestine, 142
pastoral role/power, 12, 15, 25, 49, 120, 158,
    160–62
pathological (*also:* pathologization), 23, 30, 33,
    55–56, 58, 63–64
peace and conflict studies (PCS), 7, 15, 24
peacebuilding
    everyday peacebuilding, 85
    liberal peacebuilding, 80, 83
peace-loving nations, 164
peace operations, 69
Philippines, 11, 18, 75, 91, 105–6
Pitt, B., 110–11
pluralism, 12–13, 18, 49, 73, 124–25, 148, 152
problematization (method), 17, 50–51, 151

Rabinow, P., 25, 29–30, 32
racial politics, 23–24, 91, 107, 109
Rawls, J., 61, 68–69, 124–25
reconciliation, 46, 75, 83, 86
resilience, 41, 47–50, 89–90, 93–106, 111, 117,
    155–60
resistance (anti-normalizing), 32
Richmond, O., 7, 75–76
Rohingya, 133, 144–47
rule of law, 46, 57, 62–63, 65, 72, 74–75, 78–84,
    119, 135, 139, 144

sameness, 14, 26, 31, 40, 126, 152, 163
self-care (politics), 40
self-discipline, 33, 56, 72, 130, 163
self-enforcement, 27, 30
self-governance, 27, 36–37, 75, 164
self-intervention, 129
self-reliance, 13, 47, 155
self-responsibilization, 34
social configuration, 100
social engineering (*also:* social reengineering),
    37, 57, 76, 85
social evolution (*also:* social evolutionism), 36,
    97
socialization, 16, 42
social reconstruction, 10–11, 82–83, 159
sociology of disaster, 102, 107, 111, 113
Somalia, 11, 17, 64, 100

sovereign equality, 45, 49, 66, 120, 124
sovereignty. *See* state, sovereignty
stabilization, 1, 46–47, 50, 79, 89, 117, 156, 163
state
    confession, 18, 49, 121, 126, 128–30, 132, 160
    failure, 45, 67, 70, 72, 82, 155, 159
    labeling (*see* labeling, state)
    performance, 3, 5, 14, 28, 43–44, 67–68, 78, 84, 126, 128, 145, 164
    ranking, 45, 66, 124
    recognition, 120, 123–25, 130, 156, 162
    sovereignty, 13, 31, 42, 44, 56, 63–64, 71, 76, 120, 123–24, 130, 133–34, 147, 161–62, 165, 167
    suppressive, 9–12, 15, 18, 40, 48–49, 152–53, 157, 160–61, 165
    ungoverned, 62, 64–65
statebuilding, 10–11, 14–15, 17, 38, 46, 56, 65, 69, 74–78, 82, 86, 88, 137, 155, 157–59
statehood, 1, 5, 9, 44, 56, 64–66, 77, 88, 121, 153–54
statistical (measurements), 3, 5, 27, 34
stigmatization, 4, 44
strategic alliances, 120, 155
stratification, 45, 154
subordination, 4, 33, 56, 166
supervision, 14, 29, 41, 57, 159, 164–65
surveillance, 28–29, 41, 119, 127, 153–54
symbolic interactionism, 23, 52

Taylor, D., 25–27, 29–32, 35–36
terrorist (figure of), 59
terrorist attacks, 1, 142, 147
Timor-Leste, 1, 11, 17, 75, 77, 79
tolerance, 49, 73, 83, 125, 148
Trouillot, M-R, 113

truth-telling (*also:* parrhesia), 12, 18, 120–22, 126–30, 150, 160

United Nations (UN; general), 1, 63, 70, 80, 106, 132, 144
UN High Commissioner for Refugees (UNHCR), 100
UN Human Rights Commission, 142
UN Human Rights Council, 130–33, 139, 142, 146
UN Interim Administration Mission in Kosovo (UNMIK), 75
UN International Police Task Force (UNIPTF), 79, 81
United Kingdom, 139–41, 144
United Nations Mission in Bosnia and Herzegovina (UNMIBH), 81
United States, 62, 74, 94, 108, 126, 134, 139–41, 143–44, 146
universalization, 33
universal periodic review, 18, 121, 130–35, 149, 160
US Department of State, 65, 140–41, 143

violence
    gendered, 94
    racialized, 94
    symbolic, 33, 166
violent conflicts, 2, 43, 45, 55, 62, 69, 72–73, 76, 79, 101, 155
Visoka, G., 7, 16, 75, 87, 121, 123
vulnerability, 48, 94–95, 104, 113, 116–17, 129, 164
vulnerable states/societies, 41, 106, 163

witch, 58
World Bank, 99